WO

FOR TODAY 2

Notes for daily Bible reading

**International
Bible Reading
Association**

Cover image: Photograph by Ursula Clark

Editor: Nicola Slee

Published by:
The International Bible Reading Association
1020 Bristol Road
Selly Oak
Birmingham
B29 6LB

Charity Number 211542

ISBN 1-904024-51-3
ISSN 0140-8275

Typeset by Christian Education Publications
Printed and bound in Great Britain by Biddles

CONTENTS

EDITORIAL

'The glory of God is a human being fully alive', according to the second century theologian, Iranaeus. God's glory is shown forth in a particular way wherever human beings live out their humanity fully, intensely, without sparing, gloriously. Faith should make us more, rather than less, human: more alive, more engaged with reality, more open to the multifaceted joys and challenges of life. Our cover image this year shows a man engaged in his work – cutting a piece of metal – with the utmost concentration and intensity. He is fully absorbed in what he is doing, utterly present to the moment – and, of course, he needs to be, because it is dangerous business. One moment's slackening of concentration, one slip of the hand and the metal cutter could do untold damage. As he works, absorbed in that concentrated attention, the sparks fly and an intense conflagration of colour, light and energy is let loose all around him – a lovely image of that glory of which Iranaeus speaks. He himself is largely unaware of the fire and the flare, but others see it in its full glory – just as we are probably entirely unaware of the glory that others may see in us, as we go about our daily lives, immerse ourselves in the tasks that face us, give ourselves as fully as we can to our work, our world, our relationships, our prayer. But we see that same glory flame out in others as they care compassionately, act with integrity, fight injustice assiduously, suffer courageously, serve diligently, create with originality, making more joy and peace and love in the world as they do so.

A right reading of the scriptures should nourish us, challenge us and inspire us to live life more fully, more robustly, more wholeheartedly – rather than protect or immunise us from the challenges of life. This year's notes span a wide range of contexts, issues, concerns and understandings of faith, as ever. Writers from around the globe reflect out of their own lived experience of faith, and share with us the fruits of their understanding, often gleaned through struggle and suffering. Amongst others, we hear this year from young people living out their faith in secular, multicultural Britain; from prison chaplains reflecting on what faith might mean inside prison walls; from those writing from within severe physical limitation and pain; from gay and lesbian Christians seeking to live authentically in a church which often rejects them; from countries in which Christianity is very much the minority religion as well as from others where it is the mainstream. I do not expect readers to agree with the insights or perspectives of all or even the majority of our writers: yet what shines out from all of them, without exception, is their integrity, sincerity and authenticity as they write out of their best efforts to live a life that is fully alive, drawing on the deep roots of their faith, whether Jewish or Christian. We may not agree with them but we can surely be glad for the light and the fire that shines from them, and pray that our own lives may catch just a little of that fire as we read and ponder the scriptures anew this year. As we do so, may we too come to perceive more of that glory of God of which Iranaeus spoke so many centuries ago.

Nicola Slee – Editor

Bible readings online!
IBRA's Bible readings scheme is available via our website at www.christianeducation.org.uk/ibra.htm

Acknowledgements and abbreviations

GNB Good News Bible (The Bible Societies/Collins Publishers) – Old Testament © American Bible Society 1976; New Testament © American Bible Society 1966, 1971, 1976.

NIV Scripture quotations taken from The Holy Bible, New International Version © 1973, 1978, 1984 by International Bible Society. Used by permission of Hodder & Stoughton Limited. All rights reserved. 'NIV' is a registered trademark of International Bible Society. UK trademark number 1448790.

NJB Taken from The New Jerusalem Bible, published and copyright 1985 by Darton, Longman and Todd Ltd and Doubleday & Co. Inc, and used by permission of the publishers.

NRSV New Revised Standard Version © 1989, Division of Christian Education of the National Council of Churches of Christ in the United States of America.

REB The Revised English Bible © Oxford University and Cambridge University Presses 1989.

RSV The Holy Bible, Revised Standard Version © 1973, Division of Christian Education of the National Council of Churches of Christ in the United States of America.

BCE Before the Common Era. BCE and CE are used by some writers instead of BC and AD.

* Readings from the Revised Common Lectionary. Other Lectionary readings are covered, but not in the same week.

PRAYERS

Spirit of God, fire and spark of all life:
kindle your warmth and energy in us every day as we come before you,
and grant us the courage to live life more fully, more
   wholeheartedly, more freely,
so that we may show forth the glory of God.   *Nicola Slee*

Great Spirit, whose voice I hear in the winds
And whose breath gives life to all the world,
hear me!
I come before you, one of your many children.
I am small and weak,
I need your strength and wisdom.
Let me walk in beauty,
make my eyes ever behold the red and purple sunset.
Make my hands respect things
you have made.
Make my ears sharp to hear your voice –
Make me wise so that I may learn the things
you have taught my people.
Let me learn the lesson hidden in every leaf and rock –
I seek strength not to be greater than my brother or sister,
but to fight my greatest enemy – myself.
Make me ever ready to come to you
with clean hands and straight eyes
so that when life fades with the fading sunset
my spirit may come to you without shame.
    Chi-meegwetch, Canada

Lord, may I learn to be just as pleased with me, your creation, as
you are. Help me to love my body and to cherish each part as the
lovingly fashioned gift from you that it is. Let me not look with
disdain or hate on that-part-that-would-be-so-much-better-if-only-
it-were smaller, curvier, more toned, less sagging, larger, firmer,
longer, shorter, straighter, or wavier. Let me not continually seek
out faults in your work; instead, let me wonder in the perfection of
your craftsmanship, declaring with you that yes, what you have
created is indeed very good.   *Vivian Lam*

Thank God for life, for living
Thank God for love, for giving
Thank God for death:
an ending a beginning.

Thank God for lips, for speaking
Thank God for hearts, for seeking
Thank God for weakness:
a stumbling an upsurging.

Thank God for eyes, for seeing
Thank God for soul, for being
Thank God for absence:
a longing an unfolding.

Thank God for life, for living
Thank God for death, for longing
Thank God with singing.   *Mary E Morgan, Caribbean*

That a flame may be kindled
God of power,
we pray that our lives
may be so touched by your Spirit
that dreams may be dreamt
and visions seen.

Help us to recognise
the work which you have for us,
and give us the will
to do with all our heart
whatever tasks may come to hand.   *Edmund Banyard*

God in me, God beyond me! Past compare!
O Being wholly here and wholly there!
          Angelus Silesius, 17th century German

How to use 'a quiet time'

Have a visual focus — a cross, a plant, interesting stones... Create a prayer table on which to display them with other symbols. Place on it pictures or articles from the daily news.

Use silence Relax and empty your mind of all that's going on around you. Know that God's loving presence encircles you, your family, your community and the world. Learn to enjoy God's presence. If, because of personal problems, you cannot free your mind of the day's concerns, remember that these are your prayers and offer them to God. Know that you are loved and valued, and seek the strength and peace God offers.

Read the Bible passage for the day and then the notes. Read the verses again, allowing the words to fill your mind. Try to discover their message for you and the world around you. Refer back to other readings in the theme, so that you can see how the thoughts link together. If the writer of the week's notes comes from a different culture or background from yours, ask yourself what is new and fresh. What surprising insights have come to you from his or her perspective?

Listen Remember that the most important part of prayer is to hear what God is saying to us. God speaks to us through the words of scripture, the daily news, and often through people around us — our children, our friends, our neighbours, the person who asks for help, the stranger... Frequently the voice of God disturbs our complacency, and calls us to 'Go out' and do something we've never done before!

Include the world Hold the news of the day in your mind. Enter the situation of those you hear or read about and try to pray alongside them — with them. In a wonderful way, prayer transcends the thousands of miles between us. Through prayer we draw strength from the mysterious fellowship that binds us to one another and to God.

Pray without ceasing Remember that prayer is not only 'the quiet time' we set aside. It becomes part of the whole of life, a continuous dialogue between God and ourselves, through all that we do and think and say: a growing awareness of the loving presence of God who travels with us and never leaves us.

IBRA INTERNATIONAL APPEAL

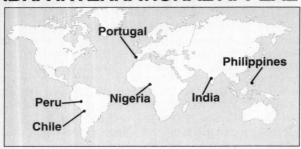

In five continents you will find Christians using IBRA material.

Some will be using books and Bible reading cards translated into their local language, whilst others use English books. Some of the books are printed in the UK, but more and more countries are printing the books and cards themselves. The IBRA International Fund works through churches, Christian groups and Christian publishing houses overseas to make these publications available.

Each year we receive more requests for help from the IBRA International Fund, with greater emphasis on helping our overseas friends to produce their own version of IBRA material.

The only money we have to send is the money you give, so please help us again by giving generously.

Place your gift in the envelope provided and give it to your IBRA representative, or send it direct to:

The IBRA International Appeal

1020 Bristol Road, Selly Oak,
Birmingham B29 6LB, Great Britain

Thank you for your help.

WISDOM
1. God's gift of wisdom

Notes on the Hebrew Bible by
Sybil Sheridan

Sybil Sheridan is a rabbi serving the Wimbledon and District Synagogue, a Reform Jewish community. She is author of Stories from the Jewish World *and has edited two books of women rabbis' writings:* Hear Our Voice *and* Taking up the Timbrel *(both published by SCM).*

The notion of wisdom pervades the Bible. From the moment that Eve is tempted to eat of the fruit of knowledge the quest for wisdom becomes part of the human experience. It can mean different things in different contexts, and in Jewish tradition there are three words that encapsulate the notion. *Chochmah* is understood in terms of native wit or intelligence, *Binah* (or *tevunah*) is the ability to make connections, and *Da'at* the knowledge gained through experience. God is the source of all three types of wisdom and God's essence embodies them all.

Saturday January 1   *Job 28:12–28*
Where is wisdom?

The passage asks about the locus of wisdom and understanding – *chochmah* and *binah*. But since humanity has no measure of it, the question can only be answered in the negative. The deep says, 'It is not in me...' and the sea says, 'It is not with me' (verse 14). Since this question does not produce results a different one is posed: from where do these concepts originate (verse 20)? Again a negative answer is given: 'concealed from the birds in the air' it is only God who knows. God then tells us what wisdom is (verse 28) – but not where it is. 'It is not in heaven, that you should say, Who shall go up for us to heaven, and bring it to us, that we may hear it, and do it? Nor is it beyond the sea...' (Deuteronomy 30:12). The subject in that passage is God's commandment, God's word – and it is 'very near you, in your mouth and in your heart'. Wisdom too is from God, and it is located within us and around us. And with wisdom comes understanding, and our ability to 'depart from evil' (verse 28).

Sunday January 2   1 Kings 3:5–14

Make me wise

Solomon is small fry in comparison to his father. King David was true and righteous and 'upright of heart' (verse 6), qualities that denote honesty and plain dealing in matters of justice. Fearing himself to be more corruptible or gullible, or maybe just cowed by the size and strength of the people he is called upon to rule, Solomon asks God for 'understanding to discern judgement' (verse 9). This is the Hebrew concept of *binah*: not knowledge or academic intelligence, but the ability to understand the true nature of a situation. 'Solomon' in Hebrew is Shlomo – a word connected to *shalom* – peace. Truth in judgement makes for peaceful settlements, and peace brings the riches and honour and length of days God promises. Rabbinic wisdom has it that 'on three things the world stands: on justice, on truth and on peace,' as it is said, (Zechariah 8:16) "Judge truthfully and a judgement of peace will be in your gates"' (Sayings of the Fathers 1:18).

✳ *You favour humanity with knowledge and teach people understanding. Favour us from your store of knowledge, understanding and intelligence. Blessed are you who favours knowledge.*   *From the Jewish daily prayer*

Monday January 3   1 Kings 4:29–34

Stop, look and listen

God has given Solomon three things: wisdom, understanding and breadth of mind. Yet it is for *chochmah* that he is known throughout the world. This wisdom, inherent in all living beings, enables him to understand the affinity of all God's creatures and he is therefore able to talk about trees great or small and animals large or insignificant. Jewish legend goes further to say he could understand the language of every creature. Wisdom here implies an understanding of the natural world, its place and importance in God's plan.

'God gave Solomon wisdom ... even as the sand that is on the sea-shore' (verse 29). The ancient rabbis suggest that God gave him as much wisdom as all Israel. This was inferred from Hosea 1:10: 'Yet the number of the children of Israel shall be as the sand of the sea' (Numbers Rabbah 19:3, a midrash or early rabbinic commentary). But the wisdom, the stories continue, was in his power of observation. It was through watching the world that Solomon learned about it and learned to communicate with its creatures.

In a world threatened to destruction by our greed, if we gave time just to stop and look and listen, then we too could gain such wisdom and an affinity with our world.

✳ *Bless us, Eternal our God, in this year with all kinds of goodness. Give blessing upon the earth; fulfil us from your goodness and bless what you have given us with good years.* *From the Jewish daily prayer*

Tuesday January 4   Proverbs 1:1–7
The need for insight
Even the wise can learn wisdom, and the knowledgeable may yet lack understanding. What they need is *haskel* – insight or enlightenment – another gift of God. This will give them skill in composing poetry and proverbs, but – more important – an understanding of the essential values of society. This Hebrew word is used only three times in the Bible, each time in connection with such values. In Jeremiah 9:24 the insightful understand that 'I am the Eternal who exercises loving kindness, justice, and righteousness, in the earth'. In Proverbs 21:15 the one who departs from such insight is contrasted with the just; 'It is joy to the just to do justice'. In our passage, the wise learn righteousness, justice and equity.

Wisdom, understanding, knowledge – all these qualities lack substance if they are not conjoined with right action, and that right action is most notably to establish justice in all of the earth.

✳ *Restore true judges for us as in former times and counsellors as at the beginning. Remove from us sorrow and sighing. Reign over us, you alone, in kindness and mercy and righteousness in judgement.* *From the Jewish daily prayer*

Wednesday January 5   Proverbs 2:1–15
Only the seeker finds
Chochmah, *binah* and *da'at*, the three kinds of wisdom, combine, and we learn here how to attain them. First, listen: 'take my words' (verse 1); then obey: 'treasure my commandments' (verse 1); then never be satisfied with the knowledge gained, but be constantly on the path to learn more (verse 2ff). Demand it: 'cry

out for it' (verse 3), seek it out: 'search for it like silver' (verse 4), and on the journey insight will be gained into what wisdom contains. 'Then you will understand the fear of God' (verse 5).

Twice before in our passages this week we have come across this phrase. But the English words 'fear' or 'awe' do not do justice to the Hebrew. With such wisdom comes a sense of God's abiding presence, God's perpetual nowness. As the poet Judah Halevi put it:

'Lord, where shall I find You? Your place is lofty and secret. And where shall I not find You? The whole earth is full of your glory.'

Know of God's eternal presence and we have no choice but to follow God's command. Recognise this and the search is over. God fills the seeker to overflowing with wisdom and with understanding. Wisdom is God's gift – but we must seek it ourselves if we are to receive it.

✳ *I have sought to come near You. I have called to You with all my heart;*
And when I went out towards You, I found You coming towards me.

From 'Lord, Where shall I find You?' by Judah Halevi
in the Penguin Book of Hebrew Verse (1981)

Thursday January 6   Exodus 35:30–35

Wisdom found in manual labour

God grants Bezalel the three types of wisdom, but here they have a specific purpose. The ancient rabbis tell us that 'with three things, the world was created, for it says, "The Lord by wisdom founded the earth; by understanding he established the heavens, by his knowledge the depths were broken up" (Proverbs 3:19); and with the same three things the Tabernacle was made, because it says, 'he has filled him with the spirit of God, in wisdom, in understanding, and in knowledge" (Exodus Rabbah 48:4). Just as God created the world, so Bezalel creates the tabernacle and all its vessels.

But God gives Bezalel one more gift – craftsmanship. God created through the word. Bezalel creates with his hands. Those who favour academic intelligence over other forms of knowledge would do well to remember that God never granted anyone the ability to do well in exams; but God did give the ability to work in metal, wood and cloth. It would appear that these kinds of gifts enable us to do God's work best here on earth.

**✳ *Let the beauty of the Eternal our God be upon us; and
establish the work of our hands on us; establish the work of
our hands.*** *Psalm 90:17*

Friday January 7 *Daniel 2:20–30*

Our strength and our weakness

Wisdom is associated with strength and both find their source
exclusively in God. Daniel, speaking in a polytheistic society,
must emphasise this – but we can be equally idolatrous in
assuming our abilities are self-generated. God gives wisdom to
those already wise, and knowledge to those who already have
understanding. Wisdom without God does exist, but is limited in
scope. It can lead to the recognition of how little we know, how
much we are dependent on God. It can lead to humility and a
recognition of how tenuous our control of our lives is.

Wisdom's connection with strength is explained by the context
of rulership here. God is king, but so is Nebuchadnezzar. His
thoughts and desires have great effect on his subjects. He must
learn to recognise them for what they are and exercise judgement
and control on how he acts upon them. We too must know
ourselves, our desires, our abilities and our place in the world if
we are to be open to receive God's wisdom.

**✳ *We give thanks to you, and declare your praise for our lives
which are forever in your hands and for our souls which are
in your charge, and for your signs which are with us every
day: morning, noon and night.*** *From the Jewish daily prayer*

Saturday January 8 *Acts 6:1–10*

Wisdom in words

The appointment of the seven is reminiscent of the seventy called
upon to assist Moses in the wilderness. God told Moses: 'I will
take of the spirit which is upon you, and will put it upon them; and
they shall carry the burden of the people with you' (Numbers
11:17). As in the wilderness, this is not granted to just any one,
but only to those whose reputation already proves them worthy.
Stephen is one such 'full of faith and the Spirit' (Acts 6:5).

But there are also echoes of Bezalel in Exodus 35 here. As in
his case, the seven are filled with wisdom for a specific task. Here
it is the ability to discern the requirements of those in need, to
judge where the limited resources should go. This is *binah* – the

15

ability to judge wisely. But Steven's wisdom extends beyond this. He, like the apostles, is able to speak of his faith, to argue his case and convince those who would do him harm. Wisdom is not demonstrated solely in right action, but in what we say and how we engage with others in conversation.

✳ *My God, guard my tongue from speaking evil, and my lips from telling lies. Make me silent when other people curse me and my soul still humble with all.* From the Jewish daily prayer

FOR REFLECTION – alone or with a group

● Think back on what has happened to you during this the first week of the year.
● How much did you fulfil God's expectations for you?
● How much did you act in wisdom?
● How can you act more wisely in the future?

FOR ACTION

Wisdom is a gift from God, but one that we must seek. Seek God's wisdom through:

● observing nature and the world around you;
● studying religious texts;
● prayer.

WISDOM
2. Wisdom, the guide of life

Notes on the New Revised Standard Version by
Jan Sutch Pickard

At the time of writing these notes, Jan Sutch Pickard was the warden of the Abbey in Iona, a member of the ecumenical Iona Community and a Methodist lay ('Local') preacher. She is a poet and storyteller, too.

The Wisdom tradition in the Bible is a rich one, expressed in different styles of writing. The idea of 'wisdom' includes both the mystery of God's creation and down-to-earth advice. In this tradition we will find Wisdom personified as a woman (the Hebrew word *chochmah* is feminine, just as the Greek word *Sophia* has become a woman's name). And before the end of the week you will discover what is 'the fly in the ointment'!

Sunday January 9   *Proverbs 1:20–33*
How long?

'Why do Christians do this? What do you believe? What does this mean?' These are questions which arise from real curiosity, and lead to dialogue. Such questions are the way we learn from each other – and learn to express the faith that is in us.

'How can you believe that rubbish?' 'What's the point of all this?' These are questions which do not really expect an answer, dialogue or fresh insights. They are scornful rejections of another point of view, claims that nothing really matters.

The Book of Proverbs asks, 'How long will fools hate knowledge?' (verse 22) and talks about 'scoffers'. Now it would be sad if we couldn't ever see the funny side of our human frailty when it comes to faith matters, or recognise that in institutions and ceremonies we can all, at times, take ourselves too seriously. It's healthy to be able to laugh at ourselves. But 'scoffers' are those whose laughter is at others' expense, making a mockery of values and deep beliefs. And all they really achieve is their own confusion, and loneliness.

✻ *God of questions, help us to listen, and to learn.*
God of joy, may our laughter not turn to mockery.
God of wisdom, take our hand and walk with us.

Her paths are peace

Malar Chinniah was a Methodist deaconess in Sri Lanka. She was one of a small group of women whose life of prayer and service to the community was based in a Christian ashram. God then called her to a different ministry – of word and sacrament. She became the first woman to be ordained in her denomination in Sri Lanka, at a time when the civil war in her country erupted again. She found herself standing alongside bereaved families, supporting young men who had been tortured and young women who had been raped. Malar will not be remembered for her sermons, but for the wisdom with which she listened to people who were trying to make sense of terrible experiences. She had no money to give away, only her full attention and her care. She had no power to make a material difference in people's lives, but she stood by them and walked with them on their journey.

This was a person who reminded those she met – Christian, Buddhist, Muslim – of our common humanity. Wisdom, in Proverbs, is imagined as a woman who embodies things we need in our lives together: sound judgement, compassion, peace.

Maybe we understand more about God by remembering a real person who displays these qualities. I have named Malar Chinniah. And you, who would you remember and name?

✳ *More precious than jewels,*
wise and gentle God,
shelter us like a living tree;
lead us along paths of lasting peace.

Better than jewels

It is said that we never forget a good teacher. Which of your teachers do you remember best? Why? Can you put it into one word? From my primary days I remember the enthusiasm of Mr Corkhill, from secondary school the encouragement of Miss Gornall.

In this passage from Proverbs, wisdom is seen as a good teacher. What is distinctive about her teaching? (Prudence, truth, discretion, good advice, insight, justice – what words are used in your version of the Bible?) This is teaching that will bring us closer to God – if we are open to learn and be changed by it. We will be enriched – in ways that are more important than money.

When the disciples followed Jesus they gave up their livelihoods, the jobs they had learned to do, and, in this risky situation, started learning all over again from Jesus the teacher. To them and to the crowds who followed him he said: 'Come to me, all you that are weary and are carrying heavy burdens, and I will give you rest. Take my yoke upon you, and learn from me; for I am gentle and humble in heart, and you will find rest for your souls. For my yoke is easy, and my burden is light' (Matthew 11:28–30). Like the mythical female figure of Wisdom, Jesus the man was a good teacher, who taught by example and whose insights and advice could change the lives of ordinary people.

✳ *Reflect on these words of Jesus. What heavy burdens have you been carrying? What have you learned, from the life and words of Jesus, that can make your burden lighter? What insights, for you, are worth more than jewels?*

Wednesday January 12   *Proverbs 8:22–36*
In the beginning
Imagine a child dancing on the sea shore, listening to the powerful music of the waves, tasting the salt on her lips as she sings back to them, smelling the kelp, feeling the sand under her bare feet and watching the soaring flight of sea-birds seeming to join her dance. Imagine her delight. She feels part of this world – God's creation. She re-creates it for herself, through her senses; she is glad to be alive and she praises God with her whole lively being.

Proverbs also reminds us of the delight of creation. The words you have just read picture God creating from the unimaginable void the universe that human beings know (or as they understood it when the Book of Proverbs was compiled): from a mountain to a grain of sand, defining the difference between sea and dry land. God has a co-worker in this task of creation, delighting God by her presence, and delighted in turn by places and people – all places, all people – as they come into being. Wisdom, the tradition claims, existed before the beginning of the world, having been created first, and the rest of creation could not have happened without her. God created the world 'in wisdom' – wisely. 'In wisdom' is also true of the way the world becomes real for us as we experience it with our senses, learn about it with our minds, learn about ourselves, using our God-given opportunities.

✳ *Imagine God still at work in the world you will see or have already begun to see about you today. Hold in your mind*

*something which has given you delight: a snowflake, flower,
bird in flight, or the taste of good food or fresh clean water,
or the face of a friend. And be thankful.*

Thursday January 13   Proverbs 9:1–12

The way of insight

As so often in the Bible, here is the story of a feast. Wisdom, a
great lady and a generous hostess, has made all the
preparations, including building a banqueting hall. Food and wine
are ready. Many folk are invited, the high and mighty and the
humble. But will they come? Because this is about more than
eating and drinking. Are they willing to 'Lay aside immaturity, and
live, and walk in the way of insight' (verse 6)? This is about the
way we live our lives.

We limit the meaning of wisdom when we use the word just for
abstract qualities or academic knowledge. It is applied in day-by-
day living. Wisdom can be the discernment that helps us through
down-to-earth but difficult situations. It relates to practical advice,
as well as being caught up in the creativity and mystery of God.

And, says the Book of Proverbs, 'The fear of the Lord is the
beginning of Wisdom' (verse 10). It isn't a fear that makes us run
away, though. It's not like the suspicion of things or people that
are different, that ends up with empty scoffing. This 'fear' is really
a respect that compels us to listen, and to respond. We could
even find ourselves joining in the feast!

✳ *O God, help us to find the grace to listen to your voice, not
   our own;
   not to scoff and scorn the feast
   that you have prepared to delight and nourish us:
   but to eat the bread which is a sign of your love,
   and to drink deeply the wine of your wisdom.*

Friday January 14   Ecclesiastes 7:1–13

Wisdom gives life

What are we to make of these short statements? They sound like
a collection of proverbs or folk-wisdom, but they may well have
been specially composed to fit together, to challenge and help the
hearer consider what is most important in life. A key word here is
'vanity', a term for which the book of Ecclesiastes is famous.
'Vanity, vanity, all is vanity' is often quoted (Ecclesiastes 1:2). But

what does it mean? The Hebrew word that is translated in many versions of the Bible as 'vanity' does not necessarily carry the English associations of self-absorption (like someone gazing in a mirror) or pride or futility, but means something like steam or mist. So it is telling us that life is beautiful, but fleeting. People are mortal. Understanding that should help us to value the moments that are important and the things that last.

By contrast, the laughter of fools is like 'the crackling of thorns under a pot' (verse 6) – thorn bushes make a noisy short-lived flame, rather like a discarded Christmas tree on a bonfire. This is nothing like the quiet joy and lasting warmth shared by friends.

A human shortcoming we will all recognise in this passage is the tendency to say, 'Why were the former days better than these?' (verse 10). Have you ever heard this said? Have you ever said it yourself?

What is more important than living in the past? Surely, valuing what God gives us and is teaching us in the present; taking it seriously; recognising sadness and loss, but also being 'patient in spirit.' This, as much as feasting and seeking fun, is a way of living life to the full. Think of ways you already do this, or could do so.

✴ *O God, help us to consider your work*
and to live in your way, with serious joy,
not in a regretful past, or an unreal future,
but in the present, which is your gift to us.

Saturday January 15   Ecclesiastes 9:13 – 10:4

The quiet words of the wise

This afternoon I went to visit Jane, a wise and gentle neighbour, and we sat talking about the blustery winter day outside, and the signs of spring: the beauty of snowdrops, and the miracle of the first lambs being born. We thought these things brought us closer to God – and we talked about people we know and books we have read that do the same. But our conversation also included things going on in the wider world, the headline stories and the pronouncements of politicians. 'We all want to know the truth,' she said, 'But they seem to think we'll believe them if they shout loud enough.' Read verse 17 again!

This passage from Ecclesiastes is a strange mixture. It starts with a story – quite a sad one, for while the poor and wise man was right and saved the city, he was forgotten. Then there are sayings which seem disconnected – although some of us will be interested to discover the source of 'the fly in the ointment' which is a common saying today. The thread that links them all is the idea of folly, which confuses and makes such a mess of our good actions and instincts. Yet the advice is to hold firm – calmness and common sense will prevail in the end.

We live in a beautiful and yet violent world, where much store is placed on military intelligence and where governments act on the belief that they should strike first, in self-defence. As you listen to or read the news today, think what these words from an ancient book mean to us now: 'Wisdom is better than weapons of war' (9:18).

✳ *In a time of silent prayer, confess to God the foolish things you have done this week; pray for the people threatened by the foolishness of world politics; give thanks for the gentle wisdom and compassion, which may yet prevail.*

FOR REFLECTION – alone or with a group

● Who are the individuals that best embody wisdom for you? How can you emulate their wisdom?
● What are the ways that lead to a development of 'the fear of the Lord'?
● How can nations and governments be led in the ways of wisdom, as well as individuals?

FOR ACTION

Pray for your local MP and for the leaders of government. E-mail or write to your MP about an issue that concerns you deeply. Share with him or her words of wisdom that you have found helpful, from whatever source.

WISDOM
3. True wisdom and false

Notes on the New Jerusalem Bible by
Joseph G Donders

Joseph Donders, a Dutch priest of the Society of Missionaries of Africa, is a professor of Mission and Cross-cultural Studies at the Washington Theological Union. He was formerly Head of the Department of Philosophy and Religious Studies Chaplain to the Catholic Students at the State University of Nairobi, Kenya.

True wisdom cannot be false. False wisdom cannot be wise. We can, however, be mistaken about what wisdom really is. It was estimated that our human knowledge was doubling every ten years even before we began to use computers. The scientific progress made since then might make us think that science itself can save us. Yet, looking around in our contemporary world, we are becoming aware that it does not and cannot do that. Our scientific knowledge can be and often is misused. No amount of it totals up to wisdom. Knowledge can be misused. Wisdom cannot.

Sunday January 16   *1 Corinthians 1:18–30*
Compassion, the wisdom of the cross
It is not the suffering of Jesus on the cross as such that is wisdom. The wisdom shown by the cross is something else. It is God's compassion shown in God's Son suffering on that cross. All of us live with the temptation to blame God for God's apparent impassivity as regards the suffering in our world. To many it seems that God – after having created us – just leaves us alone with no regard to humanity's suffering. They deny the Creator's interest in creation.

It is on the cross that Jesus, God's Son, gives us the proof that this is not true. In Jesus, God shares our human lot. The God we believe in is compassionate. In that compassion, Jesus shows not only God's understanding of our suffering but at the same time God's willingness to do something about it. It is here that we find the wisdom of the cross. We have to share in God's compassion when facing the suffering and evil in the world around us. We should be willing to do something about it, at whatever cost. It is the way of the cross, considered foolish by the world.

✴ *O God, let me, let us understand the wisdom of the cross!*

Monday January 17   *1 Corinthians 2:1–13*

Being aware of God's Spirit

Paul writes to the community in Corinth that he intended to do only one thing while being with them. He came to tell them about 'the mystery of God'. Reading his letter makes it clear that he treated that 'mystery of God' not so much in itself, but in relation to the community he addressed. He asks them not to forget that they had experienced the reality of God's Spirit alive in them. Not being aware of the Holy Spirit in our lives does not mean that the Spirit is not in us. It means that we are not living from within, from the divine power that dwells within us. It means that we are alienated, estranged from our root. We begin to prefer merely human blather to wisdom. We get crushed by our technology, strangers to ourselves, imprisoned by our ever growing material needs, frustrated in the depths of our souls.

In a concentration camp in the Netherlands, a young Jewish woman, Etty Hillesum, discovered God's presence in her inner self not long before she died in the concentration camp at Auschwitz. She added, however, that 'a lot of unimportant inner litter and bits and pieces have to be swept out first'.

✴ *Let me 'understand the lavish gifts God has given us'.*

Tuesday January 18   *Romans 1:18–25*

Reading the book of the world

When Paul wrote them his letter, the Christians in Rome were getting into greater and greater difficulties. They could not and did not want to 'worship' the Roman emperor as God. Paul explains not only why those Christians were wise, but also that the emperors and those who believed them to be god were wrong and would end up in disaster. Doing this, Paul explains how we should read the Book of the World. Ever since creation the human mind has been able to read God's presence in the world he writes. He asks his readers to see the invisible through the visible.

A famous American television preacher, the late Bishop Fulton Sheen, used the image of the universe being a windowpane, a stained glass window, through which we see the invisible God. All around us can be seen reminders and symbols of the divine reality. This wisdom is so obvious to Paul that he adds that he does not admit any excuse for those who do not see this. He even uses the word 'stupid'! Such people exchanged the glory of the immortal God for an imitation: a human being, a bird, an animal, gold or something like that. Paul's letter remains a warning to us!

✳ *God, help me to discover you, let me get your message right!*

Wednesday January 19   *James 3:13–17*
Faith that counts

James begins with a simple example of a hungry person and one who badly needs some clothing. The first one needs some food and the second one some protection against the cold. His examples are so simple that the situation is recognisable to any one of us. James' conclusion is simple. If you do not give some food and some clothing to them, what good is your faith in the good news that Jesus brought? It is just stone-dead! No wonder that from the very beginning Jesus' followers started a soup kitchen (in Jerusalem, see Acts 6:1) and a kind of clothing centre (in Joppa, Acts 9:36ff).

Excellent services, which should be rendered everywhere. But are they enough? In our days we have developed types of analysis that help us to understand better the deep causes of poverty in our world. We can do something about providing food and clothing here and there, combating in that way the symptoms of the inequity in our world. But to tackle the causes of that sad situation is really a larger task. It is a political issue! Reconnecting politics to our best faith values is what our faith asks of our political wisdom.

✳ *Dear Lord who fed the crowds, help me to understand that bread and clothing for all are spiritual issues!*

Thursday January 20   *Colossians 1:24 – 2:5*
The on-going struggle

All those of goodwill regret that the human community has not yet been able to muster the wisdom to realise among ourselves the peace promised by the angels at Jesus' birth. We do not sufficiently pay attention to what John noted in his gospel: 'that

Jesus was to die ... to gather into one the scattered children of God' (John 11:52). Though he left us that mission, we have not yet got very far with it. Paul writes to the Colossians that being engaged in that ongoing struggle of gathering humanity in the one body of Christ made him feel joyful, notwithstanding the hardships involved.

Our quest, too, should be for that fulfilment, for that wholeness. Our spirituality should join Christ's, who described himself as a gatherer, a good shepherd. Being Christ-like means taking on that gathering task and being an agent of wholeness like Paul was. This is a wisdom so deep that it is intuited by all those of goodwill. The Hopis, native Indians in America, say that we all began together; that each race went its own way and acquired its own gifts. Now is the time, so they say, for us to return, to put the pieces back together, to make the circle whole.

✳ *Lord Jesus, help me to be engaged in your gathering of God's people.*

Friday January 21   *Psalm 104:24–35*

The wisdom of creation

Praying Psalm 104, in which we praise God whose works are 'made so wisely' (verse 24), can become an uncomfortable experience. We praise God for a sea that is 'teeming with countless creatures' (verse 25) while our way of fishing is emptying the oceans. We pray that God may 'find joy in his creatures' (verse 31), while we are modifying them at our will. We acknowledge that the whole of creation depends on God, while we make it more and more dependent upon ourselves. Some will see these developments as preposterous and maybe even blasphemous. Others see them in a different way.

When praising God for his glorious creation, aren't we praising God for the way we ourselves are created, too? Aren't we equipped with the breath, the spirit our creator blew into us? Didn't we get the task of being God's co-operators? Did Yahweh not give us a task in our world and universe? God did not put us at the end of a process, but at the beginning of it.

Praising God's wisdom implies that we should use the Spirit God gave us. God's wisdom challenges us to be gentle, compassionate, healing, 'gathering' and peace-loving. This is a wisdom that recognises that everything counts and belongs.

✳ *God, send out your Spirit and help us to renew the face of the earth!*

Saturday January 22   Romans 11:33–36
Gifts and giving!
Paul expresses his amazement at the gratuitousness of God's gifts. Creation and our own existence are pure gifts. We did not pay anything for them. Nor were they only one-time gifts. Life and creation are continuous free gifts. Just think of our bodies. The lining of our stomach, our liver, in fact our whole bodily system is again and again rhythmically renewed. And in the final instance, life will prove to be everlasting! Paul admires God's wisdom and know-how in all this.

Jesus not only shows us this divine generosity in his life by giving himself up for us. He also asks us to share in this wisdom and attitude! The word 'give' occurs in the gospels over eighty times! 'Give to anyone who asks you, and if anyone wants to borrow, do not turn away' (Matthew 5:42). 'You received without charge, give without charge' (Matthew 10:8). 'Give, and there will be gifts for you' (Luke 6:38). It is a wisdom that contradicts the growing tendency to let financial profit rule. There is more to life than 'business is business'. All real values like friendship, solidarity and love remain as gifts which are beyond possession or control.

✳ *Dear God, let your Spirit, as shown in Jesus' life, flow through me!*

FOR REFLECTION –alone or with a group
● What is the wisest piece of advice you ever got in your life?
● What is the wisest piece of advice you ever gave in your life?
● What words of wisdom do you want to take from this week to live by?

FOR ACTION
Check out with a friend the wisdom of the way the two of you organise your lives, with regard to your intentions, habits, transport, diet, rest, work and spiritual life. See if you can help one another achieve a better wisdom and balance in your life before God.

READINGS IN MATTHEW

Notes based on the New Revised Standard Version by
Brian Haymes

Brian Haymes is minister at Bloomsbury Central Baptist Church, London. After 16 years in local pastorates, he taught in two English Baptist colleges. He has served as President of the Baptist Union. He is married to Jenny and they have two daughters and two grandchildren.

The community that gave us Matthew's gospel knew how to teach. The writers tell us the story of Jesus but they have ordered the material in such a way that we can focus on important issues, like discipleship, healing, parables of the kingdom and other aspects of Jesus' ministry. Matthew is aware that his teaching about Jesus is given in a world where other people think differently. So he helps us to reflect on the good news of Jesus and how we might live it out in a world of many faiths.

1. Baptism, temptation and calling disciples

From the first, Matthew shows that Jesus does not simply fall out of the sky, unrelated to anything else. Jesus has an important family history that we must recognise if we are to understand what God is doing in his life. And he does not act alone, a kind of religious lone ranger. He calls people to share what God is calling him to be and do. The opening chapters of the gospel are important for both what they tell us about Jesus and what they tell us about being a disciple.

Sunday January 23   *Matthew 1:1–17*
A surprising family tree
Matthew neatly sets out the family record. It begins with Abraham, the one called to seek with God a new country and be a new community. So Jesus is a pure Israelite, one to whom God made great covenant promises. And he is of David's line, royal, again with immense covenant promises. Jesus is introduced as the culmination of all Israel's history and hopes.

But look closely at the names. There's Jacob who was not above swindling. There's Ahab who troubled Israel with his weak leadership. These men are far from being among the good, let alone the great.

Look more closely. Matthew includes five women: Tamar, Rahab, Ruth, the wife of Uriah (Bathsheba) and Mary. Listing women was a very unusual thing to do in such a genealogy. All of these women occur in Israel's history when an unexpected but crucial turn is taken. Matthew is making a point. What do you think it is? Could it be that God is able to use families with dysfunctional members like Jacob and Ahab as well as the supposed socially weak, like Tamar and Ruth, to forward his purposes for all people?

✳ *Faithful God, thank you for never giving up on your promises. Help us to be part of your purposes for all your children.*

Monday January 24   *Matthew 3:1–12*

An urgent message for everybody

John comes striding on stage. In his dress and language he sounds like yesterday but what he says points to tomorrow. God is doing a new thing. You need to be ready. And do not think that because your parents were faithful this challenge does not apply to you. John is part of the promised purpose of God. He cries out his message in the wildernesses of the world. Get ready for God!

John knew that religious people in particular can delude themselves. They assume that such stirring talk is for others. But when John calls for repentance he means everybody, including the leaders. And repentance is serious. It is not simply saying sorry and looking crestfallen but otherwise not changing life at all. John wants to see fruits of repentance in changed lives! Something new is happening in Jesus and he wants people to be ready. All that seeks to stand against the kingdom will meet with fire!

So John has no interest in a personal following. His task is to point to Jesus. There is nothing sentimental about his message. He knows the seriousness of our condition and how only God can bring forth justice. His work is a heady mixture of serious challenge and glorious hope.

✳ *Father, may my life show that I have really turned to you as I try to follow Jesus.*

Identity and identification

Of all the gospel writers, Matthew notices a problem about Jesus being baptised. John has been calling people to baptism for repentance and the sinners were following him into the Jordan. Along comes Jesus. What is he doing here with all these sinners? John holds back from baptising him until Jesus insists. Why?

In his baptism, Jesus is given to know his true identity. The voice from heaven declares him to be God's Son. So in our baptism our identity as children of God is affirmed.

But in his act of baptism Jesus identified himself with us, with all those sinners coming in hope of new beginnings in the work of God. This is the story of his life, that he entered fully into our existence, even our death, for love of us. As Iranaeus, an early church teacher, put it, he became what we are in order that we might become what he is. So we might understand our baptism as an act of identification with him, our hope and salvation.

Today marks the end of the Week of Prayer for Christian Unity. Let us pray that all Christians may live out their baptism and acknowledge one another as brothers and sisters in Christ.

Testing experiences

It is no surprise that after the baptism temptation comes because what is at stake is the question of whether Jesus will live by this identity. All three temptations are made on the basis that he is the Son of God called to live out God's purposes. Will he trust God or not? Will he be someone or something other than God calls him to be?

And so it is for us. Temptation is often trivialised among Christians, as if it is no more than resisting creamy cakes when we are on a diet. But the real thing relates to who or, better, *whose* we are. The world in which we live is full of pressures to have our lives shaped by others, the peer group, advertisers, politicians and so on. Jesus' temptations are the church's temptations and they are strong and demonic. They call us away to live by another story, to follow another lord, to call upon another name. Jesus did not waver from the path of God's calling. He lived out his baptism and, as the writer to the Hebrews understood, because he has been through it he can help us who face the challenge of identity now.

✳ *Lead us not into temptation and deliver us from evil.*

Thursday January 27   *Matthew 4:12–17**
The heart of the message
John the baptiser is removed from the scene. The new thing is about to happen. The stage is set and Jesus is now 'up front and centre'. By picking up on an Old Testament prophecy, Matthew shows the continuity of Jesus with the purposes of God and that the message will be inclusive. It is for the Gentiles too. Already we realise the reign of God is going to be disturbing.

The heart of the message is exactly the same as John's: the kingdom of heaven is near. The message may be the same but the messenger is different. John lived in hope, pointing forward to Jesus. Now Jesus embodies the message. The hoped-for kingdom is appearing, happening, in him. We are not told at this point what the message means. Much of the rest of the gospel will spell that out. What is obvious is that this is the moment of challenge and choice. In Jesus, promise is coming to fulfilment, hopes are realised, and the gracious challenge of God is now.

✳ *Father, bless us with a deeper understanding of your kingdom that we may live wholly within it.*

Friday January 28   *Matthew 4:18–22**
Calling disciples
We ought to note that from the first Jesus called others to be with him, to follow him and become what he would make of them. His way of life in the service of God was not a private enterprise but a partnership and collaboration. He was undoubtedly the leader who calls but his life and work from the first involved relationships.

There are some disturbing aspects about this story. Matthew seems to stress the family nature of the life of the first disciples but that Jesus' call is more significant. Then there is a conflict between what Jesus calls the disciples to and their work, their occupation and income. Moreover, the response looked for is immediate! As the story unfolds we shall see that the kingdom is not here to support family interests but rather that the family must serve the kingdom. And the call of Jesus is not to make us more effective in our jobs but for our work to serve the rule of God. The story is disruptive and disturbing. The call of Jesus does not leave things as they are.

✳ *Loving Lord, you call us to follow you in the adventure of the kingdom. Help us when we are fearful at the challenge and cost of it all.*

Saturday January 29   *Matthew 4:23–25*
A glimpse of the programme
Three verbs jump out from the summary of Jesus' early ministry: teaching, preaching and healing. This is the way the kingdom shows itself:

- as a new way of looking at life that has to be learned;
- as good news to tell, news that might at first be disturbing and challenging but is undoubtedly both new and good;
- as the care and renewal not just of people's spirits but of their bodies, their whole selves.

This is Jesus' programme for his whole ministry. It becomes therefore the guide for the church in its life and work. There is perhaps one major difference. Matthew says that people simply flocked to Jesus. This was particularly true of those who were sick and longed for healing. Did they all grasp what he was about, or were they there for the healing? Who knows? Later, crowds were to call for the death of Jesus and the gospel will end not with people flocking to him but with his disciples being sent everywhere to teach, preach and heal.

✳ *Father, enable your people to follow the way of Jesus as they teach, preach and heal in his name.*

FOR REFLECTION – alone or with a group
● In what way is your identity shaped by your baptism?
● What are the serious temptations faced by Christians today?
● 'Teaching, preaching, healing'. Discuss this summary of Jesus' ministry in the light of the work of the church today.

FOR ACTION
Arrange for a group from your church to visit a neighbouring church of a different denomination to discuss with them the meaning of baptism and discipleship.

2. Teaching on prayer, fasting and faith

Chapters 5–7 in Matthew are commonly known as the Sermon on the Mount. Matthew has brought together some of the teaching of Jesus on matters of discipleship. Jesus has begun his ministry with the announcement that the kingdom of heaven is near. These chapters begin to help us answer the question of what it means to live the life of that kingdom.

Sunday January 30   *Matthew 5:1–12**
The counter-cultural kingdom

What is immediately obvious about these sayings of Jesus is how odd they sound. We do not readily think of those who mourn, the meek or the persecuted as 'blessed'. The folk who have made it in our world seem to be the assertive, the powerful, the self-sufficient and confident. What is going on?

The word 'blessed' could also be translated 'joyful' or 'deeply happy' but the notion of happiness is perhaps not the heart of the matter. The root meaning of 'happy' in our culture is related to 'chance' but the blessedness of the Beatitudes is grounded in the nature and way of God. So, for example, the peacemakers are blessed not because they strike lucky but because they act in godly ways, as children of God. People are blessed in the kingdom because they participate in the purposes of God, as they long to see right prevail, and suffer for the right, as they share the way and life of Jesus. As such, although some of the Beatitudes have a future sense, the kingdom is a present reality in which disciples live. Those who trust the promises of God and follow Jesus are 'blessed'.

✳ *Help us, dear God, to discern what you are doing in the world so that we can share your purposes of blessing for everyone.*

Monday January 31   *Matthew 5:13–20*
The people who really count

Jesus uses two amazing images. He has just been talking about those who will live differently: peacemakers, those who mourn about the world's sorrow and those who are determined to see right prevail. These people live an alternative way. And by so doing, they are salt and light. If we are ever tempted to think that the church is marginal and unimportant for the world, these pictures from Jesus suggest otherwise.

Salt and light transform situations. The small group of Christians flavours the whole world, like salt in a stew. The tiny group of disciples live differently and so become a shining light in dark places. It doesn't mean all the gloom is destroyed but that there is enough light to be a guide.

How is the church to live this way? By keeping all God's ancient laws? Jesus does not write them off but he looks for those who go beyond legalism, beyond the righteousness of Pharisees, with their negative goodness of avoiding evil. It means positively doing good in the alternative way of Jesus, a different kind of righteousness that expresses the will of God as in Jesus.

✴ *Jesus, help us realise the high calling of your people so that we really are your church in the world.*

Tuesday February 1   *Matthew 5:21–48*

Examples of living differently

Jesus gives six examples of the alternative community. He takes up the tradition of the law and invites his followers to think more deeply about these matters. We read them best not as Jesus setting us a new law but illustrating how we might get to the heart of the matter. Simple obedience to the letter may well miss the point and that is crucial because what is at stake here is not getting a high score in an obedience test but the ability to live faithfully in the way of Christ.

Take, for example, what Jesus says about loving your neighbour. It would be possible to define 'neighbour' in such a way that it excludes all those people we do not like. But Jesus calls for love of enemies, even those who make life difficult for us. Why? Because God is like that, sending precious rain on good and bad people alike. If we love only our kind of people we are just like everyone else. We are not like God whose love is for all his children. So the point is, be godly, act in the way and with the heart of God. Imitate God's indiscriminate love to all.

✴ *Loving God, help us to discern your way and to live in it.*

Wednesday February 2   *Matthew 6:1–18*

The real thing

Christianity is not a set of ideas to be discussed. It is also actions to be practised. There are things Christians do because they are

Christians. In this passage three practices are described: alms-giving, prayer and fasting. Of course, Christians are not the only people who undertake these practices. Many in Matthew's congregations would have come to follow Jesus from other religious traditions. What does it mean to give, pray and fast Christianly?

An element Matthew wants to stress is the secrecy of it all. There are ways of acting, even as Christians, that parade religious practice. We want to be seen. It does something for our reputation. Jesus is aware of this temptation and points out that if you want your religious acts to gain you a reputation you have your reward. But then your giving, praying and fasting are not the real thing. You have offered them for yourself. True faith offers gifts, prayer and discipline to God, secretly. It is not about making a name for ourselves. It is honouring God as God. It is not a false deed. It is the real thing because it is an expression of a relationship with God.

✳ *Father, forgive our hypocrisy, and lead us to that secret place where you are honoured alone.*

Thursday February 3   *Matthew 6:19–34*
Money, stress and anxiety
For all our possessions we remain insecure. In consequence, many people live with stress and anxiety that they try to relieve with having more. But crashes happen in stock markets as well as in cars. Thieves succeed in houses and banks, and moths really do not mind how cheap or expensive the clothing is. So we do all we can to protect all we have. Ironically, this does little for our sense of freedom, what with all the alarms we have to fix and the codes we have to remember.

Of course we should be prudent. We have the bills as well as the birds to look at! But where have we set our trust and hearts? Imagine, says Jesus, a world where God always affirms our human worth, our value, and gives the confidence that we are loved wholly and unconditionally, whatever the circumstances. This is the truth but it is obscured by many other demands and our eyes do not always see what is there. But if we trust the God to whom Jesus refers then tomorrow can be left until tomorrow and today can be enjoyed for the gift of the gracious Giver that it is.

✳ *Father God, save us from needless anxiety. Deepen our trust in your loving care.*

Two gates, two ways

We have noticed how following Jesus is often to lead a counter-cultural life. The claims and values of the kingdom are different to those of our society. The church becomes an alternative society, practising the way of Jesus Christ.

Jesus uses a common biblical picture to drive this point home. Before us are two gates, leading to two paths, and we must choose. But why is the way of the kingdom the narrow gate and why is the way to life hard? Here are two possible answers.

First, the life of the kingdom does not happen in a cosy religious place but out in the full claims of life. Trying to be serious about God takes us to those places where choices are hard and costly. It may mean going against the crowd and a hard choice may only be the beginning. Suppose, for example, you did decide to love those whom everyone else thought of as enemies?

Second, the gate is narrow because we are not offered several options but we are called to do God's will. Some possibilities that others may see are not available to us.

✳ *Father, keep us faithful to the vision of your kingdom and bold in our discipleship.*

Going deep to foundations

In many ways, Jesus has been suggesting through the Sermon on the Mount that our danger is superficiality. Religion lived on the surface may impress others. It may even bring us some pleasure. But it is not the real thing. The constant danger is hypocrisy, playing the part.

Bluntly Jesus says that even using the right words, singing the right songs and making the right impression may mislead. People can do all this but not belong to the kingdom. That comes down to practice. The Christian does not only talk about mercy but shows mercy. The real thing always shows itself in life.

The secret of such living is not secret at all. To the hearers and readers of the sermon there comes a final challenge. The wise person hears these words and puts them into practice. They build their lives upon the commands and promises of God. When the storms of life come, these are the ones left standing because their foundations are in God. Of course, readers of the sermon know they will encounter storms if they live this way. But in God their lives will stand because the kingdom stands.

✳ *Gracious God, help us to understand and trust your word that our lives may know and show that you are the foundation of our lives.*

FOR REFLECTION – alone or with a group

● Which of the Beatitudes seems to you to be the most significant and why?

● Prayer, almsgiving and fasting. In what ways are these corporate actions of the whole church and not simply private religious practices?

● How do you think the Sermon on the Mount engages with the stress and anxiety levels of many people today?

FOR ACTION

Prepare a series of dramas where you illustrate the truth of the Beatitudes in everyday life. Talk with your minister about using these in worship or in other ways.

ESTHER

Notes on the Hebrew Bible by
Rachel Montagu

Rachel Montagu is the Assistant Education Officer at the Council of Christians and Jews, and teaches biblical Hebrew at Birkbeck College Faculty of Continuing Education and Allen Hall. She has worked as a congregational rabbi and is particularly interested in women's inter-faith dialogue.

Esther is unlike other biblical books in style; it prefigures later Jewish folk-tales in which villains come to the horrid end they planned for others, foolish kings can be managed for their own and others' good, and Jews succeed in surviving as a minority in the diaspora. The name of God is never mentioned. Intermarriage, usually frowned on in Judaism, here saves the Jews. No wonder that Purim, the festival described in the book, is Judaism's carnival when feasting, drinking, dressing-up and parody rule for a day! Esther's historical truth has been questioned but it undoubtedly contains lessons for us.

Sunday February 6   *Esther 1:1–22*

Honour your husband – or else

After learning how each man at Ahasuerus' magnificent feast had the freedom to drink as he chose, we realise that not everyone was allowed free choice. Vashti was ordered to appear wearing the royal crown so the king could show off her beauty; traditional Jewish commentators explain her refusal as modesty – the crown royal was all she was to wear. Her unwillingness to be stared at by her husband's guests leads the so-called wise men of Ahasuerus' court to decide she must immediately be replaced as queen, lest all women follow her example and assert themselves against their husbands. Ahasuerus does not question this – perhaps because he is too stupid to realise that accepting this advice makes him look foolish, not regal, or perhaps his relationship with Vashti is only a formal one so there is no love to counterbalance his drunken rage at her defiance.

The Hebrew word used for a wife honouring her husband means both costly and precious. This stress on wifely obedience, at whatever personal cost, is reminiscent of Oscar Wilde's phrase: 'people who know the price of everything but the value of nothing'. We learn for the first time that a law once given cannot be altered, which will be important in chapter 8.

✳ *A woman of valour, who can find her? Her husband's heart trusts her and lacks no wealth* (Proverbs 31:10–11). *Eternal One, help us not to exploit those around us in ways that hurt their dignity.*

Monday February 7   *Esther 2:1–23*
Beauty in disguise
Our heroine appears – but does not reveal her identity, as anyone proud to be a Jew would normally do. The Jews must have been completely integrated into Persian society if her Jewishness was not self-evident to those around her. Feminists have questioned whether Esther should be a role-model here since she seems totally subservient to Mordechai, especially compared to Vashti's sense of her own autonomy. The plot thickens – the conspiracy and death of the conspirators show the tensions and treacheries of the court and also make possible the events of chapter 6.

The purification of the women – because they were worth it? Even the most misogynist can't imagine it really takes twelve months of anointing, sweetening and deodorising to fit a woman for the royal presence. This shows the preposterous artifice of the Persian court against which Esther's natural beauty shines. The king loves her for her grace and loving-kindness – these are moral qualities, distinct from the physical attractiveness described in verse 7.

✳ *Blessed are you, our Eternal God, who varies the shapes of created beings* (Jewish blessing to be said when one sees someone of unusual appearance). *A king of flesh and blood stamps his image on a coin, hence all coins look alike; but the King of kings put the stamp on the first man, yet no human is like any other* (From the *Mishnah* – early rabbinic literature). *Let us always be aware that everyone we meet is created in the image of God.*

Tuesday February 8   *Esther 3:1 – 4:17*
Hate one Jew, try to kill them all
This episode prefigures many later campaigns against Jews and other vulnerable minorities. Has Haman's new power gone to his head if genocide is his instinctive response to all the kings' servants

bowing and scraping but one man refusing? How dangerous a stupid ruler can be – Ahasuerus allows Haman to carry out his plan, either because he does not see any moral problem with it or because he is entranced at the idea of a large bribe for his treasury.

At London's Imperial War Museum's exhibition on the Holocaust they include Edmund Burke's aphorism: 'All that is necessary for evil to succeed is that good men do nothing'. Haman exploits the fact that Jews remain a separate group to suggest to the king that there is no benefit in tolerating them. Esther accepts Mordechai's challenge to use her royal role to save her people and asks the Jews to fast in solidarity with her and her maids. It is puzzling that the book never mentions God, nor does Esther here mention prayer as a way to seek God's help, although 9:31 links fasting and 'crying out', the word used in Exodus 2:23 for outcry to God.

✳ *Those who walk righteously speak straightforwardly, rejecting extortionate gains by violence, shaking bribes from their palms ... they shall dwell on high* (Isaiah 33:15–16). *Help us never to lose our awareness of right and wrong when we consider what we should do.*

Wednesday February 9 (Ash Wednesday)   *Esther 5:1 – 6:14*
Pride comes before a fall
Here is Haman's greatest triumph and the beginning of his downfall. Ahasuerus does not reject Esther's approach as she feared. Her modest request – for him and Haman to come to a banquet – is clearly not all she wants, yet when the king that evening again offers her anything she wishes, she asks him to come to another banquet tomorrow. This gives time for Haman to fall into a trap of his own making: the fact that he goes to banquets prepared by the queen's own hand proves his success, but he is too full of rancour at Mordechai to enjoy it. His family and friends suggest that building a gallows for Mordechai will set a happy mood for the next party. He is still so delighted with his own achievements that when the king asks him what to do for the man he delights to honour, he is certain this means himself. So he doesn't stint on the honours to be paid – reminiscent of those paid to Joseph by a grateful pharaoh – which makes it the more galling when he is told to give all that to Mordechai as his reward for saving the king.

✳ *Worship the Eternal with joy, come before God with exultation* (Psalm 100:2). *Help us never to let anger prevent us from enjoying the good in our lives.*

From tragedy to burlesque

At the second banquet Ahasuerus again offers Esther anything she wants and this time she pleads for her life, explaining that she and her people – unnamed – are to be destroyed. Again, Ahasuerus seems a few verses short of a chapter – it means so little to him that he has condemned a whole people to death that he has to ask who has done this. When the king returns from the garden and finds Haman on the queen's bed, it seems that Haman is punished for violating the queen rather than for planning to exterminate a nation. Haman had to give Mordechai the honours he planned for himself. Now he is hanged on the gallows he made for Mordechai, a characteristic biblical example of the punishment fitting the crime – compare Jacob who pretended to be his brother and then was tricked by Laban into marrying Leah not her sister Rachel (Genesis 27–29).

✳ *Look at our grief and defend our cause and redeem us soon for the sake of your name, because you are a powerful redeemer. Blessed are you, Redeemer of Israel.*

Jewish daily liturgy

Light and joy, happiness and honour

Esther and Mordechai are given Haman's property but what they want is to rescue the Jews. Because the law, however wrong, cannot be unmade, the only way to save the Jews is to permit them to defend themselves. The book of Esther is about Jewish life as a minority. Many themes in the book have echoes in later Jewish life and history: ascribing mythic powers to the Jews as Zeresh does when she warns Haman he will lose; a distinct group in society being perceived as automatically a problem. Here, rather than being a minority who live in fear of attack, the Jews are suddenly a source of fear. Later Jewish law forbade conversions for ulterior motives. The thrice-repeated 'they did not touch the spoil' (9:10, 15, 16) proves their only motive was self-defence.

✳ *The Jews had light and joy, happiness and honour, so may it be for us* (Esther 8:16, adapted in the ceremony ending the Jewish sabbath to express the hope that the sabbath's happiness will overflow into the coming week).

Lots to celebrate

In later periods of persecution, Purim (from the Assyrian for stone, the lots which Haman cast, see 3:7) was celebrated by reading Esther, feasting, giving food to friends and money to the poor. It was a reminder that God had intervened to save the Jewish people from destruction. Places where there had been an unexpected reprieve from attack kept the anniversary as a 'small Purim.'

Both in Esther and in Judith in the Apocrypha, rescue came because a Jewish woman was willing to risk her life to make it happen. Hebrew wordplay links Haman the Agagite with Agag (1 Samuel 15) – king of the Amalekite nation which had attempted to destroy the vulnerable Israelites as they left Egypt (Deuteronomy 25:17–18). There is also a linguistic link between the unusually-written letters in the names of Haman's sons and the numbers in the date of Hitler's persecution of the Jews. Thus there is a connection between all these genocides in the Jewish mind. Remembering such tragedies is a strategy to prevent it happening again.

Esther, now more assertive than in chapter 2, takes the lead in writing letters instituting Purim as a festival. The book ends with a vision of peace and good government.

✳ *It is true that you are the Eternal our God and the God of our ancestors, our deliverer and our saviour. Blessed are you who redeems Israel.* *Jewish daily liturgy*

FOR REFLECTION – alone or with a group

● The 'wise men' thought Vashti's disobedience would encourage all women to show contempt for their husbands. How much are we influenced in our behaviour by the behaviour of public figures?

● What can we do to discourage all women being stereotyped as likely to act in one particular way?

● Esther rescued her people by appealing to the king in a very tactful way. How effective are we at thinking out strategies for making sure that we succeed in our aims?

● The book of Esther assumes the need for assertive self-defence in the face of physical attack. How do we decide when violence is justified?

FOR ACTION

Try making the following traditional Purim cakes, *Hamen Taschen* (Haman's ears).

Dough

Flour — 1lb/450g
Caster Sugar — 2 oz/50g
Margarine — 2 oz/50g
Milk — ½ pint/300 ml
Yeast ½ oz/12g
1 egg
Pinch salt

Cream yeast and 1 tsp sugar. Melt margarine in the milk and when lukewarm pour onto the yeast. Pour milk and margarine mixture into the flour and salt. Knead to a smooth dough; cover and leave for 1–2 hours. Then add sugar and beaten egg and knead again.

(For those who find yeast daunting, shortcrust pastry could be used instead.)

Fillings

Poppy-seed

Put 1 teacupful poppy-seeds, ¼ pint (150 ml) water, 2 oz (50g) margarine, 2 oz (50g) each chopped nuts and raisins, 1 tbsp golden syrup and 1 oz (25g) chopped peel in a pan and cook gently until thick.

Prunes

Stone and chop 8 oz (200g) cooked prunes and add grated rind and juice of half a lemon.

Roll out dough ½ inch thick, cut into 4–inch rounds and brush edges with melted margarine or oil. Spread with filling and fold to form three-cornered cakes. Brush top with warm honey, leave in a warm place to rise until doubled in bulk, then bake at 400° F or Gas 5 until golden brown.

From Florence Greenberg's Jewish Cookery Book
(Jewish Chronicle Publications, 1964).

JOHN'S GOSPEL
1. Who is this?

Notes based on the Revised English Bible by
Joy Mead

Joy Mead is a poet and a writer who leads creative writing groups. She is involved in development education and justice and peace work. She is also a member of the Iona Community.

The first three gospels tell the Jesus story – John makes it timeless. This enigmatic guide, poet and trouble to the literal-minded is anxious to liberate his readers, to help them know themselves and the moment, become whole human beings, find their own story to live by. To do this he orders our senses by imaginative use of life-enhancing images, symbols, incantations, encounters, conversations and recognitions. Life – abundant, mysterious, fragile – is the light at the heart of this week's readings. The gospel story is presented not so much as a light to march by as one to dance in. The question, 'Who is this?' can't be answered. It must be lived!

Sunday February 13   *John 1:1–18*
In him was life

These few verses are dense in philosophy, rich in metaphor and clear in rhythm. Essentially, they are poetry. That's how they ask to be read – not as some sort of clue to a theology or, as Luther thought, a superstition to be reasoned away.

So often we have grasped and concentrated on the male 'logos' (reason, word, logic) to the exclusion of the feminine 'wisdom' (poetry, essence, imagination). Verse 18 tells us, 'No one has ever seen God' but you might look at Genesis 16:13 in which Hagar, the outsider, says, 'Have I indeed seen God and still live after that vision?' Wisdom, often the rejected one, exists before word. She is hearing into speech, the light of life, possibilities in poetry and story – sometimes reasoned away by religious institutions and people in power but carried on the margins by people like Hagar.

I think back to a morning on Iona when I stood beside the Abbey in the just-before-dawn dark. The sun came up. Suddenly, the moment and the place were luminous. Dancing light on water and land said it all: not sense or reason – but wonder, and 'grace upon grace' (verse16) appropriate to where we are living now.

✳ May we trust the light that shines out of neglected places.

Monday February 14   *John 1:19–34*

A voice crying in the wilderness

From wonder and space, thresholds and births – the big concepts of the opening poem – we move to ordinary life and local tensions. There is something poetic, and so threatening to authority, about John the Baptist, the wilderness voice. He points us to the one in whom hope, peace, surprise, wonder, anger and imagination are given flesh. That's what the gospel story is – enfleshing and transformation. And it is our story too: the matter of our lives and what matters in our lives. It is not so much a question of 'Who is this?' as 'How can the Jesus story become our story?'

The coming of the Spirit (verse 33) is about insights, dreams, longings – and imagination. The light of imagination has a profound physical effect on us. The quality and quantity of colour depends not only on the source of light but upon the capacity of our human eyes to receive that light, to really see the flower, the butterfly, the smile of a child, the tears of a stranger. Resurrection comes quietly in shining moments when we see into the heart of things and trust in life.

✳ May we use the light of imagination to see into the heart of things.

Tuesday February 15   *John 1:35–51*

I saw you under the fig tree

The Jesus of John's gospel is something of an enigmatic stranger, but there's very little that's other-worldly about him. The down-to-earth Jesus who confronts Nathanael – a worthy Israelite acting out Micah 4:4 ('Each man will sit under his own vine or his own fig tree, with none to cause alarm') – is a man who sees with his own eyes. He is pushy, and self-assured. He harangues, organises, pulls rank. Knowing Jesus and the way of peace his story offers is about engaging with the world compassionately – a process that begins (under the fig tree maybe!) with understanding ourselves.

Nathanael is called out from his personal peace under the fig tree to a wide world where people laugh and celebrate, weep and mourn together. There's a lot to be done before everyone can sit under his or her own fig tree in peace! Becoming a whole human being means recognising at a deep level that spiritual and material are inseparable. The angels of verse 51 make this connection. The ordinary physical parts of our lives are, after all, the only area for the expression of holiness.

✴ *May the light we carry within us show us where the action is.*

Wednesday February 16   John 2:1–12
You have kept the best wine till now

Flowing wine is a familiar image in Greek and Jewish stories. Amos prophesied a time when 'The mountains will run with fresh wine, and every hill will flow with it' (Amos 9:13) and there are many popular Greek stories about gods causing local streams to run with wine on festival days. Like these stories, the story of the wedding at Cana celebrates life in all its fullness: life in eating and drinking, meeting and lovemaking. It's about awakening to the mystery and wonder of ordinary life – just taste and see! Suddenly the time has come (verse 7). It all happens with a sense of beautiful spontaneous awakening. Now is the time of our lives!

This is a huge story! Asking idle questions such as, 'Was the water really turned into wine?' is to miss the point utterly. The story isn't about what happened, nor why it happened. It's about the laughing Christ and what his happening does to you. That's the question that flows through the good wine. Suddenly ordinary things, ordinary people who love their neighbours, are filled with love of life. That's what matters – that we can love. That is the light that shines in the darkness and will not be put out.

✴ *May we be surprised by the energy and miracle of everyday life.*

Thursday February 17   John 2:13–25
He made a whip of cords

Only in John's gospel is Jesus armed with a whip. And John also sets this episode – another story about the time being now – at the beginning of his gospel rather than near the end, as the Synoptics do. He has a point to make, he makes it early and he makes it with emphasis.

The 'cleansing' is a decisive threshold moment. A choice has to be made and the Jesus who makes it is angry at the misuse of people, resources and sacred space. His anger, like that of most people angry at injustice, is creative and compassionate.

Lino Pontebon is a young Philippino artist. His painting 'The Angry Christ' (which can be found in USPG and CMS's study pack,

The Christ We Share) was inspired by this story from John's gospel, and reflects the anger of his own people who have been manipulated by forces beyond their control. It's impossible to get away from the accusing eyes in the picture and the finger points like a sudden beam of light at those nice people who oppress and become wealthy on the backs of poor people. The Angry Christ points at the people in church who go on being nice while people die, suffer, are exploited, suffer racism, sexism, abuse, domestic violence, unfair trade, slavery – and more. Compassionate people do not make docile citizens. They are not nice!

✳ *May the light of creative anger awaken and enliven us.*

Friday February 18   *John 3:1–21*

The wind blows where it wills

The Nicodemus story is about one man's inability to allow his heart to be touched. No one can reach the community of God by obeying the rules alone, or by thought and reason. A born-again human being is one who weeps over evil, rejoices in goodness, loves outrageously and carries the pain and the joy of the world in healing hands and loving heart.

Jesus can't tell Nicodemus how to be 'born again'. It's not enough to study truths, they must be felt on the heart. This story is possibly the one that most lucidly turns the opening poem (in John 1:1–18) into narrative as abstracts become enfleshed in the encounter between Nicodemus and Jesus. It's about the difference between understanding a good life as obeying a set of laws and seeing it as a way of being.

Nicodemus needs the truth of the imagination. He can talk about life but its essence and mystery elude him. He is frightened of the unlimited validity of the imagination; frightened to push back the boundaries of the possible and re-dream the world. He isn't open to the moment and can't feel the answer to his own question blowing in the wind. He goes out into the darkness.

✳ *May the wind of change and the light of eternity surprise us to new birth.*

Saturday February 19   *John 3:22–36*

So measureless is God's gift of the Spirit

These few verses tell of an interesting threshold point. Jesus and John are baptising in a specific place where living water flows freely – imagery which takes us back to the wedding at Cana, as does the debate about water jars and purification (in verse 25). We are not told the reason for the debate but this gospel writer enjoys connections and knows what he's doing. If we accept that the Jesus he shows us bears witness to abundant life, that will say something about our images of God and take us into areas more universal than religious disputes. I think of Martha's confession later on in this gospel (11:27) when she speaks of 'the Son of God who was to come into the world'– a world full of struggle and suffering but also one where the light of life is given, sustained and handed on.

These verses make an affirmation about the Christ that is in Jesus, and in all people. They affirm the light and life of all things as one in mystery and wonder. This is nothing Nicodemus could learn in the law books but something he must receive from the measureless gift of the Spirit. So 'Who is this?' remains a question for all time.

✳ *May poetry like the light of a candle enable us to live with questions.*

FOR REFLECTION – alone or in a group

● John's gospel offers more questions than answers. Think about the struggle and the value of living with uncertainty, with questions that cannot be answered.

● Also think about the questions to which it's important to demand answers (the cleansing of the temple was a question).

● Think about pictures of Jesus you know or have seen. Many of them look like someone who turned wine into water rather than the other way around. Look for new and exciting images.

FOR ACTION

● Discover your own story to live by for yourself – in your own words and language.

● Read or listen to other people's stories (perhaps from asylum-seekers or refugees).

● Read *A Story to Live By* by Kathy Galloway (SPCK, London, 1999).

● Be angry at injustice wherever you see it.

● Support the Trade Justice Movement. Find out more from: tradejusticemovement.org.uk or Christian Aid, PO Box 100, London SE1 7RT. Telephone: 020 7523 2225.

JOHN'S GOSPEL
2. Signs and teaching

Notes based on the New Revised Standard Version by
Jesse N K Mugambi

Jesse N K Mugambi is Professor of Philosophy and Religious Studies at the University of Nairobi, Kenya. He is an Anglican lay scholar and prolific author. The list of some of his books may be accessed at www.action.co.ke.

The gospel of John is full of symbolism. Almost every word in the text carries much more than its ordinary meaning. For this reason, this book is perhaps the most 'theological' and the most 'philosophical' of all the gospels. In chapters 4 and 5 we encounter five words which are heavily loaded: water, well, baptism, life, death. We shall be exploring each of these words throughout the coming week and seeking to discern their deeper meaning for our own lives.

Sunday February 20   *John 4:1–15*
Ordinary water and the water of life
Jesus stops at the well of Jacob at Sychar in Samaria, where he finds an unnamed Samaritan woman fetching water. He asks the woman for water to drink. The woman is surprised, because it is not a normal custom for a man – a stranger – to ask a woman for water to drink. This request of Jesus opens up a conversation which is as revealing as it is challenging. The woman expresses surprise at the audacity of Jesus in starting a conversation with her. If Jesus had been a fellow Samaritan, perhaps the woman might have reacted differently. But Jesus makes the situation more intriguing by indicating that he has access to the 'water of life', in contrast with ordinary water drawn from Jacob's well. The woman becomes very interested in this 'commodity', and asks Jesus to give it to her, so that she may never thirst again. Quite clearly, Jesus and the woman are at different levels of understanding. In the end, Jesus reveals himself as someone who knows the background of the woman, even though the two have not previously met. The woman is so excited that she runs to the town announcing that she has met a 'prophet'. As a result of her testimony, many people believe in Jesus and become his

followers. Despite her negative public profile, she becomes a witness to the greatness of Jesus.

There is a close relationship between ordinary water and the water of life. Ordinary water will sustain our physical bodies. Symbolically, 'ordinary water' refers to the food and beverages that we must consume to ensure our biological survival. When Jesus talks of the 'water of life', he is referring to the inner disposition of the person and the sources of their spiritual life. Today, we are challenged to live beyond mere biological survival, towards eternity. Empathy is one of the virtues consistent with this challenge. Jesus did not sympathise with the woman. He empathised with her. There is too much sympathy and pity in the world today. The wealthy want to patronise the poor and give donations. But the greater challenge is to feel with those who suffer, and to rejoice with them whenever there is something to celebrate. The way of eternal life demands of us to hope with those who hope, and to mourn with those who mourn. At a time when the powerful are becoming ever more powerful and the wealthy ever more wealthy, it is difficult to come to terms with this challenge of empathy. But Jesus demands nothing less.

✳ *May God help you and me to seek after the 'water of life' which will drive us beyond sympathy and pity towards empathy and companionship.*

Monday February 21   *John 4:16–29*

The borderless community of believers

Yesterday we reflected on the distinction between ordinary water and the water of life. Today we focus on another distinction which Jesus makes in his conversation with the Samaritan woman at Sychar. The woman seeks to know from Jesus why there should be tension and conflict between believers in the same God, just because some worship at Bethel and others in Jerusalem. In his response, Jesus contrasts the imperfect present with the perfect future. The days are coming, Jesus says, when the places where we worship will become irrelevant – when the true worshippers shall worship God 'in Spirit and truth'. In this response, Jesus expresses a subtle criticism of the 'holier than thou' attitude of both communities, with their focal points at Bethel and Jerusalem respectively.

This text is also very challenging. Denominationalism has become a new form of 'tribalism' across the world. Christians boast about the worthiness of their respective denominations, as if in heaven believers will be 'housed' according to their denominational affiliation. Jesus demands of all of us to shed our denominational exclusiveness and to appreciate all people as manifestations of divine presence in the world. The text further challenges us to go beyond Christian egoism to appreciate and respect people of other faiths, other races, other nationalities, other professions, other social classes, other generations, and so on.

The text informs us that even the disciples of Jesus found it odd that he should be talking with the Samaritan woman at the well. In their view, Jesus is much too important to do that. But Jesus lived out his teaching through exemplary living. Today, many of us find it easier to live by the principle 'Do as I say, not as I do'. In practice, such teaching is not leadership; it is bossiness. Effective leaders are those who practise what they direct others to do. Lamentably, bossiness rather than true leadership has become the order of the day in our world. Jesus offers to us a better way of relating with one another — exemplary living in which we admit our weaknesses at the same time as sharing with others our strengths. Ideally, Christians should become the pioneers in the establishment of this borderless community across the whole world.

✳ *May God help us to become exemplary peacemakers, following the teaching and the example of Jesus.*

Tuesday February 22   *John 4:30–45*
Ordinary food and spiritual food
In this text Jesus makes yet another distinction – between 'ordinary food' and 'spiritual food'. The disciples bring to Jesus the food they have purchased, but he responds that he has 'other food' about which they do not know. 'My food', Jesus says, 'is to do the will of him who sent me, and to accomplish his work.' Here Jesus is contrasting the preoccupation of his disciples with normal, mundane concerns at the expense of the most important mandate – to proclaim the good news. Several years ago, a senior priest brought to my attention the distinction that we ought to make between urgent priorities, and important priorities. Too often, when we make our lists of priorities, we tend to choose according to the criterion of urgency, rather than that of importance. Jesus challenges us first to learn to determine those concerns that are important and those that are urgent. According to Jesus, the disciples got their priorities wrong. It was the

unnamed woman, whom Jesus met at the well, who got her priorities right.

What does it mean to set our priorities according to the criterion of importance rather than that of urgency? We each have to answer that question for ourselves. I share the view that too much emphasis is placed on power and profit, at the expense of human relations and human welfare. The global economy is designed to benefit the large corporations at the expense of individuals and communities. This policy is based on the principle that the large corporations are the largest tax-payers. The more profits they make, the more taxes they pay to the state. Economic growth is thus calculated according to macro-economic indicators, not according to the qualitative impact of large corporations on individuals and local communities. This 'ordinary food' approach tends to result in greater misery for the majority of consumers and greater opulence for the minority of directors and shareholders. Jesus challenges us to think more qualitatively and less quantitatively. To do the will of God means to take the most vulnerable communities as the starting point in policy formulation. We are a long way from the achievement of this ideal, but we must make the first steps in that direction. Jesus shows us the way with humility and integrity.

✳ *Dear God, show me what is really important and help me not to live my life dictated by the urgent.*

Wednesday February 23   *John 4:46–54*
Seeing and believing
Here we have yet another distinction – this time between 'seeing' and 'believing'. A senior unnamed official hears that Jesus is coming to Cana. He is aware that several months previously, Jesus had turned water into wine in the same village. The official has a son who is very seriously ill – on the verge of death. The official comes to Jesus to plead with him to perform a miracle for his son. He is not primarily interested in the good news that Jesus proclaims. His concern is mundane and urgent. Jesus can see this disposition in the official, even before they begin a conversation. So Jesus remarks, 'Unless you see signs and wonders you will not believe.' We are not told the tone in which Jesus made this remark. Apparently, the observation was a statement of the official's attitude at the time. The official replies that his immediate concern is for Jesus to heal his dying son. Jesus perceives that the official has faith, and in response,

declares that the official may go home, because the son has been healed. This is dramatic. Since the official has not come to listen to the teachings of Jesus, in return Jesus does not demand of him to stay. He has come to plead with Jesus for healing. Jesus grants the plea and allows the official to go home. On his return journey, the official meets his servants, coming to report that the child is well again, so there is no longer any need to bother Jesus. But it turns out that the son was healed at the moment when Jesus declared that the plea was granted.

In this story it is clear that believing takes precedence over seeing. The official believed that Jesus could heal, which is why he hurried to Cana to meet Jesus and plead with him. Seeing and believing are related, but believing takes precedence. When Jesus performed the first miracle, the official may not have been a believer. Thereafter, he was converted. In the second instance, when the official had his own need, he believed before he approached Jesus.

The Christian faith is sustained by believers, not by researchers compiling empirical evidence. Although empirical evidence is important, it cannot be the basis of sustainable faith. May God help us to take belief seriously, even when we do not have exhaustive empirical evidence to support doctrinal claims. Let us be like the unnamed official and believe that Jesus can heal, even before Jesus performs the miracle. God will act on our behalf, even before we ask.

✷ *Let us not be weary of praying. Without prayer our wishes and our actions cannot resonate. With prayer, our thoughts and our expectations drive us towards the hopes that kindle within us.*

Thursday February 24   *John 5:1–18*

Healing and working on the sabbath

In this text Jesus makes another subtle clarification concerning the sabbath. According to the Pharisees, all work was forbidden on the sabbath – even carrying a mat. The story is about an invalid who has been lying on his mat for thirty-eight years, waiting for some benefactor to extend a hand of support so that he might have a chance to be healed. Without immersing the invalid into the therapeutic pool, Jesus declares him healed, and tells him to take his mat and walk home. But the leaders rebuke the former cripple for carrying a mat on the sabbath! At the Temple, they ask the former cripple to disclose the name of the person who healed him. But he does not know the name of Jesus. When he was healed, the healer did not introduce himself. So he tells the leaders that he does not know the name of his healer. All he cares about is that he was ill for four decades, and has been healed. The leaders mount a campaign against Jesus, despite his works of healing.

This text reminds us that doing good works takes precedence over keeping the sabbath. It is hypocritical to neglect the things that must be done, under the pretext that it is forbidden to work on the sabbath. It is not right for anyone to suffer for any period, if anyone can prevent it. Those who would prolong suffering while claiming to be devout followers of divine law are guilty of abusing their religiosity.

There is much suffering in our world. At the same time, there is much piety. If piety prevents us from doing works of compassion, then it is like salt that has lost its saltiness (Matthew 5:13). It is of no use either to the pious or to those that observe that piety.

✳ *May God help us to do works of compassion as a priority over laws and regulations that govern denominational piety.*

Friday February 25   *John 5:19–29*

Son of man and son of God

Another distinction that Jesus makes is that between the son of man and the son of God. These two phrases have been a puzzle in Christian theology. The writer of the gospel helps us to appreciate the relationship between them. We cannot grasp the meaning of the phrase 'son of God' unless we are able to appreciate the relationship of God with the world. The works of compassion performed by Jesus are means through which we are invited to discern God's dealings with the world. Thus Jesus is 'son of God' not in the biological sense of 'son-hood', but in the sense of proclaiming divine intervention in the world. Likewise, the title of Jesus as 'son of Man' does not refer to a biological relationship but to his commitment to make right whatever is wrong in the world. These insights are corroborated and supported by other teachings in the synoptic gospels.

The way in which these profound concepts are explained in this text is remarkable. In a few sentences the reader is invited to reflect deeply upon God's expectation of us in this world. Piety and lofty theologising may make us feel good about ourselves, but such self-centred preoccupations are not enough to bring us closer to God. Rather, our commitment to making the world more humane, more just and more amicable – these are the means by which we experience divine presence within ourselves and in the world around us.

✳ *May God help us to appreciate the relationship between God and the world which has been brought into being by Jesus Christ.*

Saturday February 26   *John 5:30–47*

The testimony of scripture and the authority of Jesus

Today we consider the contrast made by Jesus between the testimony of scripture and his own authority. Jesus challenges his opponents who place more emphasis on the scriptures than on his own ministry. He observes that John the Baptist preceded him in the proclamation of God's word, but many people rejected John despite the profundity of his message. At the same time, the pious ones claimed to base their piety on the law of Moses, yet they did not keep that law faithfully. For us today, the challenge of Jesus is that we should be more concerned with doing the will of God than talking endlessly about it. Christian mission according to this challenge is not about telling others what Jesus said and did; rather, it is about showing what difference it makes to live according to Christ's teaching.

Paul's letter to the Corinthians helps us to appreciate this challenge. Faith, hope and love are important, and the greatest of these three ethical values is love. But what does love mean in practice? 'Love is patient and kind; love is not jealous or rude. Love does not insist on its own way; it is not irritable or resentful; it does not rejoice at wrong, but rejoices in the right. Love bears all things, believes all things, hopes all things, endures all things. Love never ends ... So faith, hope and love abide; but the greatest of these is love' (1 Corinthians 13: 4–13).

Jesus demonstrates this new way in his public ministry. His total commitment to empathy with the vulnerable sectors of the population has become a standard by which Christian discipleship is to be measured. Not everyone who says, 'Lord, Lord', will enter the kingdom of heaven, but only those who do what the gospel requires of them.

✳ *May God help us to work daily towards the goals that Jesus has set before us.*

FOR REFLECTION – alone or with a group

● What does it mean to you to live 'beyond mere biological survival, towards eternity'?
● What does it mean to be a 'borderless' Christian community?
● If you attempted to live according to important rather than urgent priorities, what would that mean?
● How would you describe love in action?

FOR ACTION

Find a way to share both the spiritual water of life and real water with one other or some others this week.

JOHN'S GOSPEL
3. The Bread and the Light

Notes based on the New Revised Standard Version by
Rosemary Wass

Rosemary Wass is a former vice-president of the British Methodist Conference. She is a farming partner and wife to Howard and mother of two children. Rosemary is a local preacher and has been an area president for the World Federation of Methodist Women and national president of the Women's Network of the Methodist Church.

John shares with us extra precious information about the life and ministry of Jesus. When he became a disciple of Jesus, he was a very young man. He became an apostle of an infant church and he had the good fortune to live a long life. His reflective thoughts are like a conversation. It is fascinating in this week's Bible passages to see how closely the accounts are tied to the cherished Jewish festivals. This aids us as readers, who can become almost 'witnesses' of the events, to understand something of their context.

Sunday February 27   *John 6:1–21*
Wholeness of life

In this full passage we see several important elements of life: health, food, people responding to one another. The people have heard about the miraculous healings performed by Jesus. They make a detour to try and see this man who has made a huge impression on people. They meet with Jesus and are taught by him.

Miraculously, they are also fed, with the most basic of bread – barley bread, the food of the poor – and fish. The response of the people is the growing recognition that here is their long-awaited 'king'. Jesus disappears in order to avoid this kind of acclamation. He rejects their crown. Is he perhaps overwhelmed by the people's response?

Jesus returns in the evening to his disciples, demonstrating that he is always available to those who follow him closely. He comes in an unexpected and unforgettable way. In a dark storm, he brings light to those desperate disciples, restoring a sense of wellbeing. Their response to him is obvious.

*✳ Thank you for always being available to us. Forgive us when
our expectations of you are blinkered by your reputation.
Give us open minds to see you in all your greatness. Help
us to share the signs of your love for us with others.*

Monday February 28   *John 6:22–40*

Looking backwards and forwards

I remember visiting a park the day after the Pope had addressed
thousands of people there. The place was deserted except for the
litter and those whose job it was to clean it up! The search is on
for Jesus. Yesterday he had 'free' bread – would there be more
today? No. Jesus has moved on. The people have labelled him
from his activities of the previous day. Their curiosity has been
aroused. Their persistence is rewarded.

They find Jesus – and he has them summed up before they
have been with him for long. He tries to redirect their thinking
beyond the immediate. He has won their interest with physical food
– the next course is spiritual food. His mention of the 'Son of Man'
may be a reminder of his baptism (John 1:32) but it also looks
forward to self-offering on the cross and the glory that it will bring.

When we are baffled, we search our experience to find
something that may be helpful in explaining the puzzling
phenomenon. These people knew the scriptures. They would
have heard the story many times of Moses in the wilderness
(Exodus 16). They were therefore enabled to make links between
the bread of Jesus and the manna given to Moses. The bold
statement 'I am the bread of life' (verse 35) is exciting to some of
his hearers, but for others it brings tension. This is beyond their
experience. Nevertheless, here is a source of food that will
continually give life to the world.

*✳ Thank you, Lord, for pushing the boundaries of our faith
beyond our understanding. Help us to share your bread with
others as they ask questions and search for the meaning of
life.*

Tuesday March 1   *John 6:41–71*

Tension and testing

The Jews were getting uneasy about Jesus. These leaders
thought of him as the son of the carpenter and nothing more.
They did not like what they were hearing. Claims of being

something more were intolerable, yet Jesus substantiated his claims by referring to evidence from the scriptures.

Parts of this passage are like hearing a different language! It is hard to believe and to understand. Jesus speaks variously of bread, life, descent from heaven, manna, belief, eternal life and death. All are important in this passage. Without belief, the rest cannot have any significance.

The tension was mounting. The time was coming when people would have to decide how much they could believe. There was much to discuss. How did Jesus feel at this time? Did he have a sense of failure at his attempt to share his credentials? Jesus knew that the real initiative lies with God. That must have been comforting to him.

The Jewish leaders misunderstood the teaching about 'bread' and 'body'. This is not about a 'free lunch'. It is about living bread for the life of the world.

The difference between those present is clear. The fringe followers had even less belief than most of the disciples. They found Jesus' teaching hard to accept. Jesus speaks directly to all of them. The decision is theirs.

✴ *When I feel out of my depth, give me enough faith to wait for a sign from you.*

Wednesday March 2   *John 7:1–24*

Tradition and testimony

The time of the Feast of Tabernacles is here, marking the end of the fruit harvest. After all the work, there is time for a week-long celebration (Leviticus 23:42–43). This is the time of remembering the wilderness experience of the Israelites. The brothers of Jesus urge him to use this opportunity for more signs to the people. They believe he is capable even if they do not have personal faith. Jesus' following has waned since the great feeding of the crowd. It is as though Jesus asked too much of them too soon. Jesus knows it is too dangerous. He is a hunted man. He goes to the celebrations later, but it is impossible for him to remain incognito.

Jesus teaches in the temple. His hearers are amazed. They still see him as the son of the carpenter. They cannot believe the quality of what they are hearing. Jesus leaves them in no doubt where his authority originates. Jesus uses Mosaic law to defend his own action of healing on the Sabbath. It is clear that there is a group looking for an opportunity to trap him and remove him from the scene.

✳ *Forgive us when we avoid the truth in order to be popular. Grant us courage to tell of your love and care for each one of us every day of our lives.*

Thursday March 3   *John 7:25–52*
Daring to ask questions

Who is this man? A healer, a feeder, a wonderful man? A deceiver, a prophet, a teacher, the Messiah or a man who should be arrested? All these descriptions lie within this chapter of John. There is little wonder that there is confusion, consternation and other strong emotions around.

How can he know these things? The Jerusalemites thought they knew him, but now they find he has knowledge beyond their expectations of him. Admiration changes to suspicion. The Messiah does not come from Galilee, does he? According to tradition, the Messiah would simply appear. Jesus' human origin is apparent but not his true origin in God, and whose authority he bears.

So you also have been led astray? (verse 47) – the Pharisees weigh in with mocking tones. The tension is mounting and 'arrest' is on people's lips. The temple police are reluctant. Our law does not judge people without first giving them a hearing, does it? (verse 51) – Nicodemus reminds the authorities of their own law. He is there on Jesus' behalf to see justice done.

Through all the questions, Jesus threads the promise of life-giving water – a foretaste of the Holy Spirit, using the analogy of the water being poured at the festival.

✳ *Lord, let us not lose sight of your promises to us as we live within the framework of society. When we ask questions, remind us to look for the less obvious answers.*

Friday March 4 (Women's World Day of Prayer)   *John 7:53 – 8:20*
Light of the world

The account of the woman caught in adultery is an addition included after the rest of the gospel was written. It is a powerful addition that emphasises once again the double standards of the day. The scene is set in the temple. The scribes and Pharisees bring a woman to Jesus. She is to be used by them to try and trap

Jesus. She is powerless. Again comes the question of upholding the law. But Jesus traps his prey by turning the tables and changing the focus (8:7). The woman is left alone and Jesus, deeply compassionate, releases her. On this Women's World Day of Prayer we remember women who have been abused and used as tools by others.

8:12 takes us back to the feast and Jesus continues his teaching. Just as in yesterday's passage, when he reminded people of a more powerful force of water than the one in the pool, so now he uses the image of light. In the courtyard of the temple, there would have been four golden candlesticks, giving light to everyone there. He takes this image to impart the truth of his own identity and function: 'I am the light of the world' (verse 12). This was a startling revelation for his hearers.

✳ *We pray for those who are abused in our society. We thank you for the images through which we are able to see another facet of the life of Jesus. We pray that we may share light and be bread for those we meet.*

Saturday March 5   *John 8:21–47*

Testing times

Jesus has used the things of every day to tell who he is and what it is he offers: bread, water, light. His next lesson is to tell the people of his departure. Still there is only literal hearing by the Jews. The chasm is wide between belief and unbelief, and the consequences are spelt out by Jesus. Still, the Jews hark back to their scriptures but cannot see in these very scriptures the clues to what is happening in their midst and the gift they are being offered. Jesus has tried to move them on but they refuse his invitation.

We need to remember the signs given to us by Jesus who is with us through every stage of our pilgrimage. He offers us bread and food for the journey, drink and the water of life, and light every step of the way. This is a gift to be treasured and shared, and it is to be found in relationship to the one who is source of all life and sustenance.

✳ *Loving God, for all you have revealed to us through your Son, we thank you.*
For all you have helped us to face in our life, we thank you.
For the promise of your presence with us, we praise you.

FOR REFLECTION – alone or with a group

- How much does tradition obscure the real message of bread and light today?
- For whom are bread and light good news today?
- Where do you need sustenance and guidance in your own walk with God?

FOR ACTION

Reflect on the question, 'How do I share bread and light outside the church from now on?' And decide on the first step you will take today.

JOHN'S GOSPEL
4. The world's life

Notes based on the New Revised Standard Version by
Simon Oxley

Simon Oxley works for the World Council of Churches in Geneva, Switzerland, with responsibility for Education and Ecumenical Formation. This has given him an opportunity for involvement with Christian communities and educational institutions in many parts of the world. He is a Baptist from Great Britain.

As we read the passages set for this week, it may seem all too obvious what Jesus was doing in the world and who he was. We may wonder why it was that some people not only failed to understand but felt threatened by Jesus. We should be more concerned about our own inability to see what is going on. These passages point to Jesus' power to bring light and life.

Sunday March 6   *John 8:48–59*
Dealing with difference

How do we deal with people who challenge our certainties, who make us feel fearful? Is it in the way Jesus' religious opponents dealt with him? They marginalised him by suggesting that he was a Samaritan – not one of us, coming from the wrong place. They demonised him by implying that he was possessed – not simply that he was suffering from a mental illness but that he was inherently evil. When they found that they could not dismiss him, they resorted to violence – the ultimate in self-defeating reactions.

In many countries today, asylum seekers, economic migrants and illegal immigrants experience a similar reaction. They are regarded as alien, the bringers of evil to society. To our shame, such reactions can come wrapped in a Christian guise, even though they are not at all Christ-like.

We can avoid the discomfort in our faith that difference can bring by imagining a Jesus who is too much like us. But Jesus' glory is God's glory (verse 54). Jesus' religious opponents were right to be disturbed by him, though wrong in their reaction. The question for us is how we respond to the God who challenges our stereotypes and religious preconceptions.

✻ *Help us, Lord, not to be so comfortable in our lifestyle and beliefs that we fear or fail to find you in those who are different.*

Monday March 7   *John 9:1–22**

Seeing in the light

If we do not eat the right food, if we abuse our bodies by smoking or taking drugs or if we have a sedentary lifestyle, our physical and mental health will suffer. Those of us in the privileged position of having choices in our lifestyle find this a hard lesson to learn. We know that there is a link between our behaviour and our health. However, the reverse is not true. Every disease or disability is not a consequence of sin. Jesus made it clear that the man in this passage was not blind because of sin. However, Jesus was also not claiming that the man was born blind just so that a miracle could happen later in his life. The God we discover in Jesus does not play tricks with our lives.

Jesus brings light into the world so that all that prevents humanity from living that quality of life God intends for us is revealed. He helps us to see for ourselves. The tragedy was and is that it is religious people who sometimes obscure the light.

✻ *Pray that our ministry of healing in the churches may not be judgemental but may be open and compassionate.*

Tuesday March 8   *John 9:23–41**

Seeing the reality

We should always be grateful for those who are brave enough to expose ethical or financial wrongdoing in commerce and government. They can be said to be shining light in dark places.

We rightly proclaim that Jesus opens God's love to everyone. At the same time we should recognise that he does not take an 'anything goes' attitude. The work of Jesus in the world is described (verse 39) as judgement or division. When the light of Jesus shines, we can see things as they really are. That is if we do not close our eyes or only see what we have already decided to see. Jesus does not need to pass judgement on us for we pass it on ourselves by the way in which we respond.

There is a conflict in the passage between rigid dogma and actual experience. It is easy to criticise those whose religious outlook prevents them from seeing the obvious. But what do we do when we see the light of Christ shining into dark places? Perhaps our witness would be more effective if, in addition to nice words, we could point to the results of radically transformed communities and changed lives.

✳ *Shine in our darkness, Lord, so that we may see and act.*

Wednesday March 9   *John 10:1–21*

What kind of leader?

One of the frustrations of working in the World Council of Churches is that some in key leadership positions do not pass on information from and to their churches. People in these positions are often called 'gatekeepers' as they can open or close opportunities of sharing knowledge and resources. This gives them a certain kind of power. It is tempting to see Jesus as a model of the good gatekeeper. As the good shepherd who is himself the gate, Jesus offers a totally different model of leadership to those often adopted in the churches and society. He does not send his 'sheep' out but leads from the front. He does not just take reasonable precautions for their safety but protects them himself.

Career advancement in industry, commerce, education, politics and even the church seems to work on the principle that moving into more senior positions of leadership means moving further way from active engagement – from the shop floor, the chalk face, the local congregation to a more distant office. We see political leaders on every continent who, from their positions of comfort and safety, pursue policies which put their own people and others at risk.

Gatekeepers, gates, shepherds – there is no escaping Jesus' own example of committed and sacrificial leadership.

✳ *Think of the leaders in your church, local community and nation and pray for them.*

Thursday March 10   *John 10:22–42*

Work it out

When I was at school I preferred maths textbooks that had the answers in the back. After doing an exercise, it was reassuring to check to see whether I was right. Sometimes, of course, I cheated by finding out the answer first. As someone whose work is now concerned with education, I realise that we learn very little by being given the right answer. The important thing is to know how to work things out for yourself rather than knowing some right answers.

The request to Jesus for an answer was not made out of genuine interest but in order to find an excuse to condemn him. However, Jesus' response should make us stop and think every time we want to take the short-cut of being given the right answer. Jesus tells them to look at the evidence and work it out for themselves.

Faith in Christ can never be pre-packaged and handed out as the right answer to everything in life. Our educational activities for children, young people and adults, for church members and ministers should help us work it out for ourselves. This means that our faith will be first-hand rather than second-hand. And, if we want the others to believe, our Christian life must provide evidence for them to work it out too.

✳ *In the Bible and in our living, help me to see the evidence and believe.*

Friday March 11   John 11:1–27

Life and death

We can describe many things as 'life and death' issues, for example HIV/AIDS, inter-communal violence, global warming, economic globalisation – and you will think of others. Faith, particularly in the west, is often described as a personal matter and not a matter of greater concern. The readings for today and tomorrow take us quite literally to life and death.

The raising of Lazarus is a unique story, not recorded in the other gospels and unlike the accounts of healing in John. Death was not problematic for Jesus and he made no effort to rush to Bethany to save Lazarus. Death was problematic for the disciples, not least because they had to risk their lives on the journey. Martha, in spite of the death of her brother, had seen enough of Jesus to acknowledge him as the one through whom resurrection comes.

Does this mean that we ought not to worry about life and death issues, such as those mentioned earlier, because living or dying is relatively unimportant for believers? We ought not to be in denial about death. It is a fact of life for all of us. However, neither should we be fatalistic about life. Jesus comes as the life-giver, even in the most hopeless-seeming situations. His is the voice which calls us all to life.

✳ *Pray for those who live with the threat of bereavement and death.*

Death and life

Those of us brought up with a scientific approach to life may feel uncomfortable that we cannot give a detailed and logical explanation of the raising of Lazarus. However, John's gospel does not expect us to try and account for what happened but to understand what it means.

For Martha and Mary, the desolation of bereavement, which was initially shared by Jesus, was transformed by the emergence of Lazarus from the tomb. Some onlookers believed the evidence of their eyes and came to faith in Jesus. Some opportunists, however, ran to the authorities to report him. For Caiaphas, this event threatened the very existence of the people of God and everything about his faith he held dear. For Jesus, bringing a dead man to life finally sealed his own death warrant.

This was an event in Jesus' ministry which changed everything. Jesus was now seen as the one who had power over death. For some it was good news but for others it was frightening. We are comfortable with the familiar in faith and in living. The kind of change that the gospel brings – turning the world upside down, bringing life from death – has the potential to alarm us as well as excite us.

✴ *May we not be afraid to be alive in Christ.*

FOR REFLECTION – alone or with a group

● Where have you found signs of God's presence and love in unexpected places and people?

● How do our religious traditions blind us to the needs and opportunities in the life of the world?

● How can faith help us overcome our fear of living and of dying?

FOR ACTION

Ask people who are not members of your church, or even Christian, to tell you how they see the church and individual Christians. Then reflect with others on your findings. What kind of communities and people should we be to offer evidence for belief?

JOHN'S GOSPEL
5. Jesus' farewell

Notes based on the New Revised Standard Version by
Jane Ella P Montenegro

*Jane Ella P Montenegro is a Christian Education worker of the
United Church of Christ in the Philippines. She is involved in
ecumenical empowerment programmes with and among women,
youth and children in rural and urban poor communities. Her
studies in Asian feminist spirituality have helped her in the writing
and editing of materials for the National Council of Churches in
the Philippines and Asian grassroots church women. She is a
member of the Asian Women's Resource Centre for Culture and
Theology.*

The accounts and sayings of Jesus' farewell discourses come to
us this Lent with new revelations. They shake us and touch us in
different ways. Our faith in God, Jesus Christ and the Holy Spirit
is broadly affirmed and deepened. I pray that these reflections
may nurture us to discern further the works of the Spirit in us, so
that we may become more truthful, more courageous, more
loving, more just and humble – this very day, in Jesus' name!

Sunday March 13   *John 12:1–19*
Fragrance and compassion
Rare orchids and white fragrant flowers adorned the casket of a
once beautiful and kind mother. A young nephew remarked,
'What a waste!' The daughter retorted, 'Surely at death, we want
to speak of the beauty of our mother's soul through the flowers.'

With a woman's ways of knowing and doing, Mary silently yet
bravely prepared the disciples and Jesus himself for his
impending death. Let the Master enjoy the fragrance of pure nard
while he could still smell it rather than waiting until he is wrapped
in linens. For this precious teacher would be arrested by the
temple priests at any time. Then Mary's heart would grieve
deeply. The joy of Lazarus' coming back to life was swiftly fading
away. She would miss Jesus' language that warmed her soul and
loving acts that touched her heart.

Only a light, weightless person – without negative energies as
Jesus was – could ride on a colt. He was simply overflowing with

compassion, humility and peace. So, while the people thronged about him and blessed him, the priests were angered and horrified that such a man had turned these feast days upside down.

✳ *O God, help us to respond to Jesus in a new way now at this perplexing time of our church and our country.*

Monday March 14 John 12:20–50
Children of light

A couple nurtured their children in the love of God and respect for others. But when they came to Manila, their lifestyle changed drastically. Each of them had to work for a living: laundering, carpentry, selling goods, taking care of the sick – anything, just to survive. They were also attracted by the hustle and bustle of city life: buying what's on sale, cell phone texting, movie watching and gambling. They forgot their family prayers. They became too busy. Their new language was rough and often confusing.

In the midst of poverty, ignorance, and materialism, Jesus' words came back to them again. Through the words of the preacher on the street corner they heard him say: 'Anyone who follows me will never walk in the dark, but will live his life in the light! So be a child of light wherever you are.' The preacher added, 'Let your children become the children of light beginning today!'

The couple began to look at themselves and at their own marital relationship. For indeed infidelity and hardheartedness had forced them apart. They resolved to start anew! First, they needed to forgive each other, then they returned to the family farm to take care of their ageing parents. Hopefully, they could still become the children of light, and pass on this treasure to their children, and to their children's children.

✳ *We seek your light in the darkness, O God.*

Tuesday March 15 John 13:1–30
Loving service

A bishop once attended an island conference and was led by the hosts to a special table set with flowers, silverware and napkins. He then proceeded to greet the other workers and simple folks who were cooking under the trees. 'Could I taste some of the food?' An enamel plate was filled promptly with slices of roasted and stewed seafood. Everyone felt pleased that the bishop was interested in their welfare. Eating with their bare hands, he was just like them.

This was not a normal practice. Indeed, Bishop Genotiva broke rules of decorum. He told the host that it would be better if all tables were simply set alike, with no special privileges accorded him.

By his action, Jesus brought honour to a task that may have been looked down on as menial in his culture. He had often seen women and servants washing the feet of men and their masters. This simple but needful task was to be done by the teacher-leader himself. To serve the other is to bend one's knees, lower one's body, bow one's head and remove the dirt of one's sister or brother. It is to treat the other human being with honour, respect and great attention, affirming their specialness.

✳ *O God, grant me the humility to live out Jesus' example and his command of loving service to others.*

Wednesday March 16   John 13:31 – 14:14

Greater works

The political machinations among church leaders, the abusive behaviour and immoral conduct of pastors and priests with young people and with women, the secrecy of financial procedures, the greed and deception amongst church leaders – all these signs of contemporary church life show only too clearly believers' failure to follow Jesus' commandment to love one another. Thank God, these are not the only characteristics of church life!

A son prepared his dying father to face Jesus. He said, 'Jesus will meet you on the road. He will lead you to a peaceful house where you will meet other loved ones. Don't be afraid! Jesus has promised to bring his followers home to God.' Soon the father died and the son dreamt of him. In his dream the father spoke to him, 'Son, what you said is really true!' He repeated this saying three times, looking peacefully into the distance.

I believe Jesus' promise is true because the father who died was my own grandfather. I also believe that Jesus expected his followers to do greater works than he did, as his time for working was short. There are hundreds of unknown healers and nurturers and simple folks in the hinterlands, sea coast and urban poor areas who offer their giftedness and their last cup of rice so that the sick may be healed, the children may learn to read and a nursing mother may taste good porridge.

✳ *O God, teach us to trust Jesus' words and live them.*

Thursday March 17   *John 14:15–31*

A home within us

Rosita's faith is deeply rooted. Her grandmother taught her to worship and revere God. Her farmer mother nurtured her to love and obey Jesus. Rosita only made it through the primary school. How could one poor woman, a tiller of the soil with a mechanic husband, afford to put two children through college? But Rosita is not bitter. 'All is provided by God's providence,' Rosita says.

Rosita may have had limited schooling, but she has learned other wisdom. Her whole being is attuned to the movements and sounds of creation. She knows the stage of growth when the young, sweet grains of rice become prey to certain kinds of insects. Sometimes at midnight her body senses the destructive swarm of insects on their way to the crop. From afar, she can hear their flapping wings and droning sounds. Fearlessly, she takes out her gas lamp and stick and, with exorcising prayers and clucking tongue, she wards off the rice-destroyers. If she were to be late by even a few minutes, the insects would have grazed bare the three hectares of rice in less than an hour. And so on bended knees, she cries out: 'With your protection, God, we have won again! Thank you for making a home within my life, within my family. Thank you for being here, the Holy Spirit who guides and teaches me everything that I need for life.'

✳ *May our love for Jesus make us humble and fearless, O God.*

Friday March 18   *John 15:1–25*

Becoming friends

When the church council reached an impasse on a decision regarding an erring church worker, Rosita, the only elder without any professional background, stood up. 'Let us follow Jesus' words in John 15 and remember that whoever does not abide in him is thrown away like a branch.' During difficult and shameful times, she pleaded for the council and the church staff to fast and pray, earnestly seeking God's direction.

There was relief when the disciplinary action was finally meted out. The young person who had done wrong gradually came back to participate in the church's ministry. New faces came to worship. Fresh leadership began to blossom. The healing and the reconciliation process were only possible when each one owned up to his or her responsibility and penitently asked God to forgive their communal sin.

Only as a result of this painful episode did the council members become friends among themselves. They spent more time together sharing each other's burdens and joys than had ever happened previously. Young and old, peasants and teachers, students and out-of-school youth prayed together and sought a way forward. They discovered in their own experience something of what Jesus meant when he told his disciples that he no longer wished to be in a master-servant relationship to them, but that he wanted them to be his friends.

✳ *Help me, O God, to take the risk of becoming your friend.*

Saturday March 19   *John 15:26 – 16:15*

Being right

Many who claim they are Jesus' followers are actually misleading others. A farmer holds on to a life-long eldership in church since he was one of the early pioneers in that particular church community; he refuses to follow the guidelines of the constitution which say that elders should step down after so many years. A doctor of theology gets incensed when his title is inadvertently omitted either in writing or when he is introduced at a church meeting. A deacon who is also a businessman hounds his debtors for his monthly ten per cent interest repayments right after the church service.

Jesus would probably tell them today, 'You have sinned because you do not believe in me.' The Spirit of truth most likely would say, 'You have made yourselves lords of your own lives, hence you cannot worship God nor believe in Jesus Christ.'

For the Christian, the ability to know what is right is rooted in a deep and on-going relationship with God. We cannot rest on the laurels of a past relationship. For Jesus himself, righteousness meant being intimately connected to the Father and to the Spirit of truth. For the disciples, it meant loving Jesus, believing in his Father, becoming friends with each other and trusting in the Spirit. Only in such interconnectedness and strong bonding could they ever become brave and stay confident in the face of the inevitable conflict that was to come.

✳ *Forgive us, O God, when we claim to be right yet lack the righteousness of Jesus and the Spirit of truth.*

FOR REFLECTION – alone or with a group

- What other examples can you think of from your own context of those who anoint Jesus with fragrant nard?
- Where do you see Jesus washing the feet of those who are dirty and tired in your own community?
- Can you cite 'greater works' that the women and youth in your church do today?
- What would be the signs of God in Jesus Christ 'having a home' within our lives today?

FOR ACTION

Individually or as a group, seek this week to be a child and children of light. Perform some loving service to a marginalised person, family or group in your neighbourhood.

JOHN'S GOSPEL
6. Suffering and death

Notes based on the New Revised Standard Version by
Sam Peedikayil Mathew

Sam Peedikayil Mathew has been a teacher of the New Testament for 16 years. He serves as Associate Professor and Head of the Department of New Testament at Gurukul Lutheran Theological College and Research Institute, Chennai, South India. At the time of writing, he had recently edited Gurukul Daily Devotion – 2003.

Every year during Passion Week we meditate on the suffering and death of Christ on the cross. When the suffering and death of Jesus are seen through Jesus' words and through the eyes of those who responded to the crucifixion of Jesus, we are able to gain new insights for Christian life. The meditations during this week focus on the significance of the suffering and death of Jesus for Christian life. The first two reflections draw attention to the inevitability of suffering and perseverance in the midst of suffering. The remaining five illumine the meaning of Christian suffering, drawing insights from the suffering of Jesus and the response to that suffering.

Sunday March 20   *John 16:16–33*
Without suffering there is no joy

Jesus' words in verse 16, 'A little while, and you will no longer see me, and again a little while, and you will see me', confused the disciples. When they sought the meaning of these words, Jesus made it clear that they referred to his 'going to the Father' (verse 28), which is an indirect reference to his death. Surely, Jesus' suffering and death will lead to weeping and lamenting. Although the disciples will be sorrowful at the suffering of Jesus, their sorrow will turn into joy (verse 20) at the resurrection. This experience of the disciples is compared to the excruciating labour pains of a woman in travail, whose pain will be turned to joy when she delivers a child. The disciples will rejoice when Jesus comes again and sees them. Jesus has already promised them that he will go and send another comforter, the Holy Spirit (John 16:7–8), who will continue the work of Christ. All these factors point to the inevitability of suffering and death for Jesus and consequent pain and suffering for the disciples. But the promise of Christ is that unfailing joy may accompany suffering. It is this hope of joy that gives strength to suffer.

It is the law of nature that something beautiful is created through suffering. A pearl oyster produces a pearl through suffering and pain. There can be no joy without suffering.

✳ *Lord, when we go through suffering help us to be reminded of the fact that there can be no joy without suffering.*

Monday March 21   *John 17:1–26*

Perseverance in the midst of suffering

In his prayer for the disciples, Jesus prays that they may be preserved in this world. The disciples are hated by the world since they are not of the world. Jesus is not praying to take the disciples out of the world that hates them and persecutes them. This is not a prayer for avoiding suffering, but for enduring it. It does not advocate selfish escapism, but a commitment to costly involvement. Jesus prays that the disciples may be kept in this world and that they may be guarded from evil. This implies that the disciples will have to undergo pain, suffering and even death.

Jesus' call to discipleship emphasised denying oneself, taking up one's cross and following him (Mark 8:34). Suffering is an integral part of Christian life. It is noteworthy that in John's gospel the hour of glorification is the hour of crucifixion. The life, death and resurrection of Jesus are the motivating factors for accepting suffering. Since Jesus has overcome the world (John 16:33), the disciples can undergo suffering joyfully. Thus facing suffering, rejection, and even death voluntarily and boldly, following the path of Jesus for the sake of the gospel can be embraced willingly. God's guidance and guarding are assured for the Christian in this endeavour.

✳ *Gracious Lord, grant us grace to show perseverance in the midst of suffering.*

Tuesday March 22   *John 18:1–18**

Suffering in following Jesus

When the chief priests and the Pharisees came with the soldiers to arrest Jesus, he willingly allowed them to seize him. But Peter did not want Jesus to be arrested. He reacted violently and cut off the ear of the High Priest's slave. This is because he neither wanted his master to suffer nor accepted suffering for himself.

This is evident in his denial of Jesus before a maid at the court of the High Priest (verses 15–18) and again before a slave of the High Priest (verses 25–27). Peter denied that he was a disciple of Jesus in order to avoid suffering with Jesus for the cause of the gospel. In contrast to this attitude, Jesus embraced suffering willingly and voluntarily and made no attempt to escape from it. Jesus wanted his disciples to accept suffering and made it clear that it was the will of God that he should suffer, since it was part of his mission. In fact, he made it mandatory for all those who wanted to be his disciples to take up their own cross and follow him. The path that the disciple of Jesus must travel is the same way of the cross Jesus travelled.

✴ *Loving Lord, help us to order our lives remembering the fact that suffering is an integral part of following you.*

Wednesday March 23   *John 18:19–40**

Suffering for truth

The trial of Jesus before Annas, the father-in-law of the High Priest Caiaphas, is noteworthy for a number of reasons. Jesus was questioned about his disciples and his teaching. In his reply, Jesus pointed to the openness in his mission; whatever he taught he did it openly before all in public places (verse 20). He boldly resisted and protested against being struck without any reason (verse 23). He claimed that his hearers were the best judges of his teaching (verse 21). When the Roman governor Pilate interrogated Jesus about his kingship, he replied that his mission was to bear witness to the truth (verse 37). This mission of bearing witness to the truth was done with openness and boldness, convincing the listeners.

Thus, the suffering that Jesus undertook was for the sake of truth. In fact, Jesus claimed to be the embodiment of truth when he declared, 'I am the truth' (John 14:6). Jesus referred to his teaching as embodying truth. He said, 'If you continue in my word ... you will know the truth, and the truth will make you free' (John 8:31–32). Unfortunately Pilate could not understand this because he philosophised truth and asked, 'What is truth?'

✴ *Lord, enable us to suffer for the sake of truth, as you showed us how to do in your life.*

Power and suffering

After having scourged Jesus, Pilate started questioning Jesus again. When Jesus stopped replying to Pilate's questions, Pilate asserted his own powers in an effort to coerce Jesus into responding. He told Jesus that he had full power over Jesus – to release him or to crucify him. Jesus answered that Pilate's power was given to him from above. Although Pilate did not want to crucify Jesus, finally due to pressure from the Jews, he handed him over to be crucified.

In contrast to Pilate, Jesus chose to use his power to serve others through his healing ministry. It is this choice that led him to suffering and the cross. Whereas Pilate chose to inflict suffering on Jesus to maintain his power and position, Jesus opted to serve others and suffer for others. Jesus declared that the purpose of his coming was 'not to be served but to serve, and to give his life a ransom for many' (Mark 10:45).

Jesus' attitude to power challenges us to examine the way we use our power. To be a true disciple of Jesus involves using one's power for the service of others and accepting the suffering that accompanies it.

✳ *Loving Lord, we thank you for using your power to serve others. Enable us to follow you in our use of power entrusted to us.*

Friday March 25 (Good Friday)   *John 19:17–30**

Participating in the suffering of others

At the site of the crucifixion of Jesus we find two kinds of responses to Jesus' suffering and death. The soldiers who crucified Jesus divided his garments among themselves and cast lots for his tunic. They wanted to take material benefit from the suffering of Jesus. Their aim was to make profit out of the suffering and death of Jesus. In contrast to the soldiers, we find four women and the disciple whom Jesus loved standing by the cross, empathising with Jesus. They risked their lives and shared the sorrow and pain of Jesus, thereby participating in the suffering of Jesus. Their motive for standing at the foot of the cross was not material benefit or profit. Out of sheer love and concern for the suffering and dying Jesus they remained with him and sought to support and comfort him. They proved to be the true disciples of Jesus by following him even to the cross, partaking in his suffering.

The true response that the suffering and death of Christ evokes is the willingness to share the burden of others and to participate in their sufferings in order to alleviate their pain. On this Good Friday, let us be reminded of this response.

✳ *Lord, grant us the grace to participate in the suffering of others and prove to be your true disciples.*

Saturday March 26   *John 19:31–42**

Courage in the midst of suffering and death

After the death of Jesus on the cross, two influential people showed exceptional courage in taking the initiative to give Jesus a fitting burial according to Jewish customs. It is noteworthy that the suffering and death of Jesus effected a radical change in the lives of Joseph of Arimathea and Nicodemus, who were earlier timid, secret disciples of Jesus. Now both of them no longer hid their allegiance to Jesus but declared it openly. Joseph displayed extraordinary boldness in requesting from Pilate the body of Jesus for burial and providing a new tomb for the burial. Nicodemus, a leader of the Jews who had come to Jesus by night (verse 39; see 3:1–2), brought enough linen and spices for a royal burial of Jesus.

The bold actions of these disciples of Jesus stand out in the passion narrative in John's gospel. The suffering and death of Jesus on the cross enabled them to overcome their cowardice and fear. Finally they proved in public that they were true disciples of Christ.

In fact, no one can remain a secret disciple of Jesus, precisely because one has to follow Jesus in public as well as in private life. The cross beckons every follower of Jesus to identify fearlessly with the cause of Jesus and stand boldly for the values of the kingdom of God, which Jesus came to establish.

✳ *Gracious Lord, help us to identify with you and your cause courageously even in the midst of suffering and death.*

FOR REFLECTION – alone or with a group

● What do you think are the reasons for the tendency to avoid suffering for the sake of the gospel?

- Think of different ways in which your power can be used for serving others. What do you think are the consequences of such an exercise of power?
- What are the various ways in which you can actively participate in the suffering of others?

FOR ACTION

Where are you most aware of Christ suffering in the lives of others at this time? Decide what you will do to offer Christ solidarity and support through participating in the suffering of these, his brothers and sisters.

EASTER FOR ALL
1. Hurry, everyone – he is risen!

Notes on the New Revised Standard Version by
Barbara Calvert

Barbara Calvert is a Methodist local preacher who came to Paisley, Scotland, in 2001. She taught RE in secondary schools in Gloucestershire and Herefordshire for ten years, then worked for Christian Aid as area co-ordinator for the three counties of Gloucester, Hereford and Worcester, during which time she visited Israel/Palestine, Uganda, Haiti and Jamaica. While living in Paisley, she became chaplain to international students in the three universities in Glasgow, where she is also completing her MTh in Practical Theology at Glasgow University. Locally, she works to raise the awareness of justice and peace issues in the church and community.

I read this saying on a poster on a friend's wall: 'God give me patience, but please hurry'. The readings for Easter week express this sentiment the other way round. For the most part they are stories of hurrying. But they contain within them the pause which enables the resurrection to be experienced. The hurrying to the scene or with the news is a natural response. But the reception of the resurrection involves a patient reflection.

Sunday March 27 (Easter Day)   *John 20:2–6**
Action in stillness
Early in the morning, Mary Magdalene sees the empty tomb. She runs to tell Simon Peter and the other disciple. The two disciples set off for the tomb at a run, the other disciple out-running Simon Peter. It is easy to imagine them arriving at the tomb panting and out of breath.

Today, like Mary and the two disciples on that first Easter Day, many Christians throughout the world will have risen early. Others will have been keeping vigil all night. At dawn some may gather for worship out of doors, perhaps meeting together on a hill to witness the sunrise. Imagine yourself hurrying up a hill, arriving at the top panting and out of breath but anxious not to miss the awe-inspiring moment as the sun rises on Easter Day. If we don't hurry we will miss the moment. But equally we will miss the moment if we don't then stop and gaze. In perfect silence the sun rises. The moment is in the stillness.

So stop hurrying for a moment now. Be still, stand with the disciples in the empty tomb and gaze at the 'linen wrappings lying there'. For it is not in the hurrying response of Mary and the disciples that God's energy and power are revealed. They are revealed in the absolute stillness of the linen wrappings.

✳ *God, help me to find you in the stillness of your activity.*

Monday March 28   *John 20:11–18**
Presence in the ordinary
One Monday morning, I was at home on my own when the telephone rang. It was a woman from our church who wanted to speak to the minister; so I asked if I could take a message. She told me that yesterday afternoon her husband had passed away so she would like the minister to call about the funeral. Had I heard her correctly? She had just telephoned to announce her husband had died a few hours earlier and her action and words were so calm and matter-of-fact that I almost missed what she was telling me. But how do you relate matters of life and death?

The few verses of today's reading in John's gospel relate the news of Christ's resurrection. This astounding news is revealed not with trumpet and fanfare but through Mary Magdalene's calm, ordinary and dignified actions. She weeps, she bends over, she looks, she speaks, she turns round, she turns again, she sees a man she mistakes for the gardener. The extraordinary is almost obscured in the ordinary.

In the simple ordinary actions of our daily lives we too are called to witness to the extraordinary, to the presence of the risen Christ in our midst.

✳ *God, help me to find your presence in the ordinary.*

Tuesday March 29   *2 Kings 4:25–37*
No short cuts
This is another story where the truth is revealed in quiet simplicity in contrast to frantic human activity.

Following the death of her son, the woman saddled her donkey and told her servant to 'Urge the animal on' (verse 24). She is hurrying to Elisha when he sees her from afar. Elisha tells his servant Gehazi to run and meet her. The woman grabs

Elisha's feet and pours out her distress. Instead of going to the son immediately himself, Elisha attempts a short-cut. Elisha gives Gehazi his staff, instructing him to go and lay it on the boy to revive him. But it doesn't work! Only when Elisha gives the living warmth of his own body to the boy is the boy's life restored.

In our own spiritual journeys, we find that there are no short-cuts to the life that God wants to give us. When we feel that we are being invited to do something with God, it won't work if we try to send someone or something else. Like Elisha, we have to give of our whole selves. When we do, then we feel God's life-giving warmth, flowing through us, and we open our eyes upon God.

✳ *God, help me to avoid the short-cut and give myself to you.*

Wednesday March 30   *Luke 15:11–24*
Impulsive action
Once I spent a weekend retreat with a group doing the Myers Briggs personality tests. First the tests determined who were the extroverts and who were the introverts amongst us. A simple task we were given soon suggested the accuracy of the tests. The extroverts rushed off impulsively to start the activity, while the introverts quietly thought it through first.

Maybe the prodigal son was an extrovert! His actions were certainly impulsive. He takes his father's money, leaves home, squanders the money and soon finds himself living in squalor. But then he acts on an impulse again. He decides to return to his father. And how does his father react? Impulsively! The father rushes out to greet him even before the son has confessed his wrongdoing.

As we learned on our weekend retreat, it is neither right nor wrong to be an impulsive person or a reflective person. Particular circumstances often require reflective, thoughtful, prayerful action, but sometimes impulsive action is what is needed. Impulsive actions result in the prodigal son's downfall, but his forgiveness also comes about as a result of impulsive love.

✳ *God, bless my impulsive actions that they may be signs of your grace.*

Thursday March 31   *Romans 10:11–13*
Love in action
In a spirit of pessimism, it can sometimes seem that the Christian faith has spent the last 2000 years denying the truth of these

verses! Paul clearly states here that 'the same Lord is Lord of all' (verse 12) and yet frequently the church has acted against whole communities of people. In an attempt to justify slavery, it was argued that black people did not have souls – no question of them 'being saved' then. Women likewise were inferior, but in a spirit of generosity, it was suggested that women could possibly be saved, but only through the faith of their husbands! And what about people of other faiths, how could they possibly be saved?

It would be wrong to simply spiritualise Paul's words. Generous love is love that gives life to all. The injustices of poverty, oppression and prejudice are life-denying and it is scandalous that so many people, in our modern world, are denied even a chance for life.

2000 years ago Paul recognised the necessity of extending the gospel beyond Judaism. What does Paul's message of God's overwhelming love for all mean for us today?

* *God, may our lives reflect your overwhelming love for all.*

Friday April 1   *John 21:1–8*

Action for justice

This has always been one of my favourite Bible stories – the disciples seeking solace in fishing, a cold and disappointing night followed by the warmth of the rising sun, a fantastic catch of fish and then Jesus on the beach cooking breakfast. What could be better? But besides being a great resurrection story this passage suggests many other things to us.

It suggests that Christ appears to people as they go about their secular activities. It suggests that Christ cares about our daily lives. Jesus could have just appeared on the beach, which would have been amazing enough for the disciples. But Jesus is concerned about the disciples' disappointing night's fishing, and allows them to experience the joy of pulling in full nets.

Today, the greed of the 'high tech' factory fishing industry is denying many traditional fisherfolk the joy of hauling in nets of fish for feeding their families. The seas are being emptied of fish through the use of sonar soundings and nets half a mile wide. We too must act to show our concern for the daily lives of those who struggle for survival. Through the Trade Justice campaign, supported by organisations such as Christian Aid, we can act so that all might enjoy the fruits of the earth and the seas.

* *God, may your justice flow through all my actions.*

Prepared for action

A couple of years ago we spent Easter week on holiday in Andalusia. On the journey there, my husband broke his collar-bone, so, rather than travelling around as we had intended, we stayed put for a week in a lovely village in the mountains. The village was small and we, with one arm in a sling, were rather conspicuous. People soon came to recognise us and we came to recognise them, especially the village pharmacist who lived next door, whom we had cause to call on once or twice. We would pass him in the street and smile and exchange greetings. By the end of the week we had observed that his pharmacy was not officially open for many hours each day, but that he was there and ready to offer his services whenever needed. He did not rush around or engage in frantic activity trying to convince himself and others of his own importance, but he was a quiet, reassuring presence in the village ready for action when required. Ever since then, whenever we have found ourselves engaged in frantic but not always necessary activity, we have said to one another: 'Remember the pharmacist'!

For each of us, our calling to follow the risen Christ will be different. Peter's call to follow Christ would end in martyrdom. The calling of the beloved disciple was to witness to the truth of what is written in John's gospel. Twice Jesus says in this passage, 'What is that to you?' Our role is to be ready for whatever response Christ requires of us.

✳ ***God, lead us to act in response to the call of the risen Christ.***

FOR REFLECTION – alone or with a group

● How do you discern when it is the moment for stillness and when the moment for urgent action?

● Do you consider yourself a reflective person or an impulsive person? What do you learn from this week's readings about the importance of both characteristics?

● Who has exemplified for you the love and availability of Christ, as the pharmacist did for me? Who or what do you need to 'remember' when you are tempted to become too frantic?

● What action towards justice are you being challenged to engage in this Easter?

FOR ACTION

Practise stillness in action this week by stopping at many moments to attend to the presence of God in your everyday activities and in the people you meet. Use some of the stillness and waiting to pray for others.

EASTER FOR ALL
2. Women with Easter tidings

Notes on the New Revised Standard Version by
Gaynor Harper

Gaynor Harper is an Anglican lay spiritual director, living and working in the Gloucestershire countryside. Firmly rooted in her lifelong tradition of Anglicanism, she has for over 20 years been involved in women's creative liturgy groups that explore faith on the margins of the mainstream.

Last year, one of my closest women friends died. I have been shocked and disturbed by the depth of my grief. She was a woman of great faith: humble, strong, kind and holy, someone who radiated the joy of love through her very being. This week we will read about women whose actions or message enshrine aspects of the Easter news. In the different biblical passages, I detect clearly the qualities shown by my friend. As we grow up in our faith, we are each called, gently and compassionately, to become more like these women.

Sunday April 3 Luke 24:1–11
Look for the living

I am an Associate of a contemplative Anglican community in Wales. The women in this reading remind me of the sisters there. In my busy life, rushing around, they prompt me to stop and pray, and then to get on with the important tasks. The women taking the spices to the tomb were simply getting on with a loving task. They didn't know how they were going to roll away the heavy stone guarding the tomb, and yet they went anyway in faith that what will be will be.

The sisters at the convent I go to are always busy getting on with the practical day-to-day activities of keeping a large community going, looking after the more elderly sisters, gardening, preparing food, farming, looking after guests, seeing spiritual directees, washing up, managing the library and so on. And throughout the day, from early in the morning, they stop, pray, listen to the Bible, take the Eucharist and keep silence. This is dedicated hard work in which prayer and action are woven together. Like the women in today's passage, they are exactly where they need to be.

As I move through my life, I want to try to be more like them, staying put and praying, getting on with simple practical tasks, and not searching always for more exciting places to be. Can I live like this? Can we live like this? There are so many opportunities to travel, to explore, to taste and see. But if we stay still with what is around us, we may become aware of the angel's voice. There is something deep and true about carrying on performing the simple rituals that bring us close to God and give us great inner peace.

✳ *God, help us to hold on to what we know to be true, and to seek you among the living.*

Monday April 4   *Exodus 1:15–17*

Fear God?

Whose are the voices we listen to? Powerful people who tell us what to do? Those who threaten, or bully, or cajole? Or the quiet voice, which is sometimes drowned out in the clamour of our lives?

The Hebrew midwives would surely have been afraid not to do what the king wanted, but they were more afraid of doing wrong by God. Their brave and daring act of defying the king's ruling changed the course of history for the Jewish people. They remind us that some actions can bring about unimagined repercussions.

Rosa Parks is known as the 'mother of the civil rights movement'. In 1955, in segregated Montgomery, Alabama, she sparked the Montgomery bus boycott by refusing to give up her bus seat to a white passenger. A year later, as a result of this brave act, the Supreme Court ruled that segregation on buses was illegal.

The Hebrew midwives, in spite of their fear, were able to do the right thing. As a consequence, the baby Moses, who would grow up to lead his people out of enslavement and oppression, was allowed to live. Who knows what consequences your right action today may have in the future? Small acts of defiance can set in motion enormous change.

✳ *God, help us to listen to our innermost voice and be guided to take right actions from a place of calm, reflective prayer. We pray for the courage to stand up for what we believe in, and to meet oppression with strong, non-violent dignity.*

A gentle and quiet spirit

This reading, to a feminist, seems to say two things: one challenging, the other liberating. The first reaction I have to the passage is to be reminded how different the world is today from the one in which these words were written. If the husbands do not believe the word they may be won over without words by the behaviour of their wives. Perhaps a more modern interpretation would be to suggest to all of us the need to respect the integrity of our life partners and close friends. The command is to be pure and reverent. Dignified spirituality, maybe, rather than arguing a point.

But there is a second point. We all age. Women especially are under pressure to look perfect, to be thin, adorned, gorgeous, and yet here we have a call to the unfading beauty of a gentle and quiet spirit. What a relief! It's okay not to keep up with the latest fads and fashions – not to be 'beautiful' as the world regards beauty, all plastic surgery, expensive clothes and immaculate make-up – but to cultivate inner beauty. I welcome hearing in our holy scriptures that women have a special part to play in helping all humanity to develop this inner spiritual beauty. God values a gentle and quiet spirit. In everyone.

✳ *God, help us to develop our inner lives and not to be insecure about our appearance. Help us not to judge others by looks, but to encourage and recognise prayerfulness in all people.*

Blessed are the peacemakers

Sometimes we have to humble ourselves, perhaps even grovel like Abigail in this story, for the greater good. True humility is a strong quality, and it is different from enforced abasement. There is a strength in the one who can admit their mistakes and set aside their own wellbeing for the greater good of others. Abigail's action of abasing herself prevented bloodshed and issued from a strong self, not a weak one. Her action reminds me of the Easter story. Jesus knew he did not have to go all the way to the cross; he could have chosen to avoid it, but, like Abigail, he chose to abandon himself and endure suffering and shame for the salvation of others.

Self-love and self-sacrifice are difficult themes today, particularly for oppressed peoples. We rightfully strive to love ourselves: we are told by modern psychology that this is a good thing that leads to greater love for others. How does this then fit with a sacrificial love that eats dirt and grovels in order to save others? In order for us to find meaning today within the duality of modern psychology and our ancient faith, we need to see the purpose of true faith as linked with high self-esteem. We can take risks in the name of our God when we believe whole-heartedly both in God and in our own sense of self. When we have a strong self that we treasure, we can offer it both to others and to God to be used. If we grovel or take risks from a position of powerlessness and low self-esteem, we will merely reinforce our own as well as others' oppression, and this helps no one.

✳ *God, may we learn the true humility of faith in action.*

Thursday April 7   1 Timothy 5:16

Duty of care?

The women in this passage are charged with looking after their elderly relatives. This is good advice, especially since, if they don't look after them, nobody will. The reading raises several questions for me. Does this tell us something about community? How can we care for our ageing population? How can we be cared for as we get older, without being patronised or left to fend for ourselves? Do we only need to care about our blood relatives, or are other people important, too?

I listened to a radio documentary recently, about two secular eco-communities in rural England. It seems there is a small, but growing, movement away from individual houses with their own washing machines, cars and TVs, towards communal ecological communities. Maybe this is a positive movement, calling us to be more environmentally careful and to care for each other, as we get older. Certainly it is not new. But perhaps the appeal is stronger? A group of my women friends are planning, in their old age, to live together, separately but with some shared facilities. We remember Jesus' command that we should love one another; this includes a duty of mutual care. How do we exercise this command?

✳ *God, help us to seek out new ways of being your church. Help us to grow into community with others and to open our hearts to ways of responding to your need. As we grow more deeply in love of one another, let that love flow into the hearts of those who need it most.*

Friday April 8   *Joshua 6:22–25*
I believe, help my unbelief
Did Rahab know this was the right thing to do? Because of her action she and her family were saved, but Jericho was destroyed. Rahab's faith seems so sure.

The Russian poet and former political prisoner Irina Ratushinskaya wrote much of her remarkable poetry in captivity. She said once that she knew people were praying for her beyond the prison walls, feeling their prayers as a warm blanket when she was freezing, hungry, and alone. I feel there is a connection between Rahab's faith, when her whole city was about to be destroyed, and Irina's, enduring in appalling hardship.

I am moved whenever I hear of people who have believed God loves them in and through the most challenging circumstances. My understanding of faith is not, 'If I pray hard enough, bad things will not happen to me,' but 'God is with me in the suffering'. The Easter message is one of trusting God in our unbelief, knowing that God will love us and show us the way, even when the future looks uncertain, as it was for Rahab and Irina – and as it is for us.

✳ *Lord, we believe; help our unbelief.*

Saturday April 9   *John 4:28–29*
Living waters
The Samaritan woman would have been surprised, perhaps shocked, at this Jewish man speaking to her. He does not lecture her, but has a conversation. Her action in this passage spurs her friends and family to meet Jesus. We see an example of Jesus cutting through social, religious and gender barriers to spread the good news. This may be a foretaste of the women proclaiming the Easter message, as we read at the beginning of the week.

I like to think of myself as a liberal. And yet as a lesbian Christian feminist, I feel most comfortable worshipping with those who support me, love me, protect me and serve my own belief system. So the reading challenges me to cut through the boundaries, as Jesus and this woman did. I need to listen to Christians who use different forms of worship, or who hold different opinions from me, on all sorts of issues. Obviously, I long for unconditional love and support from my fellow Christians, and I do not want to bare my throat to the sharp knife of prejudice, but equally I must not dismiss fellow believers or fellow human beings, or I am guilty of the same prejudice. I want to be open to God in all sorts of people. Maybe I have the most to learn from people with different backgrounds and life experiences from my own. Maybe we all do.

✳ *God, help us to let go of rigid belief systems and be open to the truth. Let us hear your voice in those around us, especially in those we are reluctant to hear.*

FOR REFLECTION – alone or with a group

● What message or action can we show to others this Eastertide that points to the truth of God's liberating grace?

● The women in these Bible stories show qualities of faith, humility and compassion. How can we embed these qualities in our daily lives?

FOR ACTION

Take time each day to refresh yourself spiritually, by being quiet and alone with God. Build community in whatever way is right for you by expanding the walls of your home and your heart to include others.

EASTER FOR ALL
3. Young people living the Easter message

Notes based on a variety of translations by
Young people from Birmingham, UK

This week's notes have been written by a group of young people from Anglican churches in Birmingham, UK: Natasha Manyuira, aged 17, who describes herself as 'an active ambassador for Christ' with a flair for writing; Catherine Overend, aged 16, who says, 'I enjoy talking, eating chocolate and worshipping God'; Rosie Shakespear, aged 16, who is chair of the Bishop's Youth Council for the diocese of Birmingham and owns a horse called Benson; Jim Houghton, who is also a member of the Bishop's Youth Council; and Joshua Wilson, aged 13, who likes running, playing his clarinet and worshipping God.

Young people don't always get a good press in the church. Churches which struggle to attract young people or keep them involved in the life of the church bewail their absence, but churches where young people are present do not always seem to know how to include them positively in the ongoing life of worship, decision-making or service. Yet where young people's presence, experience, insights and struggles are welcomed into the centre of church life and witness, they bring a vibrancy and reality to the rest of the church community which is a precious gift indeed. As the notes written by the Birmingham young people this week demonstrate, young Christians' faith is alive, dynamic, searching and vibrant. Those of us who are older have much to learn from them about the living reality of Easter faith – as well as our own experience and insights to share with them.

Sunday April 10   *1 Samuel 3:1–21*
Simple obedience

Samuel lived a simple life in the temple, ministering before the Lord under Eli. He was reverent and obedient, and was not doing anything special or out of the ordinary when God spoke to him. Samuel can teach us a lot about the sort of life we need to live as Christians. Like Samuel, we should be open to God and his word, and come before him as we are – not influenced by others and with no pre-conceived ideas or agendas (verse 7). In verse 10, Samuel says, 'Speak, for your servant is listening'. He recognised God and humbled himself before him, listening to what God had to say. As a result, God stayed with Samuel as he grew up, protecting and guiding him (verse 19). Note that God only started to speak to Samuel after Samuel had first acknowledged him. We too should take time to come before God, respectfully and unassumingly, acknowledging his presence and waiting for him to speak and to reveal his will for us.

✳ *Lord, I pray that today you will help me to dispel any pre-conceived ideas that I may have about you. Help me to come before you with an open heart, ready and willing to listen to your voice and receive guidance from you.*

Monday April 11   *1 Samuel 17:33–50*

The battle belongs to the Lord

Have you ever heard the song 'In heavenly armour we'll enter … the battle belongs to the Lord...'? It's true! The fight does belong to God! So why are you trying to take matters into your own hands when the Lord's got your back covered? Don't you know that the same God who created the entire universe can also handle every battle you go through? Trust God! Accept that you need God's help. Learn from David's experience when he totally relied on God.

For a period of time, cash flow was scarce. I tried really hard to find a means of income but there were barriers. Halfway through my turmoil, it clicked. Of course – God dried my wells for a reason! He wanted me to realise that I didn't trust him. All I was doing was burrowing deeper into my problems. I was too blind to involve God. I had no choice but to bow down and accept total dependence on him. When I did, he said, 'You do not know how blessed you are!'

If you are struggling, confide in Jesus. You will win the battle not by your own strength but by his, which is so powerful! When the trust finally kicks in, he will bless you so much you won't even know what to do with yourself. So what if the battle seems impossible? Be like David, and cry out bravely that you won't back down because the Lord Almighty has already won the battle!

✳ *Father God, you are amazing in the way you are prepared to fight for me every step of the way. Be my strength and provider when I can't see a way out. Help me to trust you wholly.*

Our God is an awesome God

We join the story as Abraham, the father of God's chosen people, is reaching the end of his days. In order to continue God's great promise (Genesis 12), he is searching for a wife for his son Isaac. In the verses before we join the passage, Abraham has commanded his head servant (who would dearly like to please Abraham) to go back to his hometown in order to find a girl from the family of Abraham and to bring her back to the new land. Clearly the servant is somewhat sceptical of this request and asks the sensible question, 'What if the woman is unwilling to come back with me to this land?' It is easy to imagine his train of thought as he journeys back to the land of the family of Abraham – 'I'd better please the old man by going, but no girl's going to come back with me'.

Reading on we find a prayer in verse 12, which rings true for many of us. The servant, desperate to please, isn't sure how he is going to go about the job of finding a wife for Isaac and asks God for help (no doubt with a slight scepticism in his voice). However, our Lord God is more than up to the task of finding a girl for Isaac and answers the servant's prayer in such a dramatic way that he has no choice but to choose that girl.

The question raised here is why did God answer this man's prayer so dramatically yet in our lives God so often seems to be distant when we cry out in such a way? The answer given by this passage is that God has promised (in Genesis 12) that from Abraham will come a great nation and God does not go back on promises. Hence the servant is praying in line with God's will and Abraham sends the servant out in line with God's will. The servant is not praying for a Ferrari, but for a wife for Isaac so that God's chosen people may continue to increase in number.

We see in this act how God works on two levels, in one fell swoop confounding the scepticism of the servant and keeping his promise to Abraham. But the most important point raised by the passage is the way in which God works through humans to work out his eternal plans. We are an integral part of God's plan for salvation; it is neither God working on his own, nor us on our own. So let us thank God for considering us special enough to be involved in his plans and promises for the world.

✳ *Dear Lord, thank you that you never fail to keep your promises and that you are utterly faithful. We thank you that you hear all our prayers, and though you may not always answer them as we expect, we know that you answer all prayers. We thank you for the privilege of being part of your plan, and that you continue to use us. Help us this day to live in the light of knowing you, and to make decisions accordingly.*

Wednesday April 13   *2 Kings 5:1–15*

All out for God

If I told you to jump in a muddy puddle a few times because it was a miracle cure for spots, you'd think that I was having a laugh at your expense. Read the passage and think about how you would have felt at each stage in the story.

Naaman certainly thought that Elisha was playing a joke on him when the prophet wouldn't come out to meet him but told him to wash seven times in the water in Israel to cure him of his leprosy. He got pretty angry, thinking it was a pointless and belittling exercise.

And the King of Israel was terrified when he heard that Naaman was coming to be healed. Who was going to make him better? He certainly couldn't! Elisha told the king to chill out; he knew that God would have something up his sleeve. And God did. When Naaman was obedient (after a bit of moaning and groaning), he was healed.

Sometimes we have to go all-out for God even though we think that what is being asked of us is a bit strange or risky. The servants are the best example of an amazing all-out attitude in this passage. Note that it is a servant girl who first suggests to Naaman, through his wife, that he go to Elisha for healing and later it is Naaman's servants who encourage him to go and do what Elisha has commanded. All of them could have lost their jobs or even been killed for saying what they thought.

Today let us try and think like the servants about what God wants us to do, however odd or hard it may seem. Let us pray to become more like the servants who were obedient to the will of God.

✳ *Show us how to go all-out for you, dear God, and not to be ashamed to do what might seem foolish or strange to others.*

Thursday April 14   *Jeremiah 1:6–10*

God equips those who are fearful

In this passage, Jeremiah is called by God to be a prophet of the nation. However, when God calls him, Jeremiah says he is too young. He is afraid of God and of what he is being asked to do. So he comes up with an excuse: that he is too young. We, too, when we are asked to do something by God, can be afraid. But instead of turning away and making lame excuses, this is precisely when we need to turn to the Lord.

God answers Jeremiah's cry, comforting him and giving him confidence. He tells Jeremiah not to be fearful of others because God will be with him, speaking to him and through him. We can learn from Jeremiah's experience. When we feel fearful or lacking in confidence we should turn to God. When we need comfort, God will comfort us. When we need help, God will help us.

✱ *Lord, I pray that when I am in need, you will help me. When I have no confidence in myself or in you, show me how marvellous you are and that I can trust utterly in you.*

Friday April 15   *Daniel 3:13–30*

Hot stuff!

The story of Shadrach, Meshach and Abednego provides us with another biblical example of being sold out to God. They trusted in God so much that they were willing to be chucked in a fire because they knew that he would protect and honour them. In the Street Bible, a version that uses the language of the street, verses 17 and 18 are paraphrased as follows: 'If we were chucked into this blazing oven, the God we work for could pull us out alive. He'll rescue us from your cruelty, King. Even if he doesn't and we fry, there'd be no regrets – no way are we bowing down to your gods or your overgrown gold action man.'

This is a really cool (or should I say hot?) example of trusting in God no matter what. It is unlikely that many of us will ever be asked by a king to bow down and worship a huge gold statue of them on pain of death, although some readers of these notes may live in countries where it is a dangerous thing to worship the living God. However, for all of us there is the temptation to worship other things, other goals or other people who want us to worship them. For example, at school I could be asked by one of the school bullies who are in the 'in' crowd to nick food for them, at the expense of being beaten into a pulp. If I say yes, even to some small act, I am selling my soul and worshipping them rather than giving my obedience and worship to God.

Take some time out to think about who or what you might be worshipping instead of God. Think of the consequences if you stop doing the things that you are doing. Ponder over whether you can trust God enough to worship him alone, even if it means changes in your own life.

✴ *Father, I pray that we can all trust enough in you to be fully sold out to you like Shadrach, Meshach and Abednego. Give us the confidence to make changes in our lives so that we can be sold out to you alone.*

Saturday April 16   *1 Timothy 4:11–16*

No, you are not too young!

Have you ever felt that you are too young to lead? Have you ever thought that your role in church is insignificant? At some point in our lives we've all wondered how we can show others we are keen to be used by God. The key to the matter is, listen to the Holy Spirit! It's no good sitting down and moping, wondering how you can contribute when you should be first consulting God's Spirit for guidance.

Older Christians may have general views that young people are troublemakers and are too noisy. We have to break that stereotype. The only way to stop this kind of thinking is for young people to set a different kind of example. The witness of a young person living fully for God is a very powerful thing. It will make others want to improve their ways of living.

We all have spiritual gifts and we must be prepared for the Holy Spirit to use us, whoever we are, young or old. God is calling you. How can God use you when you are stuck in the frame of mind that you are too 'young' or not 'wise' enough? Or too 'old' and not 'active' enough. Or too poor and not wealthy enough. Or too uneducated and not clever enough. Stop thinking that way because you are ignoring the potential in you. Exercise your God-given gifts by focusing on God's word and God's ways, and be ready and willing to be used. Do whatever tasks you are given wholeheartedly and then others will see your progress and be inspired.

Being a Christian is for life. Therefore we must keep watching ourselves and stay true to what we believe in.

✴ *Lord, I want to be an example to others. Help me to recognise my spiritual gifts and use them for your glory.*

FOR REFLECTION – alone or with a group

● What kind of attitude does your church have to young people? Are they fully involved in the life of your church? On the margins? Or missing altogether?

● What can you do, individually or collectively, to encourage the faith of young people?

● What gifts and insights do young people bring to the life of the church?

● How have you been encouraged or challenged by the young people's thoughts in this week's notes?

FOR ACTION

Reflect on what you can do to encourage and support a young person this week – in your family, in your neighbourhood or in your church.

EASTER FOR ALL
4. Can men believe the Easter news?

Notes based on the New Revised Standard Version by
Mark Pryce

Mark Pryce is an Anglican parish priest currently working in Smethwick, an inner-city multi-ethnic area in the diocese of Birmingham, UK. His work in spirituality and pastoral care includes a special emphasis on gender issues, particularly men and masculinities, and he has written a book exploring these issues: Finding a Voice: men, women and the community of the church *(SCM Press, 1996).*

'Can men believe the Easter news?' The short answer to this question is a resounding 'Yes!' History and personal experience reveal that both women and men have faith in Jesus. Yet the faith of each person and community is shaped by particular circumstances and conditions, and one formative aspect is gender – the ways in which man is man and woman is woman in any given historical context and social culture. The 'gender regime' will set certain norms for men and for women which shape their attitudes and behaviour, including spirituality and religious practice. In any culture, the given norms and limits of masculinity will give rise to particular spiritualities for men. These masculinities will shape the ways in which men may receive the gospel message and give expression to their Christian faith, and also present particular obstacles to faith and believing.

What masculinities do we see operating within the New Testament? Did the gospel of Jesus challenge some of the presuppositions and practices of masculinity as it operated in his day and in the time of the early church? Does the Easter news present a fresh challenge to masculinities in our own time, and to the stifling complacency or injustice arising from them? These are the kinds of questions you may like to have in mind as we explore this theme.

Sunday April 17   *Mark 16:9–14*
Memories of failure
Mark's version of the Easter events is that Jesus' disciples are full of fear and unbelief. The experiences of both women and men

are taken into account. Both are profoundly disturbed by the resurrection of Jesus. The women respond with terror and secrecy; the men with incredulity and stubbornness. Mark's gospel records these memories of failure as part of the Easter message.

Yet the risen Christ commissions these same disciples to carry the good news. Surely one of the most powerful evidences of the resurrection is that these first disciples do not hide their history of fear and unbelief, but tell the true story as a witness to the sheer grace of the risen Christ. The male disciples do not claim to have been more discerning than the women, or to have been any less afraid, or to have been any quicker in believing the resurrection experiences of their fellow disciples. They do not set up a hierarchy of blame or create any kind of spiritual rivalry. They even admit that the risen Christ admonishes the apostles for their lack of leadership. Such honesty suggests a new community in Christ, a community of equality and mutual respect between men and women.

✳ *O risen Christ,*
give us your power to trust one another,
and to accept the new life you create among us
as women and men of faith.

Monday April 18   *1 Corinthians 15:1–11*
Recognising God's grace
Here Paul's attitude towards others shows the quality of relationships in the new community which is formed around the resurrection experience. This is an attitude of mutual respect and humility rather than self-assertion and domination. Here Paul puts into practice a masculinity which does not insist on independence or separateness. He acknowledges that he has received the gospel from the teaching and instruction of others. What understanding he may possess, and what missionary work he has been able to achieve, has been the product of interdependence within the body of the church. He acknowledges the faith of others – many others, both women and men – and that he has gained from their experience of the risen Christ. He expresses his own sense of unworthiness to be an apostle, not because he is crippled by shame for past transgressions, but in an attempt to witness to the grace of God at work in his own life. He does not regard his preaching and evangelism as his own achievements, a kind of spiritual territory which he must control or

defend; rather, he sees the growth of belief and understanding as the power of God's grace working in human lives, as it has worked in his own.

✳ **Lord, show us the power of your life**
at work in others and in ourselves,
that we may know the richness of your grace.

Tuesday April 19 Mark 8:31–34

Seeing with God's eyes

Here is another memory of failure, recalled in the light of the resurrection, in a way that expresses the nature of God's kingdom. For God's reign is one of justice and peace in which the old powers of domination have been exposed as corrupt.

Jesus' teaching about his rejection and death at the hands of the religious authorities offends and angers Peter. For him, to be excluded or made weak in the eyes of others can be nothing else than defeat: a humiliation from which there is no recovery. Like many men, Peter fears exposure, ridicule, loss of status and respect. To go to the death of the cross cannot be the will of God. Peter has confused patriarchal power with the reign of God. Jesus teaches that within God's plan of salvation there is glory which surpasses the false power of human authority. For in God's eyes, those who embrace exclusion and humiliation in the cause of Christ are beautiful and victorious. It is God who confers true and authentic honour, not men.

✳ **O Christ,**
who was lifted up upon the cross in ridicule and shame,
give us eyes to see where true glory lies.

Wednesday April 20 Hebrews 11:4–12

Faith heroes

The writer to the Hebrews commends faith as the indispensable basis of believing in God. In chapter 11 he presents a 'great cloud of witnesses' (12:1), men and women of faith from Israel's history, to encourage the faith of those who follow Jesus in the present time. In this early part of the chapter, Abel, Enoch, Noah and Abraham are commended as role-models for a life of trust in God. These men are more than venerable patriarchs from a religious past; they are men who listened to God, respected his will, and took risks in responding. Their great 'achievements' as holy men were rooted in their faith in God and in his action in their lives. Their strength as individuals was to co-operate with God, even when that seemed crazy or dangerously disruptive.

In a world where role-models for men and boys are influential, who are the contemporary role-models for the power of faith to change us and strengthen us? What men do you look to as faith heroes? How do you model faith for others? Does your trust in God go just far enough to keep you feeling comfortable and safe, or is your faith heroic?

✳ *God of the past, be present to us now.*
Open our ears and strengthen our minds,
that we may hear your call and obey your will.

Thursday April 21   Acts 26:1–9, 19–29
The light of faith
Faith in the risen Jesus blew Paul's life apart. Once he had received that blinding revelation on the road to Damascus, all his former certainties crumbled; his status as a religious leader within Judaism fell away. He who had once been a persecutor now became persecuted and despised. The implications of faith in the resurrection mean the sacrifice of so much he previously held dear, including a traumatic shift in his identity and his inner conviction. But the light which Jesus brings for both Jew and Gentile cannot be denied, and Paul now sees by this light, walking the difficult path the light reveals.

What new light does Christ shed on our lives? Are there losses which we are called to suffer for the sake of gaining Christ in our relationships and communities?

✳ *Christ our light,*
show the love you have for those we fear and hate.
Illuminate our minds
and reveal to us the extent of your justice.

Friday April 22   Luke 24:36–43
Touch me and see
For the frightened disciples the resurrection of Jesus is still an abstract idea. They are weighing up in their minds the evidence of other people's experience. They are trapped in fear and shock. Jesus comes among them and gives the greeting of peace: he brings resolution and a connection with his new being. He invites

them to step beyond their fear and to touch his body. He asks them to let go of ideology and to make sense of his physicality – not just in a cerebral way, but through the medium of touch.

Sometimes men are trapped in the realm of the cerebral, cut off from the reality of the body – from their own physicality or the physicality of others. Sometimes men are so caught up in their own psychology – in refusing to admit fear, or weakness, or stifling the emotional dimension of their lives – that they do not attend to physical pain in themselves or others. Sometimes the dynamic of the group in which they find safety will prevent them from reaching out and touching that new life which they long to know for real. Is the risen Christ inviting you to reach out and touch a new reality?

✳ *Lord Christ,*
in you there is new life.
Help us to overcome our fears
and to touch the new way of being that you embody.

Saturday April 23   *John 20:24–29*

Acknowledging our wounds

By touching his wounds Thomas comes to know that the figure who stands before him is the risen Christ. The one who has come to them is the same man who actually suffered the pain and torture of crucifixion. Resurrection has not vanished away the past, but takes it forward into a new future.

Many men hide their wounds so as not to be vulnerable to others. They conceal any scar which might tell of shame – that they were bullied or hurt or defeated in the past, for example. Thomas knows Jesus to be Lord because he does not hide the suffering he has endured. He is not ashamed of what he had to bear at the hands of others, and so he brings new life for all who follow him.

Are there wounds from the past which you are hiding from others? Are there experiences of humiliation about which you still feel ashamed? Do you despise those who are scarred by the brutality of others? Can you see in Christ the power of one who acknowledges his wounds and takes them forward into a new freedom?

✳ *Lord, you know our secret hurts and our hidden*
humiliations.
Take away the tyranny of our past.

Give us strength to move forward into new life
where there is mutual respect and safety in our
relationships.

FOR REFLECTION – alone or with a group

● Reflect on how your gender has shaped the way you think of yourself and the way you have received faith.

● What are some of the stereotypes of masculinity you have received?

● How does Christian faith challenge role-models of masculinity which operate in wider society?

● What gifts do men bring and live out in the community of your own church?

● How can those gifts be better celebrated?

● What are the wounds and the struggles that men in your family or church may find it more difficult to own and expose to others?

FOR ACTION

Pray for a specific man you know who is struggling in his own life and needs the grace of God to own his wounds or move on from his past. Decide on one practical way in which you can show support and offer solidarity.

REMEMBERING
1. God remembers...

Notes based on the Revised Standard Version by
Lesley G Anderson

Lesley G Anderson is the Senior Ministerial Tutor and Warden of Methodist students at the United Theological College of the West Indies, Jamaica.

Scripture records many occasions when God remembers the covenant made with the people and with certain representative individuals. This act of remembering is important, because God's relationship with the people is one marred by much sin, struggling and suffering, and God needs to remind the people of the covenant they freely entered into. This week explores some of this 'remembering' in stories relating to Noah, Abraham, Sarah and Rachel. The covenant, pact or agreement with God will indeed be abused, forgotten or broken by the people, but God will 'remember' it and seek to heal, forgive and restore because of his unfathomable love for them. The word 'covenant' appears 200 times in the Old Testament. Jeremiah (31:31–34) speaks of a new covenant which is to take the place of the covenant of the exodus. This new covenant has been introduced by Christ (1 Corinthians 11:25).

Sunday April 24   *Genesis 9:1–17*
God promises life
Today's lesson is a reminder that the promise of life is a promise to all of us: a promise confirmed by the oath of God which can never be reversed (Isaiah 54:9). God blessed Noah and promised him life and happiness and the enjoyment of the fruits of his labours (Genesis 5:29). This promise of life tells us that human life is sacred and more precious than the life of a 'beast' (verse 5). This promise of life was given after the flood as a new covenant of salvation from death and destruction. It assured Noah of safety from ruin. It was a covenant of peace and of reconciliation with God.

Let us remember God, who promised us life and sent Jesus Christ to die on Calvary's cross that we might have not just life, but eternal life. Let us remember God with honour and serve God all the days of our lives.

✳ *Lord, you remember us in our times of trouble; may we now live to honour you and enjoy your promised life.*

God promises joy

Abraham was old and Sarah was barren. God made them the promise of a son. Abraham laughed with joy. Our Lord Jesus said of him: 'Your father Abraham rejoiced that he was to see my day; he saw it and was glad' (John 8:56). Sarah rejoiced in God's promise, 'even when she was past the age' (Hebrews 11:11). A son was born and his name was Isaac, which means, 'laughing'. There was much joy at his birth (Galatians 4:27–28). The name was to be a reminder for ever of an event which made Abraham and Sarah laugh with joy and wonder. Ishmael, which means 'God shall hear', was also a living reminder that God heard the prayer first of his mother Hagar and then of his father Abraham.

Some years ago I visited the country of Haiti and hardly anyone was laughing. Life was hard and difficult for the people. On a more recent visit, I saw people laughing. The suspicion, division, turmoil and unrest in the country were overshadowed by the conviction that 'God is for us' (Romans 8:31). Jesus Christ hears our prayers and gives us the power to live, to be, to become, to forgive, to love, to serve, to rejoice (Philippians 4:4).

✳ *Lord, you are the joy and love of my life. Without you, there would be no reason to rejoice. Keep me happy and laughing.*

God promises miracles

God heard the prayers of Rachel as he heard Noah's. God remembered her plea that she might not die childless. She wanted a son to keep her name in remembrance. By God's grace and favour, she received a son and named him Joseph. His name has a double meaning, meaning both 'taking away' shame and 'adding' to her a son. For women in this ancient patriarchal culture, to be left childless was to be excluded from the promises of God. Rachel bore a son, continuing the line of Abraham, the seed in whom all nations should be blessed. Joseph was to Jacob the 'son of his old age', younger than the ten sons that Leah and the handmaids had borne him. Joseph was promoted over them all, became lord over his brothers, became their saviour and deliverer and a father to Pharaoh and to all the land of Egypt. We see in Joseph the 'adding' of blessing to blessing, and the heaping of honour upon honour.

A Brazilian friend of mine got married and for fifteen years longed for a baby. Finally the miracle came. She now has a beautiful baby boy, a constant reminder to her of God's boundless love and blessing. Childless or child-bearing, God has given to each of us his beloved son, our Lord and Saviour Jesus Christ. This gift to us is unspeakable, in whom alone there is redemption and abundant life, now and for evermore.

✶ *We give you thanks, O Lord, for the miracle of your son, who gave his own life on the cross as a gift for our salvation.*

Wednesday April 27   *Exodus 2:23–25*

God promises deliverance

After a period of time, the king of Egypt who had sought to kill Moses died. His successors continued the cruel oppression of the children of Israel. The death of the king, however, gave them some needed time to pray and cry to God for help. In their affliction the Israelites cried unto the Lord (1 Samuel 12:8); they repented of their sins which had brought evil upon them and prayed fervently for deliverance and redemption. God knew of their condition, their humiliation and sorrow. He remembered his covenant with them. This does not mean that he had previously forgotten it, but that the opportunity had now come to fulfil his merciful purpose of delivering them. They were afflicted, but not cast away; chastened, but not rejected.

In our own time and world, oppression and cruelty continue apparently unchecked in many places. Criminals seem to run free and wild in many communities whilst people stand by in weakness, coldness and apathy. Recently in Jamaica, people were known to have stood still while a killing of another human being took place. No one wanted to get involved! One of the saddest funerals I had to conduct in Belize was that of a mother who had been killed by her son. He wanted money to buy drugs and she rightly refused to give it to him. Instead, she paid the ultimate price – the sacrifice of her life – in order to save her son from drug addiction.

When I remember the life, death and resurrection of Jesus and his gifts of salvation and liberation to others and myself, like Charles Wesley I wish I had a thousand tongues to use them all to praise him! In our times of suffering and affliction, Jesus will hear our cry. In him all our needs are met.

✶ *O God, deliver us from cruel heartlessness and apathy. Save us from oppression.*

God promises help
God knew and bore all the sorrows and sufferings of the people. In their affliction 'he was afflicted' (Isaiah 53:7). The day of their redemption and liberation was in his heart. God sent Christ, who humbly submitted himself, taking 'the form of a servant' and 'becoming obedient' (Philippians 2:7–8) to the state of bondage and affliction, even to the point of the cross. He poured out his blood, in the depths of our affliction and misery, to break the chain of evil. The result is, we are free – liberated to serve God.

God is the great 'I AM WHO I AM'. God is the one and only true God. All blessings flow from God. God is the source of eternal life, whose name is 'holy' (Psalm 30:4) and who is 'to be remembered throughout all generations' (verse 15). God will not forget his covenant with Israel nor his love for her. He will pity and restore her.

With life being so difficult for so many of us, we have become consumed with our own problems. When this happens, it is easy to forget the burdens, sorrows and concerns of others, particularly in Africa, Asia, the Caribbean, Latin America and the Pacific. When we reach out to the suffering poor to give them bread, the thirsty to give them water, the naked to give them clothing, the homeless to give them shelter, and those with HIV/AIDS to give them medical care, we give to Jesus (Matthew 25:31–46). When we think of all that we have and remember how Jesus has given us so much, we are inspired to show his love to others.

✴ *Lord, help us to reach out in love to help each other in times of need.*

God promises forgiveness
Growing up as a child in my parents' home in the Republic of Panama, I knew what it was to be punished for wrongs committed. In today's passage, we read that God punished the people of Israel. This led to repentance and confession of sins, both their own sins and those of their ancestors. It was a moment of both humility and self-humiliation. Coming to God as they did, they discovered the promise of forgiveness and mercy. God promised once more to 'remember' the covenant with them (verse 42).

I have always been deeply moved by the story of the father's love for his son who left home to live in a far-off country, which became his land of hardship. He experienced such waste of life and acute famine, until 'he came to himself' (Luke 15:17). He remembered his loving father and a wonderful home. He repented, turned around and retraced his steps back into the arms of his beloved father, who celebrated his return. He who was lost had been found. He who was dead now lived again. God does not desire the death of a sinner!

✳ *Forgive our foolish ways, O Lord, and restore us to yourself – giving us new life.*

Saturday April 30   *Ezekiel 16:59–63*

God promises a new relationship with his son, Jesus

Jerusalem will enjoy a new relationship with Samaria and Sodom. They will become her daughters instead of her sisters. This new relationship will not be dependent on anything relating to the past but only on the grace of God. God's love will remain steadfast. He will have pity on Jerusalem and restore her to himself – offering her love, pity and forgiveness.

God remembers the covenant he made with his people, despite their disobedience, and restores them to himself. Likewise, Jesus Christ is able to do for us what we cannot do for ourselves. He is able to make all things new. He is able to cleanse us from all unrighteousness. In times of sickness, he heals; when we repent, he forgives; in our pain and sorrow, he offers us comfort. When in our distress we cry out to him in mercy, he gives us strength to persevere. God promises us a new relationship with his son, Jesus, who freely broke his body and shed his blood for us all!

✳ *O merciful God, we are grateful for the new relationship we have with your son, Jesus Christ.*

FOR REFLECTION – alone or with a group

● How can we assist people to understand that all persons are made in the image of God and are precious in God's sight?
● What is the difference, if any, between God's covenant with Israel and the covenants we make with each other?
● How binding is a covenant?

FOR ACTION

Read again the biblical passage and commentary for Wednesday April 27. Consider getting involved in one or two crime prevention groups in your community in order to encourage a greater commitment to the wellbeing of your neighbourhood.

REMEMBERING
2. Memories are made of this

Notes based on the New Jerusalem Bible by
Helen Cameron

Helen Cameron is a Methodist Presbyter who is involved in ministerial formation in an ecumenical setting and also in local ministry. She is the mother of three small children.

There are personal memories, and memories held collectively by families, communities and nations. The people of God, too, hold memories of central and symbolically important events like the Exodus, the time in the wilderness, the death and resurrection of Jesus, the birth of the church at Pentecost and so on. This week we reflect on some of these memories and consider why we find some memories easier than others to remember. What we wish to forget is as important as that which we are glad to recall.

Sunday May 1   *1 Corinthians 11:23–32*
Do this as a memorial

Paul begins by declaring that he is handing on a tradition that he received from the Lord. This emphasises how central to the early church were the accounts of what Jesus had said and done. Indeed, such traditions and stories handed down from those who had been present were the beginnings from which the gospels grew.

Jesus invited those of his friends present at his last meal to remember him whenever they broke bread and drank a cup of wine. Paul is reminding the people who belong to the church at Corinth that this memorial meal is about Jesus and his sacrifice. Paul has had reports that this meal, which for early Christians, as for us, is about Jesus' sacrificial death, is being abused. Paul wants the church at Corinth to remember that in sharing in this memorial meal they recall his sacrifice, made for them and for all. He died for all; therefore they need to remember that they are all called, as a community, to share in his sacrifice. Paul reminds them they are now part of a covenant community; those for whom Christ died. It is then not just the bread and wine which are transformed but their lives. They will be broken and blessed and shared – for others.

✴ **Loving God, may this meal unite us and not be a source of hurt and division.**

Monday May 2   Luke 22:14–20
The Passover meal
Luke divides the story of the last supper into three parts. There is Jesus' vow of abstaining from future Passover suppers (verses 15–18), his interpreting the significance of the bread and wine (verses 19–20) and finally (in verses 21–23) there is the prophecy of his betrayal. This structure and form in the story is significant and mirrors the shape of the traditional Passover narrative shared in the Passover meal.

In the Christian understanding of the Passover experience, the people are brought out of slavery to freedom, not from a place, Egypt, but through the power of the cross of Christ. What Jesus offers is a new and radical, even shocking re-interpretation of an old memory and understanding. So Jesus doesn't invite his followers to repeat the Passover meal but gives them a new commandment to 'do this in remembrance of me'. He has become the way of freedom.

Jesus tells his friends there is a time of waiting to come, they are to wait with longing, not for next year in Jerusalem but for the new Jerusalem of the kingdom of God, inaugurated in him. In eating his meal he will be present to them.

✴ **Jesus, take us, bless us, break us, and may our lives be an offering to you.**

Tuesday May 3   Psalm 95:1–11
Hard times
The Christian church has long used this psalm (known as the *Venite*, from its first word in Latin), as a call and guide to worship. The key to the power of the psalm is that, in remembering and praising the greatest attributes of God which make God worthy of praise, the psalmist is unafraid to visit a time of difficulty and testing for the people of Israel. The psalmist laments that the people are not listening to God and have hardened their hearts towards God just as they did at Meribah and Massah. These place names refer to incidents during the great Exodus journey through the wilderness when people lost hope in Moses and God and wandered away. The people doubted that God and his

servant Moses could save them; they lacked trust and faith in God's purposes for them.

It is easy looking back to remember only the good times. All my childhood holidays were in Scotland and I can now only remember hot days, swimming in rivers and lochs. My head tells me it must have rained sometimes, but my heart whispers only of long sunny, carefree days. The psalmist is keen for the people to remember faithful and faithless days.

✳ *Lord, remember us who are sometimes faithful and at other times faithless but always your children, always your own.*

Wednesday May 4   *Isaiah 49:14–16*
Hard to forget
This passage is part of a longer section in the form of a lament and is part of the second Servant Song in Isaiah. Zion laments that she is forgotten and God replies that she will never be, indeed cannot be, forgotten. The metaphor of a human mother forgetting about her child after birth or when she is breast feeding, is chosen deliberately to emphasise how much more God loves us, even more than a mother loves her children. There are times mothers might want to forget their children and can't! They are never far from our hearts and minds. So, too, we are unforgettable and never out of the circle of God's remembering and care.

When children are lost through stillbirth, miscarriage or infant death, when memories of a well-formed person with an individual and separate identity can be faint, a mother (and father) still finds it hard to forget. We are God's and never forgotten.

✳ *As a child at your breast, so you love us, feed us, nourish us. We pray for those whose children have died, for those who long for children but do not have them. Help us all to remember that nothing is lost, no one is outside the embrace of your love.*

Thursday May 5 (Ascension Day)   *Acts 1:6–11*
Nothing is lost
Whenever family members come to stay with us, my children always insist on the whole family gathering to wave them off and wish them a safe journey. As we live a long way away from grandparents and aunts and uncles, these visits are treasured and the departure is never easy.

An abiding visual image of the Ascension represented many times in Christian art is a group of desolate disciples looking longingly heavenward. It is easy to imagine the feelings of loss and emptiness the disciples felt. However, at this very moment the angelic witness reminds the disciples of the ongoing divine activity. This is not an end but a beginning. God is at work in and through them even more powerfully than when Jesus was physically present among them. All that they are will be taken and transformed by the risen and ascended Christ, blessed by the Spirit of God at work in the world. The church will be born. A time of sadness and regret is transformed by the power of God into a time of anticipation and excitement.

✴ *Risen and ascended Lord,*
let us see our flesh as holy
just as you are holy.
  May we be your body
  given for the world,
  blessed and broken.

Friday May 6   *Luke 24:13–32*

Stranger and friend

The structure of this resurrection story is fascinating. Cleopas and another disciple encounter a stranger on the road to Emmaus. There is an opening conversation followed by the 'stranger' expounding scripture. The climax comes at the supper when the 'stranger' takes bread and blesses it, breaks it and shares it with them. At this key moment their eyes are opened and they see the risen Jesus.

The account makes it clear that this is not just about human recognition or that Jesus' bodily form post-resurrection is not recognisable. This is God at work. Verse 16 is clear that the disciples' eyes were prevented from recognising him. This allows Cleopas, not knowing he is speaking to Jesus, to witness powerfully to Jesus' ministry, his death and the women's account of the empty tomb. Only when Jesus takes, blesses, breaks and shares the bread are their eyes opened. This is a moment of revelation. Until this point Cleopas can only tell of what others have said to him: now he knows for himself that Jesus is risen.

✴ *Give us the power and wisdom to discern your presence in friend and stranger.*

When we forget

There are various anointing stories in the gospels (Mark 14:3–9; Matthew 26:6–13; Luke 7:36–50; John 12:1–8). In all these stories the anointing of Jesus is undertaken by a woman and takes place at a meal, but the accounts vary in other details. In Mark an otherwise unknown woman anoints Jesus' head and is not portrayed as a sinner. In entering during the meal and breaking a jar of nard over Jesus' head, the woman has performed an act of great significance and symbolic importance. To anoint the feet, as Luke and John describe, is the job of a servant or a slave. But to anoint the head is to call a person to God's service, to consecrate him or her for a special task. The unknown woman at Bethany was performing a prophetic act; she recognised and proclaimed in her act that Jesus was the Messiah.

The response of the disciples and the acts of Judas and the chief priests are to be contrasted with her actions. The teller of her story states that her deed will be remembered throughout the whole world – the only place in the gospel where any one action or deed is singled out in such a way. To the church's shame we have forgotten to tell this story of a woman who was a prophet and powerfully prepared Jesus for the task he had to undergo. She is a model of true discipleship, but we have forgotten her.

✳ *Great God of love,*
  forgive us what we fail to celebrate;
  forgive us what we choose to ignore;
  forgive us our reluctance to learn from women.
  In your love, remake us.

FOR REFLECTION – alone or with a group

● Why does the celebration of the Lord's Supper divide us from one another?

● The church makes much less of a celebration of the Ascension than of Christmas and Easter. Why is this?

● Why has the church failed so dismally to honour the woman of Bethany who anointed Jesus?

FOR ACTION

Organise a shared fellowship meal with local Christians of many denominations. Consider if there are people of other faiths you could invite.

REMEMBERING
3. Called to remember

Notes based on the Revised Standard Version by
Salvador T Martinez

Salvador T Martinez is an ordained minister of the United Church of Christ in the Philippines and an International Associate of the Common Global Ministries Board (Disciples of Christ) and the United Church of Christ in the USA. He resides in Chiang Mai, Thailand and is appointed to teach theology and ethics at the McGilvary Faculty of Theology, Payap University in Chiang Mai. He also serves as a volunteer in the HIV-AIDS and prison ministries of the Church of Christ in Thailand.

This week's readings explore the idea that the people of God are called to remember – to remember God, our heritage and those on the margins. 'Remembering' is part of being human. The ability to remember sets human beings apart from animals. Although we sometimes talk of animals as being able to remember, what they do is instinct-based rather than representing a real ability to remember. I have seen people who have had shock treatments and lost some of their memory, and it is an awesome process to behold. Seeing people in situations like this makes one realise how important the past is as a part of one's identity, and why amnesia is always called a sickness, not an asset. A person without a memory is only half a human being, and this is true religiously as well as in every other way.

In the Bible 'remembering' is both a divine and a human attribute. God remembers his people, his covenant and the iniquities of the people. Recollecting the past is a very important activity for the people of the Bible. It is an important principle of religious life: 'My soul is downcast within me; therefore I will remember you' (Jonah 2:7; see also 2 Peter 1:12–15; 3:1).

Sunday May 8 Galatians 2:9–10
Remember the poor
If there is one way to characterise the ministry of Christ, it is his passionate concern for the poor and the downtrodden. It is a tradition he himself inherited from the prophets. For Jeremiah, 'to defend the cause of the poor and the needy' is what it means to

know God (22:16). Jesus is equally emphatic in his declaration that the poor will inherit the kingdom of God (Luke 6:20). And in the parable of the sheep and the goats, Jesus identifies himself with the least of the brothers and sisters and condemns those who call him 'Lord' but have no concern for the poor.

At the start of Christian Aid Week, it is well for us to heed the teaching of the Apostle, to remember the poor. To do so is to know God and to identify with Christ himself.

✳ *For the rich blessings that you have given us to enjoy, gracious and compassionate God, we are deeply grateful. Forgive us when in our gladness and thankfulness we forget our less fortunate brothers and sisters. Many are homeless and in need of warm clothing and daily food. May we not rest in our comforts until we have done our very best to provide food and shelter, comfort and cheer to as many as we are able to care for.*

Monday May 9   *Psalm 105:1–5*

Remember God's works

The psalmist calls upon the people to 'give thanks to the Lord, call upon his name', sing praises to him and tell about his wonderful works. The demand is not without a basis. God's people are to do so in gratitude to God for his compassion and grace. God has done marvellous works and miracles for the people. As we read on in this chapter, the miracles referred to are the plagues brought upon Pharaoh and his people in order to deliver Israel from bondage (verses 29–36). Because of the great privilege they have received from God, their responsibility, in gratitude, should be equally great. This is likewise true of the Christians who are made free in Christ.

✳ *Creator God, you have done wonders in our lives. May we not forget that we are bound to you and to one another: our strength gives strength to others, our hurt brings hurt to others, our weakness causes others to weaken. May we be mindful of the needs of others as you have been mindful of our needs and have given so graciously, even of your very self, to us. Help us to proclaim your great work and compassion through our prayers and through selfless service.*

Remember the Sabbath

Tropical fruits, such as mangoes, bloom once a year. With the use of chemicals, however, farmers can induce the fruit trees to bear fruit out of season. The practice has dire consequences. It shortens the life of the trees. Human beings, animals and all creation need rest. The commandment to keep the Sabbath has a purpose for the whole of creation, not just for humanity. It points to the dignity of all creation. Human beings and other creatures should never be used beyond their limits. In the creation story, even God rested on the seventh day! The fourth commandment, like the commandment to 'honour your father and mother,' is not a prohibition ('You shall not'). It is stated positively (see Deuteronomy 5:16). It must also be interpreted in the light of Mark 2:27–28: 'The Sabbath was made for man, not man for the Sabbath. So the Son of Man is Lord even of the Sabbath.'

✳ *Dear God of the Sabbath, forgive us for being too busy to take time to rest and enjoy the beauty of your creation. Help us to appreciate time to rest and use it to ponder your love and grace. At the same time, we ask your forgiveness for the times we have made the Sabbath an excuse to do nothing. Teach us to manage our time and energy so that we may use them to the fullest for our neighbours' gain and to the glory of your name.*

Remember God's word

The story of Joshua is commemorated in rituals, festivals and stories passed on from one generation to the next for several hundred years. In the past the Joshua story was misused as a pretext for colonising and evangelising a 'lesser' group of people. However, there are great lessons in the Joshua story about God. God is a liberator! God is passionately concerned and enduringly faithful to the poor and oppressed peoples. God will do everything in God's power and grace to bring about a society where the poor and oppressed will have a place ('an arena of freedom', as Walter Brueggemann puts it in his book *The Land*) – a place to live a peaceful and productive life where all can enjoy freedom, justice and peace.

✳ *O God of all nations, we pray for the leaders of our nation and all nations, that they may be sensitive to the urging of the Spirit within to rule justly, to use their energies to establish justice and peace, to meet unkindness and animosity with goodwill, to inspire belief in goodness and righteousness, to seek ways to meet the needs of the poor, to listen, speak and act with understanding and respect, to shun political gains and to think only of the people's good.*

Thursday May 12   Isaiah 64:1–9

Remember God's ways

One of the industries the city of Chiang Mai is proud of is its pottery making. The city has several pottery factories which make products ranging from ordinary ceramics to exquisite green celadon. Whether it is just an ordinary ceramic plate or a beautiful green celadon vase, every piece is made out of common black or red clay. There is no beauty in the clay itself until it is formed into something beautiful by an expert artisan. The transformation is simply marvellous to behold.

'We are the clay, you are our potter; we are all the work of your hand' (verse 8). In the most distressing of times and circumstances, our remembrance of God's loving and forgiving ways will see us through. God will 'not remember our sins for ever' (verse 9). 'Like clay is in the hands of the potter, so are you in my hand' (Jeremiah 18:6), is the promise of God.

✳ *God of grace and God of mercy, thank you that we come before you with the assurance that all our sins are forgiven and forgotten. Grant that we may also have the grace to love those who have caused us irritation and pain, to forgive our enemies even when we are attacked, and to forgive the misunderstanding of our friends. Keep us always willing to forgive, to forget, to bless and to love the unlovable. O mould us and make us after your will.*

Friday May 13   Colossians 4:15–18

Remember the prisoners

It must be of utmost importance to the apostle to ask to be remembered in prison, since he writes this request in his 'own hand', rather than dictating through an amanuensis (cf. Philemon 19; Ephesians 3:1; 6:20). I often join a ministry to visit foreign prisoners in the provincial jail in Chiang Mai. The inmates have been found guilty of various crimes, from travelling with a fake passport to drug trafficking. Their sentences vary from one to several years. They are lonely, all the more so because they are imprisoned in a foreign land, away from their families and friends. Most of them appreciate a visit from someone and some of them have come to know Christ through these visits. One such inmate appealed to the judge to transfer his fellow inmate's conviction to him because he felt that his friend, who had a wife and two children, deserved freedom more than he. 'Greater love has no one than this, that he lay down his life for his friends' (John 15:13).

✳ *O eternal and most merciful God, how thoughtlessly we have regarded our freedom. While we take it for granted, others are deprived of it and long to be free. Help us to remember those who languish behind bars for whatever reason, whether they deserve it or not. In your mercy bring them comfort and hope, that in suffering and strain they may look forward to the peace and justice that only you can give.*

Saturday May 14   *Revelation 2:1–7*

Remember from where you have fallen

The call to remember 'the height from which you have fallen' is addressed to the church in Ephesus, the first Christian church and an important centre of early Christianity. Paul had his headquarters there for at least three years. The church built up a great reputation because of its deeds, hard work and perseverance (verse 2), all apparently done in 'love.' But once it had abandoned its 'first love', everything came to naught. 'Love' is what the church needs to recover today. Without love, what the church does will not reflect God in Christ. Love is the basis of the church's existence. 'This is how we know what love is: Jesus Christ laid down his life for us' (1 John 3:16).

✳ *We thank you, God, for your mercy and love which have brought us out of the depths into which we had fallen. We implore your forgiveness. Help us to see ourselves in the light of the cross so that, being freed from sin and from aimlessness, our minds will be renewed and our hearts spirit-filled and we will be victorious over all things through Jesus Christ our Lord and Saviour.*

FOR REFLECTION AND ACTION – alone or with a group

● Think of the possibility of losing your memory. How do you think you would feel and manage?

● Think of people who have lost or are losing their memory because of Alzheimer's disease, amnesia, or plain forgetfulness due to old age. Do you know of any such persons? Pray for them; better yet, pay them a personal visit and help them to do things that they can no longer remember how to do.

● Try to remember all the persons who have made a difference in your life, for better or for worse. Thank God for all of them and pray for forgiveness for the wrong and pain you may have caused others.

FRUIT OF THE SPIRIT
1. Love

Notes based on the New Revised Standard Version by
Louie Crew

Louie Crew is Professor Emeritus of English Literature at Rutgers, the State University of New Jersey, USA. He is the founder of Integrity, a gay and lesbian ministry, and serves on the Executive Council (like the Archbishop's Council) of the Episcopal Church. He is the author of over 1,460 publications and maintains extensive Anglican pages at http://newark.rutgers.edu/~lcrew/rel.html

Our readings this week take a hard look at the subject of love. Whole industries seem at times bent on debasing the word – with sappy songs, with greetings cards, with advertisements to sell myriads of things. Christians ourselves often throw the word 'love' around glibly. Comedian Garrison Keillor has a delightful anecdote in which a pastor who thinks he loves everybody steadily gives the wrong names to the couple whose marriage service he is conducting. Theologian Carter Heyward warns us: 'Love without justice is cheap sentimentality.'

Saint Francis said, 'Preach the gospel at all times. If necessary, use words.' Paul emphasises that same imperative about 'Love' in calling it a fruit of the Spirit – something we manifest only if the Spirit gives it to us as a gift, not something we can manufacture. Love's presence or absence in our lives is a litmus test to whether we have been with Jesus.

This week's reflection and action suggestions are incorporated into the readings as we go along.

Sunday May 15 (Pentecost)   *Galatians 5:22*
The fruit of the Spirit is love
The Bible says nothing explicit about many of the major moral issues of our time, and when it does seem to, sometimes it sends mixed signals. For example, pacifists and militarists alike cite scripture to support their ideologies. Much of the Hebrew scriptures describes God as war-like, taking sides and giving victory to his followers and brutal death and destruction to their enemies – even to innocent women and children. The same scriptures envision a new Jerusalem and a world in which swords are beaten into farm equipment, a world in which war will be no more.

Enemies of Jesus frequently tried to trip him up in scriptural arguments. 'What is the greatest commandment?' lawyers asked him. 'To love God with all your heart, mind, soul and strength, and the second is like it, to love your neighbour as yourself. On these two hang all the law and the prophets' (Matthew 22:37–38; Luke 10:27). In other words, if a scriptural law or a scriptural witness does not lead us to love God and to love our neighbours, that law or witness fails to meet Jesus' test. The writer of Galatians puts it another way: if we want to know whether we are living as God wants us to live, we will show the fruit of the Spirit. And the first fruit listed is love.

✳ *God, I name those near to me whom I do not love as much as I love myself. Reveal to me how I might this day behave towards them so that by my actions they will know that I love them. Please use the same standard in forgiving me that I use in forgiving them.*

Monday May 16   *1 Corinthians 13:1–3*

If I do not have love

In February of 2002, I attended a consultation on gay and lesbian Christians in the Anglican Province of Brazil. The primate organised the gathering as part of his response to the commitment all bishops made at Lambeth 1998 to study the question of sexuality and to listen to the experiences of gay and lesbian Christians. He and several other bishops were among the church leaders who listened for three days as Brazilian gay and lesbian Christians told their stories. On the last morning one very introverted bishop, who had said almost nothing during the week, spoke up: 'There is something wrong with this conference. The gays and the lesbians have taken all the risks. We straights have sexual histories too, and I am going to tell you mine.'

You could have heard a pin drop. He continued: 'I am enormously grateful that when I was 14, the Anglican Church received my mother as a prostitute. Because her conversion was real and deep, she understood that she was not being made better than other prostitutes, but being called to love them. Even to this day I count as important members of my family many of her former co-workers.

'And there is more. In my late teens, my first cousin and his male lover came to live with us. Much of what I know about the love of God I learned from the way those two loved – not just each other, but all whose lives connected with theirs.'

Christianity is not primarily about respectability, nor about correct attitudes, nor even about correct behaviour. First and foremost, it is about love.

✳ *What would the church look like if it became a safe place for sinners?*

Tuesday May 17   1 Corinthians 13:4–7

Love is kind

My partner and I were conspicuous as an interracial gay male couple in our small town in rural Georgia, especially when we took out a joint cheque account. We said the marriage vows in the *Book of Common Prayer* on 2 February 1974. A few months later, I received a letter from my parish church asking me to worship somewhere else 'more in sympathy with your concern for homosexual persons'. I continued to attend – not to offend them, but to honour the One who issues the invitation for absolutely everybody.

At that time Ernest was a hairdresser, and in our kitchen he did the hair of many of the poorest black women in the county. They told us everything going on in the community, far more than we wanted to know. About two years after the vestry's letter, one of his customers called me downstairs from my study. 'I have something delicious to tell you,' she said. 'Dr Brown's (not his real name) mistress is going to have a new baby for him.' (Dr Brown was a key member of the congregation.) I called a gay priest friend in Chicago to tell him. 'Should I send Dr Brown a Father's Day card?' I asked and giggled. 'You'll do nothing of the kind. This is not about you. This is about a new life coming into the world. If you care at all, you will offer yourself to be a sponsor for the child in baptism. Otherwise, leave well enough alone.'

'Love is patient; love is kind … It does not rejoice in wrongdoing … It bears all things … endures all things' (verses 4, 6, 7).

✳ *John Heywood is credited with saying, 'If you haven't got anything nice to say about anybody, come sit next to me.' What is the latest piece of gossip I have heard and possibly relished? What quiet, loving action can I take to counter the malice?*

Wednesday May 18   1 Corinthians 13:8–13

Seeing fully

Mirrors in the first century were primitive by modern standards, and failed to reflect much of the detail. 'For now we see in a mirror, dimly' (verse 12). That's quite an admission for the apostle Paul, and he lived much closer to the opening events of Christianity than we do. It was not until the fourth century, after many battles among Christians about what the faith means, that the church formulated the creeds; and battles about doctrine continue to be waged with all sides claiming a certainty of being right that Paul himself disavows. Paul holds limited but clear certainty. Against all the other claims, faith, hope, and love are important, but the first two pale completely before love.

I can pass the creed with a lie-detector, but would not want to belong to a church that required one. When the thief on the cross next to his asked Jesus to be merciful, Jesus did not ask him to recite the creed first, but rewarded him for his simple compassion: 'Today you will be with me in Paradise' (Luke 23:43). Many who stumble over the creeds live more lovingly, hence more faithfully, than I do.

At the heart of the Maundy Thursday service is the claim *Ubi caritas et amor, Deus ibi est* (`Wherever love and charity are, there God is'). If we want to know whether God is in a decision, we have to look at whether the decision empowers love.

✷ *'When I became an adult, I put an end to childish ways' (verse 11). What does adult faith look like? What childishness still prevents me from experiencing mature faith?*

Thursday May 19   *Luke 7:27–36*

God loves sinners

A disciple needs to turn off the tremolo when reading scripture. Pious muzak deafens us to scripture's boldness. We risk dehumanising Jesus.

Jesus took on our humanity for a purpose. He did not spend all of his time in the temple. He spent much more time in the streets and at parties – so much so that the religious leaders mocked him. 'The Son of Man has come eating and drinking, and you say, "Look, a glutton and a drunkard, a friend of tax collectors and sinners!"' (Luke 7:34).

I don't know much about the righteous, but being a sinner, I know a lot about. I know no sinner who would invite someone back to dinner who insulted the guests on the first visit by telling them how bad they were. Jesus repeatedly ate and drank with sinners, even with the despised tax collectors – Jews who were willing to serve as agents of the Romans who occupied Israel at the time. When he encountered the Samaritan woman, whom most Jews would have considered 'poor white trash', he spent little time on her sin and most time on her thirst.

At his installation as Presiding Bishop of the Episcopal Church USA, Frank T Griswold quoted Archbishop Helder Camara of Olinda and Recife, Brazil: 'Let no one be scandalised if I frequent those who are considered unworthy or sinful.'

God loves sinners. So ought we. Such are we.

✳ *Have a party and invite some of the 'wrong sort of people'.*
Expect to see Jesus.

Friday May 20   *2 Corinthians 6:3–7a*
Servants of God
Let us now praise caustic Christians,
the champions of justice in all generations,
through whom God has restored the flow of mercy.
Some have nailed theses to the church door
with prophetic power.
Some have started new universities to
challenge the prevailing notions.
Some have overturned tables at the temple,
demanding alms for the poor, the sick,
and the destitute before we buy organs and stained glass.
Some have worn dresses to be priested for gender justice.
Some have yanked off masks to proclaim their loving gay
   unions.
Some have demanded of the white authorities, 'Let My
   People Go!'
Some have marched through tear gas and police dogs,
defying orders from prelates and judges.
Some have destroyed draft files
and burned plans for nuclear destruction.
Some have organised unions and co-operatives.
Some have fought to redistribute God's bounty justly.
All these won notoriety in their own generation
and were the scandal of their times.
Many have sat in jails rather than recant
or say that the earth as we know it
is at the centre of the universe.
Others have died.
Many there are who have left behind them no name,
but a legacy of hope restored, conflict resolved,
injustice rectified, lives redeemed.

Their victories are the inheritance of future generations.
Their line will endure for all times.

✳ *If you were on trial for being a Christian, what would be the evidence used to convict you?*

Saturday May 21   *Ephesians 5:25–33*
Loving the body

I wangled an invitation to speak about AIDS at one of the best fee-paying schools in New Jersey. The chaplain got cold feet and persuaded the history teacher to sponsor the presentation as part of his series on public issues. 'I'll never be invited back,' I told the audience, 'so I might as well speak without restraint.'

'Imagine you are in bed with the most beautiful person in the world,' I told the teenagers. 'Do you like that fantasy?' Obviously they did. 'Now imagine that you are both naked. Do you like that?' They did. No one was asleep, especially not the nervous faculty members. 'Now imagine that as you almost touch, the other person says, "Oh, one thing first. Love is about trust..." – and while speaking, retrieves a pistol from under the mattress, opens the chamber, and asks you to confirm that you see no bullet.

'"Show me that you trust me and take the pistol and point it at my temple and fire," your companion directs.

'What's wrong with this picture? Love is not about trust. In Newark where I teach, the gun is loaded. One out of every 4.5 males aged 21–44 is HIV positive. Use a condom.'

'You saved lives tonight,' the history professor said as we walked to the reception. 'Why else would I leave the comfort of home and come all the way out here to sport gay stigma?' I replied.

✳ *'For no one ever hates his own body, but he nourishes and tenderly cares for it, just as Christ does for the church' (verse 29). God did not turn out the lights while making each of our body parts. Name them, and thank God for each, especially those we are not supposed to talk about.*

FOR PRAYER

Hold in your prayer any whom you find difficult to love, including groups who challenge or threaten your own understanding of faith.

FRUIT OF THE SPIRIT
2. Joy

Notes based on the New International Version by
Wanja Knighton

Wanja Knighton was born and brought up in a rural village on the foothills of Mount Kenya. She was educated there and went to receive her degree at St Andrew's College of Theology and Development, Kabare. She is now married and living in Oxford, UK, working for the world development charity Oxfam.

The pressure of globalisation on culture around the capitalist world makes of time a commodity and values every thing and every person in terms of what they can achieve or produce. Each fruit of the Spirit, however, is a quality which cannot be assessed in such terms, and cannot even be recognised within such a market economy. The fruits of the spirit are qualities and characteristics which may never lead to fame and for which there is no price in the market. That is not to say that they are not precious, but that they are beyond money or price. They cannot be bought or sold, manufactured or achieved by human effort. They are the gift and the work of God in us. The first fruit of the Spirit and the greatest is love; yet joy comes a close second, and is the hallmark of the Christian.

Sunday May 22   *Galatians 5:22*

A slum with a difference

Mathare is a slum in Nairobi with a dirty river running in the middle of it. There are no toilet facilities and the only drainage system consists of gutters running through the small alleys. Houses are made out of mud, sticks and rusted tin roofs. Thuggery, drugs and alcoholism are the order of the day. However, meet a Christian living in this harsh conditions and you will realise there is an inner joy inside them even when the world around them is in shambles. They are not angry with God for the harsh conditions they are living in but have found their joy in knowing Christ, a joy no thug can steal or spoil.

Like the Christians in Mathare slum, may we never lose the focus of our joy, Christ, a joy that no one can steal away.

Monday May 23   *Isaiah 12:1–6*

God is great

This is the shortest chapter in the book of Isaiah, but it is full of joy and praise. For a moment the writer looks away from the dire and threatened position of the kingdom of Judah and looks at things from a larger perspective – the perspective of the last day.

Looking backwards it is often much more possible to see what God has done for us than when we simply focus on the present. People of faith can praise and rejoice, recognising God's saving hand as they look back on the events of their lives and discern God at work there.

When we drink water from the wells of salvation we will be truly happy and overflowing with divine enjoyment. This is none other than to be filled with the Spirit. So joyful are we that we are ready to make known the saving name of Jesus among all nations; for we know that Jesus did not die for one tribe or race alone but for every tribe and tongue on the whole earth. So all God's people in every nation want to shout aloud and sing for joy.

* *Lord, we pray for every tongue, tribe and land on this earth that all peoples may know the saving grace of Christ and be filled with joy.*

Tuesday May 24   *Isaiah 35:1–10*

Road of joy

The crocus is a pretty little flower that comes in due season following the wastes of winter or the lack of vegetation in a dry season. In the Middle East and Africa, when the rains come to a dry and arid land, new growth appears on the bare ground within a matter of days. How lovely then are the first flowers! In the previous chapter the day of the Lord's vengeance has come upon the kingdom of Judah laying it waste, so that it contains only stones of emptiness. Here in chapter 35, the prophecy follows immediately, announcing that the desert shall rejoice. The place in which there is no joy shall become full of joy. That which is dry desert shall become as lush and verdant as Lebanon, the best-watered place in the Middle East – complete with misty cedar forest!

There was a road called the King's Highway running north and south through the whole land of Israel that was made for trade and used by the superpowers of Egypt, Syria, Babylon and Persia. In Isaiah's vision, this road is replaced by the way of holiness. Only the redeemed will travel that road, the way to the kingdom of God – and those travelling along it will not be able to stop themselves singing for joy.

The jackal is a cunning thief in African traditional stories. He robs most families of their joy by stealing their chickens while they are asleep. All such predators and thieves will be banished from the road of joy that Isaiah sees.

✳ *Lord, give us wisdom to overcome the jackals of this world and to experience the fullness of your joy.*

Wednesday May 25   *Luke 10:17–20*
Joy of Christ
The earthly mission and movement of Jesus seem to reach a high point here. The seventy-two disciples commissioned to go through the towns and villages of Palestine return with joy, having witnessed many marvels and signs: they report that even the demons have submitted to them in Jesus' name. Jesus seems to share their joy, and speaks of a great victory over Satan. He sees, in the ministry of his disciples, the same activity of rescuing people from the grip of Satan that he has already witnessed in his own ministry. Even though he must go to the cross in his confrontation with evil, he knows that there will be others to continue the Spirit-inspired ministry of overturning evil and bringing in the reign of God.

In Africa a living may be made out of manipulating spirits but this power is not to be the motivation of the Christian disciple. The reward for overcoming evil is that we and ours are saved from the deceits of power opposed to God.

✳ *Lord, give us the joy of sharing in your work of overturning evil and setting the captive free.*

Thursday May 26   *Luke 24:44–53*
The jumping song
When I was in secondary school, Sunday services were never the same if we did not sing a song we called the 'jumping song'. This was a song which involved much beating of drums, dancing,

jumping and singing with joy as we praised God. There was one particular song which was very much liked – a song which talked about Emmaus, of how the Lord has given us bread and of how our eyes and minds have been opened to his presence, as were the eyes of the two disciples at Emmaus.

A closed mind will not understand the scriptures. We need the presence of Jesus to open our minds in order to be able to attend to what we read and to bring insight to the text. As the disciples were fired up by the living presence of Jesus who interpreted the scriptures to them and received a transformed sense of direction and hope, so we too will find new energy, hope and direction when we allow Jesus to speak to us through the scriptures. This is the blessing of Jesus that gives the greatest joy and issues in continual praise.

✳ *Lord, we pray that our minds will not be overcrowded with activities that block out your joy. Pierce our closed minds and speak to us your liberating word.*

Friday May 27   *Colossians 1:9–14* ·

The mango tree

During the dry season in Kenya there is one domestic tree that remains green. My grandmother told me that during former times if the mango tree branches were breaking with the weight of fruit, this was a sign to all that a drought was on its way, stopping the fields yielding a harvest. The mango tree normally has ready fruit during the driest and hottest months of the year in Kenya. So the mango tree not only gives a sign of the famine to come, but also offers to sustain and make good the earth.

God deals with his people like the mango tree. Out of the dominion of darkness God redeems us to bear fruits of great endurance, patience, thankfulness and, above all, joy. God does not save us primarily so that we might acquire ministries but so that we might bear fruit.

There is no more joyful sight in an African village than a mango tree full of children in its branches plucking the sweet fruit and letting the juice run down their bodies as they enjoy its sweetness. What a lovely image of the enjoyment God intends for the redeemed!

✳ *Lord, help us to bear fruit so others may enjoy the gifts you have given us.*

A parable from Africa

Once upon a time Wango'mbe was taking care of his herd in the fields. He owned a lot of goats and cows. Goats are any leopard's target and one day, a goat's kid wandered off from the rest of the herd. The leopard was quick to attack the helpless, feeble creature. Without wasting any time, Wango'mbe set off quickly to save the helpless kid, with a spear in one hand. Courageously he saved the animal, and so there was great rejoicing in the village.

No one likes to lose anything they have. No herder likes to lose a single animal from his flock, since each one is part of his livelihood. How much more precious is the life of a single human being. Joy in heaven is great when one human life is redeemed and saved from destruction. This does not happen through human effort or righteousness but when we repent and cry out for the Saviour's aid. We may be lost to ourselves but if we are willing to be found then we can be saved not only for this life but also for everlasting life.

✱ *Pray that we will have the courage to look for those who are lost and extend to them the saving hand of Christ.*

FOR REFLECTION – alone or with a group

● Has the achievement-focused culture of today clouded your real source of joy?

● Do we seek power for ourselves in our Christian life or do we seek to serve God and thereby discover his joy?

● Do you bear fruit even during the most trying times of your Christian walk?

● What new joy have you perceived this week in the scriptures?

● What does it mean to you to be 'saved'? Do you experience joy in this knowledge, or do you need to know that joy renewed?

FOR ACTION

Make a conscious effort this week to celebrate God's gifts with joy. Look out for every sign of God's joy. When you find it, enjoy it and share it with someone else!

FRUIT OF THE SPIRIT
3. Peace, patience

Notes based on the New International Version by
Norman Taggart

A Methodist minister who has worked in Ireland, India, Britain and Sri Lanka, Norman Taggart lives in retirement in Lower Ballinderry, close to Lisburn. He was ordained in the Church of South India. In 2003 his wife, Margaret, completed her 2-year term as President of the Methodist Women's Association in Ireland.

These notes were written towards the end of 2003, a year in which my wife and I joined with thousands of others in protest against the Iraq war and I wrote a book in which I discussed the record of the churches in 'the Troubles' in Ireland. Conflict may be hidden, yet apparent to a discerning eye. It is a reality in many families, churches and countries. The gospel speaks directly to every form of alienation. Peace and patience are robust spiritual realities, whatever the circumstances. They are the products of faith in God, commitment to Christ and life in the Spirit, and are relevant during and after conflict.

Sunday May 29   *Galatians 5:22*
Peace, patience and inner conflict

Verses 16 to 21 present conflict more in terms of internal personal struggle than as a war against an enemy. It takes place within each of us, in the clash between our selfish selves and God's Spirit. We need to acknowledge evil in our own hearts, and allow the Spirit to triumph.

The character produced by the Spirit (verses 22 and 23) includes peace and patience. In summary, it is Christ-likeness. The closer we draw to Jesus, the more we depend on the Spirit, the more like Jesus we become. The challenge is to 'live by the Spirit' (verses 16 and 25), to 'belong to Christ Jesus' (verse 24) and 'to keep in step with the Spirit' (verse 25). When a firm or business comes 'under new management', it sometimes seems to make little difference. Only the name changes. Dubious practices continue. In the management of our lives, it should be 'all change' with our wills surrendered to Christ (verse 24). But transformation takes time. We need patience.

✳ *Open our eyes, Lord, to the evil within our own hearts. Help us to believe in your power to change us.*

Monday May 30   Revelation 12:7–12
Peace, patience and conflict in heaven

Today's reading presents a very different perspective on the epic struggle between good and evil. Couched in highly colourful language, perhaps JRR Tolkien's trilogy *The Lord of the Rings* – in book or film form – may help to make it more accessible to some people. The titles 'devil', 'Satan', 'the ancient serpent' and 'the great dragon' are used in attempts to personify the evil adversary of God and humanity. Satan and his cohorts engage Michael and his angels in a 'war in heaven' (verse 7). Satan is defeated by Jesus' atoning death, by God's word and through the faithfulness of martyrs determined not to submit to his authority. Satan is hurled from heaven to earth where for a time he 'leads the whole world astray' (verse 9). But his 'time is short', and his final overthrow is assured (verse 12).

Until Satan's final defeat, our task is to witness to God's kingdom and to act on Christ's authority. Two churches did this together in Colombo in the 1990s, one Anglican (aptly called Saint Michael and all Angels!) and the other Methodist. They provided medical care for the poor, placed some unemployed people in jobs and rehabilitated young men caught up in conflict.

✳ *Help us, Lord, to confront evil and to witness by word, deed and example for peace and righteousness.*

Tuesday May 31   Ephesians 2:13–18
Peace, patience and 'traditional' conflict

According to this key New Testament passage, peacemaking is a high-risk activity. First, it required Jesus to confront and destroy 'the barrier, the dividing wall of hostility' (verse 14) between Jew and Gentile, a highly divisive conflict in the ancient world. Second, peacemaking caused Jesus to lose his life, through crucifixion. Third, the implications of peace and reconciliation had to be explored. Jew and Gentile became 'one new man', yet 'in this one body' it is 'both of them' who are reconciled to God (verses 15–18). Cultural, historical, religious and other differences did not disappear. Was their continuing role for good or ill? There is no higher calling than to be committed to the unity of the church and its mission in the world. What can we do locally, nationally and internationally to build trust and encourage people to destroy the barriers which divide?

✳ *Father, make us one for your glory and for the sake of the world.*

Wednesday June 1   *Isaiah 26:1–4*

Peace, patience and armed conflict

Notice the strong words in this short passage – salvation, faith, peace, and righteousness. We should avoid simplistic applications. True, the Lord will 'keep in perfect peace' the person 'whose mind is steadfast' and who trusts in God (verses 3 and 4). But if the city is in danger of attack it needs to be 'a strong city (with) its walls and ramparts', and its gates open to host 'the righteous nation' (verses 1 and 2). 'Might' needs to be coupled with 'right'. Spiritual and moral values are never secondary. Salvation is for cities, nations and individuals.

Some years ago I spoke against a loyalist paramilitary group in Northern Ireland, for taking unilateral action in a divided society and presenting it as part of a peace strategy. Calling for cross-community action, I suggested that Christians – whether Protestant or Catholic – had to give a lead to a divided community by 'practising love, forgiveness and trust' and working with others for peace. My call provoked many responses, for and against – with some threats. A senior church figure rang to say I was 'on my own'. Not so, 'for the Lord … is the Rock eternal' (verse 4). He, the strong one, keeps 'in perfect peace' those who trust him. With him, we are never alone. In the Bible, peace is real even when life itself is at risk. Or is this naïve?

✳ *Thank you for your words, Lord, 'peace I leave with you; my peace I give you … do not be afraid' (John 14:27).*

Thursday June 2   *1 Thessalonians 5:12–14*

Peace, patience and church conflict

According to CS Lewis, it takes all sorts of people to make a church. For a realistic picture of a local church, read today's passage through to verse 24. These church members were a mixed bag. They included hard workers and shirkers, troublemakers and timid people, bossy and weak people. What advice does the writer offer? 'Be patient with everyone' (verse 14). Don't give up on any, or cut them down to size. Should this be our line too, in the workplace, the church, and the home?

Jesus' disciples often disappointed him, but he always gave them another opportunity to listen, learn and grow. How many chances has he given us? He never loses patience or despairs of us. This is comforting and challenging in our roles as parents, grandparents and church members. We should remember it especially when leading people to Christ and 'discipling' them.

✳ *Loving Lord, you have been so patient with us, and you have needed to be! Help us to be patient with ourselves and with others.*

Friday June 3   *Luke 13:6–9*

Peace, patience and judgement

Jesus' parable is a wake-up call, a sharp reminder that true religion is more a matter of positive than negative goodness. A fig tree was thought to mature within three years, so a tree that had failed to produce fruit within that time seemed unlikely ever to be productive. In the parable the fruitless tree is viewed as using scarce resources to no good purpose. The owner of the vineyard orders it to be cut down. The vineyard keeper asks for more time. Perhaps by loosening the soil, adding fresh nutrients and providing extra care, he will be able to turn things around.

In the Bible a fig tree is sometimes a symbol of God's people. The application is plain. The parable warns of judgement, and yet dramatises hope. God's patience and mercy are not in doubt, but those who fail to produce fruit must face the consequences. Jonathan Swift's eighteenth century claim, that we have enough religion to make us hate and not enough to make us love, remains uncomfortably true for Ireland and elsewhere. Whatever the difficulties, the challenge is to look to Christ, to live a life of love and to create community.

✳ *Centre our lives on you, Lord. Fill us with your love. Help us to reach out to others, and to seek to build community.*

Saturday June 4   *Romans 12:14–21*

Peace, patience and persecution

This reading is directly relevant to Northern Ireland and other areas of conflict. It refers to wrong attitudes and relationships within the church and society. Notice the striking contrasts – love and revenge, evil and good, brother and enemy, cursing and blessing, and peace and affliction.

'If it is possible, as far as it depends on you, live at peace with everyone' (verse 18). But often everything does not depend on us. It is difficult, for example, to see how we can live at peace with those who make no secret of their hostility towards us, and refuse to be reconciled. 'Do not be overcome by evil' is a timely warning. 'Overcome evil with good' is a challenging gospel alternative (both in verse 21). The passage shows us how to attempt this: by doing what is right, seeking to live at peace, leaving vengeance to God and supplying the needs of enemies (verses 17–20). A victim in our Irish Troubles said, 'It's difficult.' To which I replied, 'No, it's impossible.' It is only possible for those who are being renewed by Christ and his Spirit (Romans 12:2).

✳ *In conflict situations, Lord, help us to listen, learn and try to meet evil with good. Against all the odds, give us a harvest of goodness.*

FOR REFLECTION AND ACTION

Ideally with at least one other person, visit an individual, family or group whom you know to be resentful and hurt due to unresolved conflict. Spend time with the person or group, patiently listening and learning. If appropriate, discuss whether some form of follow-up might be attempted. Finally, if you cannot pray with them, pray for them and for others caught up in conflict.

FRUIT OF THE SPIRIT
4. Kindness, generosity

Notes based on the Revised English Bible by
Elizabeth Salter

Elizabeth Salter began her ecumenical journey in Geneva in 1956, working for the newly-formed World Council of Churches. Some 34 years later, after four children, widowhood, commitment to development concerns and six years as Moderator of the International Division of the British Council of Churches, she returned to the WCC, within the Commission of the Churches on International Affairs (CCIA). Her main involvement was with churches in many war-torn countries, wrestling with issues of peace and justice. A Quaker, she is convinced that peacemaking lies at the heart of the gospel message, and not on its fringes. She set up the WCC's Programme to Overcome Violence, now a Decade (2001–2010) to which every member church is committed. In retirement she writes, travels and has fun with her eight grandchildren.

If the everyday values of society in Galatia were anything like those in western society today, then the fruits of the Spirit listed by Paul were unfashionable intrusions. Some of us might question Paul's insistence on the incompatible demands of body and spirit (developed by the early Greek Gnostics), but the world's crying need to recognise, take to heart and make its own the particular gifts of the Spirit is a challenge to us all. Kindness and generosity, in a society obsessed by its material wants rather than needs, by competitive impulses fed by business and media, and by the constant urge to succeed, are in short supply. Yet they are given to us freely by the Spirit of God to share with others. And the fruits of the Spirit are not handed out parsimoniously; they are a generous package. How they might transform our lives is a voyage of discovery.

Sunday June 5   *Galatians 5:22*

Unlimited resources – for all

In verses 19–21 Paul has listed a set of undesirable characteristics, immediately recognisable in our modern world. Can we acknowledge some of them in ourselves? Next comes a set of attributes that are quite astonishing in their completeness:

can anyone be that perfect? The point is that they are gifts, freely conferred by the Spirit of Christ. We are at liberty to accept them or to refuse them, but they are vital components of life in the Spirit.

Kindness and generosity can, of course, come and go, as the mood takes us. But here it is not just a question of making gestures. A chicken and a pig were taking a morning stroll together. After a while, the chicken said, 'I'm hungry. Let's go home and have some bacon and eggs.' 'All very well for you,' replied the pig. 'In your case, that's just a gesture. For me, it's total commitment.'

Total commitment means a change of heart, a turning around to see the world from a completely different angle. A brother of the Taizé community in France once offered me, as a gift for my Vietnamese daughter, an exquisite set of statuettes, given to him by a Vietnamese friend. 'How can you bear to part with it?' I asked. His reply was simple. 'Things must circulate,' he said.

✳ *Lord, help me to realise that letting go of what we hold dear, and sharing it with others, is often the way to fullness of life.*

Monday June 6   *Romans 2:1–11*
No favourites
Nobody's perfect. Do we sometimes behave as if we resent the fact that they aren't? That can include us. Even if we start to accept our own imperfections, it's easier to be kind and generous to those we love, or admire, or just like. But what about the awkward squad? The bored teenagers, skateboarding under my window and throwing their litter into my garden? The smelly old tramp sitting next to me in the train? Refugees with different customs and multiple needs? Traditional enemies, in Israel/Palestine, for instance, locked in an endless cycle of hatred and mistrust?

But reflect on what consistent kindness and generosity can do to transform relationships. The writer of the book of Deuteronomy reminds us that, as God is 'no respecter of persons' (Deuteronomy 10:17), and 'shows love towards the alien who lives among you', we too must be inclusive in our concern for others. I once met a German woman who, learning that I was a Quaker, flung her arms around me, her eyes filling with tears. 'At last I have someone to thank,' she said. 'Quakers came from Britain to Germany after the war with food for the starving. They saved my father's life.'

✳ *All-caring God, free of favouritism, may we too know how to seek justice for all, and to reach out to those who are hard to love.*

Tuesday June 7　　　　　　　　　　　　　*Colossians 3:12–17*

Generosity unlimited

This tremendous passage says it all. Maybe we feel on reading it as Alice Walker did when reflecting on Martin Luther King's espousal of non-violence – that it is 'a burden too noble to bear'. Yet Paul is writing from prison to a group of new Christians in a hostile environment! The garments he describes as being perfect for them are precisely what they and we need to show Christ's love to fellow men and women – compassion, kindness, humility, gentleness, patience.

In July 1991 I visited Christians in Albania with a delegation from the World Council of Churches. Since 1967 all Albanian faith communities had been banned, and it was only a short while before our visit that restrictions on them had been lifted. The people were desperately poor; they had suffered unimaginable persecution and deprivation. Yet when we travelled south to visit isolated Christians and to be present at the handing back, after 25 years, of their vandalised church, we were lovingly greeted with gifts: crocheted mats, a bunch of mountain herbs and a small bag of hazelnuts. Out of their poverty, they generously shared with us the best they could provide. I shall always be thankful.

✳ *Loaves and fishes, small coins in the Temple treasury, a bag of hazelnuts: may my own offering, Lord, be as generous as that of the poorest of the poor.*

Wednesday June 8　　　　　　　　　　　　　*Romans 12:6–13*

Do it cheerfully!

It's well known that babies and children are far more likely to flourish if they experience large doses of unconditional love. When we applied to adopt our little Vietnamese daughter, the social worker would come round unannounced, often when I was preparing a meal, the four children creating an impromptu band from the saucepans and wooden spoons they'd filched from cupboards and drawers. 'Wonderful!' she would enthuse. 'Just how it should be!' She meant, of course, that encouraging my daughter to be part of family fun was far more important than a neat and tidy kitchen. Even though she didn't linger to clear up the mess, I knew she was right.

How often do we think of our Christian service as 'solemn duty'? Why is it that many people outside the church wouldn't come inside even if you paid them, because they see Christians as depressing killjoys? Paul places great emphasis on leading our lives as Christians with a light touch: charity without grudging, helping others cheerfully, mutual affection, 'aglow with the Spirit', hope keeping us joyful, practising hospitality.

Psalm 145 reminds us that the Lord 'watches over all who love him' (verse 20). Are we aware of God's quiet, unfussy watchfulness in our living and loving?

✳ *Generous God, may the gifts you have given me be used generously too, joyfully and with the lightest of touches.*

Thursday June 9   *2 Corinthians 9:6–15*

More than enough to spare

When spring comes, I am each year overwhelmed by the generosity of nature. Walking in the high Alpine meadows that surround my home in France, I am surrounded by a profusion of wild flowers, tall grasses, rich pastures. The cows that have for months been confined to fields and barns can at last roam over the newly-green mountainside: we in turn enjoy delicious cheeses, butter, milk and cream. We often – especially if we live in urban areas – take this generosity for granted, not just the plentiful riches of nature, but her sights and sounds and scents as well. Do we take enough time really to appreciate God's gifts in the world about us? Maybe it is only when they are taken from us, for whatever reason, that we begin to appreciate the generosity of God's world.

We in turn are called in this passage to follow God's generous example, 'overflowing in a flood of thanksgiving' (verse 12). Not just sharing what we have with others, but taking time to allow others to share with us. Like the teacher with a crowd of little boys in an Edinburgh park; one of them lingered to stroke the bark of a beautiful tree, his eyes shining. 'Feel it, Miss!' he called. 'Isn't it lovely – just like velvet.' Such gifts of wonder must be celebrated!

✳ *Teach us, generous God, to give without reluctance, and with no sense of compulsion. As you provide unstintingly for us, may we too be alert to the world's needs.*

It's not fair!

It may well be that you feel this passage is not addressed to you. 'Rich in this world's goods'? Hardly, what with the mortgage, the rising cost of living, clothes for the children, holiday expenses and all. But hold it! Did you know that 1.3 billion people live on $1 a day – or less? Three billion live on $2 a day. The World Bank is gracious enough to call that 'absolute poverty'.

Such poverty, with all its attendant evils – lack of adequate food, healthcare, education or shelter – should, as Sam Kobia, General Secretary of the World Council of Churches, has written, be included in the continuum of 'intolerable conditions in history: slavery, colonialism, apartheid'. He goes on to say that the plight of the poor becomes 'so morally and spiritually repugnant that the greater part of humanity rises up to struggle against it'.

Are we rising up? We may be generous in our giving to charity, but do we protest about the structures that keep the poor in poverty? Do we tell those in power that such domination is intolerable? The movement that brought Jubilee 2000 to life must not be allowed to lose momentum as it calls for debt relief for poor countries. Groups such as the World Development Movement keep the issues on the political agenda in the UK. Christians need to speak up alongside all those who care – and act.

✳ *Caring God, teach us each day to care enough, as we act to meet the needs of those who bear the burdens of injustice. May we bring closer your kingdom of unreserved generosity.*

Life after death

When I read this passage, I feel a twinge of envy – envy that Peter was nearby to raise Tabitha to life. I recently attended the funeral of a dear friend, François, a Rwandan Anglican priest, killed in a car crash. At 39, he leaves a wife, four small children and a parish that mourns his death, as do many in Rwanda, where his parents and many family members were murdered in the genocide, and in Ireland, where he exercised his ministry. His overflowing energy, generosity and self-giving seem buried with him in the cold ground where he was laid. There was no miracle to raise him to life, or to return him to those who loved him.

Or that is how it feels. Yet his enthusiasm, his sense of fun, his love, loyalty and deep commitment to the gospel were shining beacons in a world that desperately needs such unconditional generosity. None of that is lost, but remains in the many lives he touched. His 7-year-old son wrote, 'Daddy was very good, and the best'. Thanks to François's ministry, as with Tabitha, 'many came to believe in the Lord' (verse 42). We cannot explain his tragic death, but we can find strength and inspiration in his life and witness.

✳ *Loving God, may we have the courage and insight to say, If we accept good from God, shall we not accept evil? Though he wounds, he will bind up; the hands that harm will heal' (Job 2:10; 5:18).*

FOR REFLECTION – alone or in a group

● Recall someone who has shown you particular kindness or generosity. How did they offer it? Were there strings attached? Did it make a big difference to your life? Did their action inspire you to act like them?

● Has God been generous to you? How?

● How can you share that generosity?

FOR ACTION

There are many calls on our time and resources. Make a list, prioritising them individually, and, after discussion, as a group. Take time to consider the implications of this list, and the action you are taking or might take, individually or collectively, to make a difference in God's world.

FRUIT OF THE SPIRIT
5. Faithfulness

Notes based on the Jerusalem Bible by
Jo Ind

Jo Ind is a writer based in Birmingham, UK. She works as a journalist for The Birmingham Post *and also contributes to* The Independent *and* Third Way *magazine. Her first book,* Fat is a Spiritual Issue, *is on eating disorders. Her second,* Memories of Bliss, *is about sexuality and spirituality. Her enduring interest is in the connections between theology and the body.*

In the West, faithfulness is a fruit of the Spirit that is going out of fashion. The rate of divorce is continually rising. In business, companies are employing staff on short-term contracts so they do not have to invest in people in the long term. Products that we buy are no longer designed to last a lifetime. Obsolescence is built into the design. CD players, mini-disc players and DVD players are discarded as soon as the next technological breakthrough comes onto the market. It is a culture in which doing what is right for now is valued over commitment through thick and thin. The West is suspicious of faithfulness. Why is it considered a virtue? What is the point of someone hanging on in there for its own sake, when she could be moving on to a person or a situation that better meets her needs? These are good questions and ones that should be taken seriously. There are indeed times when we mistake 'faithfulness' for putting up with a situation that is far from healthy. Discerning when we are being rightly faithful and when we have got stuck in a rut takes skill. But it is a skill we need to cultivate because, whatever the messages of our culture, faithfulness is a fruit of the Spirit and always will be because God is faithful to us. Our God is a God who will never let us go. To grow in God is therefore to grow in our capacity to be faithful.

Sunday June 12   *Galatians 5:22*
Faithful to…

In many ways faithfulness is like patience or endurance, the fourth fruit of the Spirit. Both carry a sense of carrying on when the going gets tough. The difference with faithfulness is that it suggests a relationship: we are faithful to someone or something. In the Jerusalem Bible this seventh fruit of the Spirit is translated as 'trustfulness.' To be faithful is to be worthy of trust, without which there can be no happy relationship. Tomorrow we will be looking at five verses from the book of Ruth. Why not read the whole book today, or make a decision to read it at some point this week? It is almost an allegory of faithfulness.

✳ **Lord, help me to trust. Help me to draw into your heart and rest in the knowledge of your faithfulness to me. May I communicate your faithfulness to all whom I meet and in all that I do.**

Monday June 13   *Ruth 2:8–12*

Faithful to friends and family

Much is made of the love of Boaz for Ruth as revealed in this text and Boaz does indeed prove to be an honourable man. But this story belongs to the women. The primary faithfulness is between Ruth and her mother-in-law, Naomi. It is this faithfulness that has so much impressed Boaz (verse 11) and which creates the happy ending to what could have been a bleak tale.

The story begins with a famine in Judah, which meant Naomi and her husband, who was from Bethlehem, had to leave their country with their two sons and settle in Moab. The two young men married Moabite women, Orpah and Ruth. After about ten years all three of the men in the family had died, leaving Naomi and her daughters-in-law destitute. It was the custom in Israel that a childless widow would marry the brother of her deceased husband, but Naomi had no more sons so she believed the best hope for Orpah and Ruth was to return to their mothers while she made her way back to Judah. Orpah kissed Naomi and did just that, but Ruth clung to her mother-in-law and made her powerful vow of faithfulness to her (1:17–18). Ruth went with Naomi back to Bethlehem, though her chances of finding a husband there were slim because she was a Moabite and foreign women were prohibited from marrying Israelites. Once there, Ruth went out to gather corn, and by chance ended up in the fields of Boaz, a rich relative of Naomi's deceased husband. Today's verses are the words said by Boaz, after he had spotted Ruth in the fields. Happily Ruth ended up marrying Boaz and having a son. The son also brought joy to Naomi because technically he belonged to her, as it was her husband's land that was sold to Boaz as part of the marriage contract to Ruth. The women of the neighbourhood said to Naomi, 'The child will be a comfort to you and the prop of your old age, for your daughter-in-law who loves you and is more to you than seven sons has given him birth' (4:15).

* *Give me the heart of Ruth, O Lord. May I be faithful to my friends and family. May I go where they would go. May I share with them their journeys home. Thank you for those who are entrusted to my heart. May I never abandon them.*

Tuesday June 14   *Luke 12:42–48*
Faithful to the master
These are chilling words that add another layer to our understanding of faithfulness. They are the perfect counter to any notion of faithfulness as a static quality. Being faithful is not about making a decision once and for all and sticking to it. The call in this passage is to be alert, to be constantly responding to God's trust in us. God is faithful in entrusting us with his world. Our faithfulness in response is to care for God's world. There is no scope for going to sleep on the job.

Think of your relationships, your gifts, your talents, the various communities to which you belong and your wealth. How much faith must God have in us to have entrusted us with so much? How can we respond to such faithfulness?

* *Make a list of all that God has entrusted to you. Hold those things before God in grateful appreciation. Ask God how you can live them more completely.*

Wednesday June 15   *Psalm 119:30–37*
Faithful to the law
The idea of being faithful to the law of God is perhaps more natural to Jews and Muslims than it is to Christians. Christians too often perceive honouring of God's law as the ugly legalism that earned Jesus' rebuke, but that is not what the psalmist is expressing here. If you struggle with the overtones of seemingly authoritarian words like 'rulings', 'decrees', 'commandments' and 'statutes' it can be helpful to replace them with the softer word, 'ways'. Far from a legalistic faith, the psalmist has made a conscious decision to be faithful to the ways of God (verse 30) and is asking that they be written in his heart.

* *Summarise this passage in your own words. Make it your prayer for today.*

Faithful to the message

Passages in the Bible that begin by asking slaves to submit to masters are likely to evoke difficult feelings, most of which are healthy. It takes a little discipline – and faithfulness – to look behind what Paul might be saying here. Paul wrote this letter to Titus, whom he has left responsible for the church in Crete, which was in urgent need of correction. This letter was to encourage Titus in his task of bringing the church to order, hence its practical and specific tone. The instructions for slaves come at the end of a passage (2:1–10) in which he is explaining to Titus how all the different members of the church should be behaving. Though we no longer find slavery acceptable, Paul is showing how no one, whatever his or her social situation, is exempt from being faithful to God's message (verse 11).

Do we do anything that does not lead us to God (verse 12)? If it doesn't lead us to God, then why do it?

* *Examine your past week and ask yourself what things moved you away from your sense of the presence of God. Imagine walking past those things and moving on nearer to the heart of God.*

Faithful to each other

Paul's urging that this, his favourite, church should stay united is all the more moving for the knowledge that he was separated from them through being in prison. The church at Philippi was being persecuted, so there was an urgent need for its members to cleave together. Being faithful to the gospel is not just an individual endeavour. The gospel is something we live as a community. Being faithful means sticking together. This can be excruciatingly painful at times when people within churches are deeply divided. It takes great grace to say of those with whom we disagree: 'You and I are together in the same fight' (verse 30).

* *Dear God, I remember your church throughout the world. Thank you for its life in so many cultures, in such different circumstances. Give us a heart that is faithful to the gospel and faithful to each other, that we might truly be a sign from God.*

Faithful to the end

For those who live in regimes where they are in fear of their lives, these words are potent in their simplicity: 'Even if you have to die – keep faithful' (verse 10). This passage is saying that faithfulness is more important than life. It is saying that our faithfulness to God is life.

Not all of us are facing death on a daily basis, but we will each have to face it one day. Our ability to trust in the loving faithfulness of God when that day comes will be dependent on the extent to which we have practised faithfulness in our more ordinary lives. To practise faithfulness is to prepare for our death.

✳ *Dear God, the one who hugs and holds us and is eternally faithful to us. Teach us to let go into you each day that we might let go into you on our last day.*

FOR REFLECTION – alone or with a group

● Where do you experience others' faithfulness to you?
● Look back over your life and call to mind all who have demonstrated to you the faithfulness of God. Give thanks for them.
● In what ways does the culture in which you live value or despise faithfulness?

FOR ACTION

Make a point of expressing your appreciation to someone who is faithful to you. Bring to mind someone who is suffering as a result of broken faith. Pray for that person, write them a letter, phone them or visit them to express your solidarity with them. Hold them faithfully in your prayer over the coming months.

FRUIT OF THE SPIRIT
6. Gentleness, self-control

Notes based on the New Revised Standard Version by
Nicholas Alan Worssam SSF

Brother Nicholas Alan is a member of the Anglican religious community, the Society of Saint Francis. He has been involved in various types of work in the community's houses, and is at present living at a monastery in Worcestershire, England.

On 8 May 1373 a young woman, only 30 years old, lay in the agony of an illness that had brought her to the point of death. She received the last rites of the church, and a priest held before her a crucifix, saying: 'I have brought you the image of your maker and saviour: look upon it and draw comfort from it.' The room grew dark around her, except for the cross which seemed to her to glow with light. She began to lose all feeling in her body, and felt she was about to die. Then suddenly she was released from all pain, and experienced a series of revelations of the love of God. She pondered these visions for the rest of her life, and wrote them down in one of the first books written in the English language. The notes and prayers this week are based on her writings. (For a modern version of her book, see *Julian of Norwich: Revelations of Divine Love*, translated by Clifton Wolters, in the Penguin Classics series).

Sunday June 19   *Galatians 5:23*

I desired to suffer with him

When Julian was a young woman she asked God for three things: the first was to know the sufferings of Christ more clearly; the second was to experience this suffering physically; the third was to receive the wounds of contrition, compassion, and longing for God. The first two requests passed from her mind, but the third stayed with her continually. In her sickness unto death she truly experienced the sufferings of Christ, but what stayed with her was the overwhelming certainty of God's presence and love in the midst of her suffering.

This love of God within her overflowed in the gentleness of her spiritual writings. The Greek word in Galatians 5:23 is *prautes*, which can be translated as meekness, gentleness or humility.

This is the quality of those who are blessed and will inherit the earth (Matthew 5:5), a meekness shown by Jesus riding a donkey into Jerusalem (Matthew 21:5), and who humbly invites us to learn from him and shoulder his yoke (Matthew 11:29). Julian is overwhelmed by the humility of Jesus, the king of heaven dying for love of her on a cross. 'If I could have suffered more, I would have suffered more,' Jesus says to her in her Revelations, 'it is a joy to me that my passion was for you.'

Gentleness is born of compassion, of sharing with another in their sufferings. It is born of the wisdom of humility.

✳ *God of your goodness, give me yourself.*

Monday June 20   *Ephesians 4:1–6*

Behold, God's handmaid!

In this passage from Ephesians, gentleness is linked with humility (*tapeinophrosunes*). In the Greek language this word for humility was used negatively, as a slavish, ignoble quality. The followers of Jesus turned it around, celebrating the humility of God in his Son. Mary is not ashamed of her 'lowliness', singing in her Magnificat of the God who has lifted her up among the lowly (Luke 1:48); and Paul proclaims the Christ who 'humbled himself', emptying himself to take on human form and die on a cross (Philippians 2:6–8).

Julian sees the wisdom and truth of Mary's soul as she receives the greeting of the angel, and stands with her again at the foot of the cross, sharing her love for the dying Jesus. In realising her lowliness, Mary attains greatness and nobleness of heart. 'And so, by this ground of meekness,' says Julian, 'she was fulfilled with grace and with all manner of virtues, and overpasses all creatures, as to my sight.' 'For all who exalt themselves will be humbled, and those who humble themselves will be exalted' (Luke 14:11).

✳ *You are enough for me, O Lord.*

Tuesday June 21   *1 Peter 3:13–16*

See! I do all things!

For many people, fear is an undercurrent to their lives. Its swift, cold waters can paralyse our hearts and minds. 'Do not fear what [others] fear,' Peter tells us, 'and do not be intimidated.' The knowledge of God brings freedom from fear, and this was something Julian knew in abundance. 'See! I am God: See! I am in all things: see! I do all things! ... How could anything be amiss?' These words fill her with confidence. In her hermit's cell in Norwich she knew about the pain of the world as the black death ravaged Europe and people came to her window for counsel and comfort. And God's words to her still resonate today: 'All shall be well and all shall be well and all manner of thing shall be well.'

But is this the end of all fear? Not quite. In today's passage we read, 'Always be ready to make your defence ... but do it with gentleness and reverence' (verses 15–16). That word for reverence in the Greek is *phobos*, the same word earlier translated as 'fear'. Gentleness is not about giving in to others out of weakness: there is no being intimidated here. Rather it is a godly fear, the beginning of wisdom (Proverbs 1:7), reverencing God who meets us in each other and always acts for our salvation.

✳ *If I ask for anything less than you, I remain in want.*

Wednesday June 22   *Titus 3:2–7*

The courtesy of God

In her sixth revelation Julian looked up to heaven and saw in her mind's eye our Lord as a lord in his house, with all his dear servants and friends whom he had invited as to a banquet. 'I saw the Lord royally reign in his house, fulfilling it with joy and mirth, himself endlessly gladdening and giving solace to his dear friends, full homely and courteously, with marvellous melody of endless love radiating from his blessed face.'

In today's passage the word translated 'gentle' is *epieikes*. The letter of James associates this word with being peaceable, a willingness to yield, being full of mercy and good deeds (James 3:17). It is the opposite of drunken or violent behaviour (1 Timothy 3:3). Aristotle defines *epieikes* as 'the indulgent consideration of human infirmities'. It is about applying the spirit rather than the letter of the law, acting out of mercy rather than strict justice.

God, says Julian, always shows us his mercy. He looks on us with pity, not with blame. And when he welcomes us to heaven he thanks us for all that we have done and suffered. 'And the more loving souls see this courtesy of God, the more willing they are to serve him all the days of their life.'

✳ *Only in you have I all.*

The true lasting joy that is Jesus

Julian tells us: 'Truly it is the most joy that may be, as to my sight, that he that is highest and mightiest, noblest and worthiest, is lowest and meekest, homeliest and most courteous: and truly and verily this marvellous joy shall be shown us all when we see him.'

Rejoice! The Lord is near! The nearness of God's presence is truly the source of all Christian strength and joy. This is God's humility, God's gentleness: being found in human form in Jesus, and being found now in our own human lives.

And yet there is still work to be done. 'For as long as we be meddling with any part of sin, we shall never see clearly the blissful face of our Lord.' The more we sin, the farther we are from this sight, but though we may feel we are in hell, 'our Lord God holds us and enfolds us for tender love that he may never leave us.' In this there is both joy and sorrow: joy because our maker is so close to us, and sorrow because our spiritual eyes are so blind and we are weighed down by sin. But by the grace of loving our eyes are opened, and at last we will see him clearly, face to face.

✳ *Ah! Lord Jesus, King of bliss, how shall I find rest?*

Our kind mother, Jesus

The spiritual life is a battle. It is a wrestling with demons, a fight to the death of the self. *Egkrateia*, or 'self-control', is the discipline that harnesses the passions of greed and hatred, the desire and aversion that almost pull apart the soul. In 1 Corinthians 7 Paul uses this word for the virtue of chastity – the faithfulness of commitment to God in either celibacy or married life.

Julian sees in God the holding together of all aspects of reality, and in particular the reconciliation of masculinity and femininity. 'For as truly as God is our Father,' she says, 'so truly God is our Mother.' God is the power and goodness of fatherhood, the deep wisdom of motherhood, and the great love of the Spirit uniting all. The motherhood of God she sees especially in 'Jesus, our true mother' who bears us in creation, and brings us to rebirth in endless life, tenderly feeding us of himself in the sacraments of his body and blood.

Self-control is not a denial of our humanity but a reconciliation of the energies of our disparate selves in the unity of the Trinity. It is a thankfulness for the passion that unites us with the passion of our Lord.

✳ *Good Lord, I thank you; blessed may you be!*

Saturday June 25   *Titus 2:1–8*
Love was his meaning
At the beginning of Julian's *Revelations* she has a vision of a hazelnut in the palm of her hand, and wonders what it may be. God answers, 'It is all that is made.' Julian continues, 'I marvelled how it might last, for methought it might suddenly have fallen to nought for littleness. And I was answered in my understanding: "It lasts and ever shall for that God loves it". And so All-thing has being by the love of God.' Julian says that we need to realise the littleness of creatures and all that is made, so as to love and have God who is unmade. For we seek rest in things in which there is no rest, rather than in God the All-mighty, All-wise and All-good.

The word *sophronas*, here translated as 'self-controlled', can also be translated as 'prudent', 'serious' or 'of sober judgement'. It is the state of being of the man once plagued by a legion of demons, now healed by Jesus and 'in his right mind' (Mark 5:15).

Prudence is a matter of perspective. It is the giving up of immediate pleasure for the enjoyment of a longer-term good. This wisdom enables us to see through the confusions and pain of life to the patient presence of God. It attunes our ears to the single word that God has spoken since the dawn of creation: love.

✳ *You are my heaven.*

FOR REFLECTION – alone or with a group
● How have you experienced the gentleness of others in this past week, and in what ways have you been gentle towards them?
● Who in your life has been an example of humility, and how might you learn from their example?
● In what way is God calling you to greater self-control?

FOR ACTION
Make a conscious effort to look for the joyful presence of God in all things this coming week and beyond.

READINGS IN MATTHEW

Notes based on the New Revised Standard Version by
Julie M Hulme

Julie M Hulme is a Methodist minister following a call to live the ministry of word and sacrament as a life of prayer. This is expressed through preaching, teaching and writing on Christian spirituality, and also through art. She lives in Birmingham, and is married to David, who is also a Methodist minister. They have two daughters.

3. Healing encounters

All joy, all praise, all adoration spring from our glimpses of God's eternal and endless grace. God's love is higher than the heavens, sturdier than the mountains, more profound than the ocean's depths (Psalm 36:5–9). And it is out of this abundance that God heals through Jesus, who, filled with God's compassion for suffering humanity, expressed that love to the full. Jesus followed love wherever it led him. He embodied both God's desire that all people should have abundant life (John 10:10), and humanity's decision to choose the life that God provides (Deuteronomy 30:15–20).

Sunday June 26   *Matthew 8:1–4*
God is life – Jesus chooses life

Is Jesus able to heal? Does Jesus want to heal? These questions can haunt us as we approach Jesus, seeking the abundant love of God.

The man suffering from leprosy recognises Jesus' power, but he is less sure of Jesus' desire to heal. Forced by his society to live as an outcast because of the disease, he has lost confidence in the benevolence of humanity. Human fear has magnified his pain. Leprosy has made him suffer; excluded from the life of his people, he has suffered twice over.

Jesus' response is immediate and emphatic. God is abundant love. God longs to heal us, to make us whole, and to remove all that distorts or destroys us. So how can God's Son do otherwise? By touching him, Jesus not only heals the disease but also restores the man to human society.

* *Read Psalm 100.*

* *O God of abundant life, we thank you for the life you have given and the love we have received. We ask for your loving strength in dealing with our difficulties. Help us in all things to choose life in the name of Jesus, who was filled with your longing to make us whole.*

Monday June 27   *Matthew 8:5–13*

God's life is for all

Was Jesus only able to heal those who met him? Was his healing power only for Jews? As we ask Jesus to touch our wounds, these questions – and others – may trouble us. But here Jesus shows us that God reaches out to heal anyone, anywhere.

God's grace is not daunted by distance, and responds to the smallest measure of faith, wherever it is found. Wherever there is honesty, humility, obedience and trust, then God's love is at work, and can create change. God's love will work amongst any who understand the nature of faith.

So we can have courage in asking God for healing, and confidence when prayer is offered today in the name of Jesus Christ. God's people are those who recognise the word of grace wherever and whenever it is spoken, and who trust in its life-giving power.

* *Read Psalm 95.*

* *O God of abundant grace, we thank you that your life and love are for all people, in every age and place. Help us to hear your loving word in both the heights and the depths of our experience, in the name of Jesus, who was filled with your longing to make us whole.*

Tuesday June 28   *Matthew 8:14–22*

God's life is for those with empty hands

As we show Jesus our wounds, our fear may grow. How can I be sure that God longs to reach out to me (Psalm 8:3–4)?

We cannot be sure. We can only act as if it is true. And not because we feel worthy of God's love, but because God is good, and God loves us. We come before God with empty hands, but God looks upon us only with love.

Jesus himself had nothing to offer his disciples that would shelter them from the hardships of the road ahead – no headquarters, career structure, financial security or influence with the powers of this world. Furthermore, the pain of the world is urgent, insistent and infinite. It soon overwhelms our resources. Our skills and strength are soon exhausted. We have nothing to give but our confidence in the abundant, healing, gracious love of God.

✳ *Read Psalm 51.*

✳ *O God of abundant mercy, we thank you for the compassion you pour into the depths of our hearts, cleansing and renewing our spirits. Help us to offer you our empty hands, that our hearts might be full of gratitude, faith and love. We ask in the name of Jesus, who was filled with your longing to make us whole.*

Wednesday June 29 *Matthew 8:23 – 9:1*

God leads us through fear to faith

These stories resonate with fear. It is fear that prevents us seeking God's abundant life: fear of death or grief, loss or turmoil; fear of being different or of accepting new responsibilities. We think, 'If that happens, I cannot cope with it!' Fear is the enemy of faith.

The world is full of forces we cannot control, some of them indifferent to us, some of them hostile to our wellbeing. They can appear overwhelming. But we can choose how we respond to them. We can trust that, whatever the evidence to the contrary, God loves us. If we are threatened, God loves us. Whatever is taken from us and whatever is done to us, God loves us. And because we are loved, we can choose life and create peace – even when we are surrounded by terror, despair, destruction and death.

✳ *Read Psalm 93.*

✳ *O God of abundant peace, we thank you that, whatever we face today, you still care for us. Help us to tell you our fears, so that we can make a creative response to our difficulties. Help us to act as if we have courage, in the name of Jesus, who was filled with your longing to make us whole.*

Thursday June 30 *Matthew 9:2–8*

God's life flows through us

Can God heal others through my intercession? Can my prayers release the abundant life of God?

We cannot save our friends, but we can offer God our fear for them, and allow God to turn that fear into faith. For why do we fear for them at all, when our sovereign God loves them so much more than we do? What is it about their situation that unsettles us? Why do we feel their pain as our burden? Why are we consumed with anger, anxiety or guilt?

As we examine ourselves, we are shown where and why we fail to trust in God's abundant love for ourselves and for others. We learn to love as Christ loves. And, understanding this, we are indeed used by him as channels of healing grace. For it was the faith of his friends that brought the paralysed man to Jesus, to be healed by a love that works from the inside out.

✳ *Read Psalm 148.*

✳ *God of abundant compassion, we thank you for our families and our friends. Help us to offer you our fears for them, entrusting them to your steadfast love, in the name of Jesus, who was filled with your longing to make us whole.*

Friday July 1   *Matthew 9:9–17*

God's life reshapes our priorities

Why does Jesus bother with these people? They seem to be beyond help. But a doctor goes to the sick, even if there is nothing he or she can do. The Pharisees had all they needed to enjoy abundant life, if they but knew it. So Jesus went to those who had nothing. Love led him: he followed. This offended the Pharisees, but God's thoughts are not our thoughts (Isaiah 55:8–9). God's life re-shapes our priorities.

Love is creative, offering space for renewal, even where renewal seems impossible. Love makes room for new ways as well as cherishing traditions honed by devotion, experience and time. We foster both, learning how to use old and new together – how to encourage an outpouring of creativity, then use the wisdom and experience of the tradition to refine and deploy the ferment for the benefit of individuals and the re-shaping of communities.

✳ *Read Psalm 96.*

✳ *God of abundant hope, we thank you for both old and new in the church. We pray for those who have experience but less energy, and those who have energy but less experience. Help us all to offer ourselves again to your renewing power, in the name of Jesus, who was filled with your longing to make us whole.*

God's life breaks taboos

Can God break down walls of fear?

Jesus reached out to others even when this made him 'unclean' according to his religious tradition. He challenged ideas in his culture as to who could be regarded as holy and worthy of God's attention. He did this because he was full of God's unceasing, overflowing compassion. He saw how powerful taboos surrounding blood, for example, trapped women in their suffering. Love does not want to see anyone isolated and desperate. This is Jesus' understanding of holiness, service, worship and mercy.

Jesus sees faith in those who besiege him, even if they do not see it themselves. He expects to find life in a situation, because he assumes that God is ahead of him, pouring out blessing. It is tragic that those who are steeped in the words of God cannot see God's grace in the world.

✳ *Read Psalm 102.*

✳ *O God of abundant power, we thank you that you set free those who are imprisoned by fear. Help us to offer you all our pain. We pray for those who are in anguish, in the name of Jesus, who was filled with your longing to make us whole.*

FOR REFLECTION – alone or with a group

● Where in your life do you see evidence of God's abundance?

● How does God help you face your fears, and live despite them?

● What are the ideas in your culture that exclude people from the fullness of life that God intends them to enjoy? How can these ideas be challenged?

FOR ACTION

Take action this week to share God's abundance with another person.

INTERNATIONAL BIBLE READING ASSOCIATION
1020 Bristol Road, Selly Oak, Birmingham, Great Britain B29 6LB

ORDER FORM for 2006 Books

Name: _____

Address: _____

_____

_____ Postcode: _____

Telephone number: _____

*To qualify for 2006 books at these special IBRA readers' prices, this order form must be used (photocopies not accepted). Your order will be dispatched when **all** books are available. Mail order only.*

Code	Title of book	Quantity	Unit price	Total
ZYW63	Words for Today 2006		£7.00	
ZYL61	Light for Our Path 2006		£7.00	
ZYL62	Light for Our Path 2006 *large print*		£7.00	
ZYL63c	Words for Today 2006 *on cassette*		£7.00	
ZYL61c	Light for Our Path 2006 *on cassette*		£7.00	
PRI43	Prisons and Palaces		£6.75	
ZYD0989	Discovering Christ *Advent & Christmas*		£8.00	
ZYD0994	Discovering Christ *Ascension & Pentecost*		£8.00	
ZYD0999	Discovering Christ *Lent & Easter*		£8.00	
ZYO0990	Online to God		£6.25	
ZYL0781	Living Prayers For Today		£15.50	
ZYM0902	More Living Prayers For Today		£15.50	

❏ I enclose a cheque (payable to IBRA)

❏ Please charge my MASTERCARD/VISA/SWITCH:

Card no: _____

Issue no (Switch): _____

Expiry date: _____

Signature: _____

Total cost of books	
UK postage included Overseas – add £3.00 airmail per book	
Donation to International Fund	
TOTAL DUE	

*Payment in **Pounds Sterling**, please.*
Please allow 28 days for delivery.

The INTERNATIONAL BIBLE READING ASSOCIATION is a Registered Charity

International Bible Reading Association

Help us to continue our work of providing Bible study notes for use by Christians in the UK and throughout the world. The need is as great as it was when IBRA was founded in 1882 by Charles Waters as part of the work of the Sunday School Union.

Please leave a legacy to the International Bible Reading Association.

An easy-to-use leaflet has been prepared to help you provide a legacy. Write to us at the address below and we will send you this leaflet – and answer any questions you might have about a legacy or other donations. Please help us to strengthen this and the next generation of Christians.

Thank you very much

International Bible Reading Association
Dept 298, 1020 Bristol Road
Selly Oak
Birmingham B29 6LB
Great Britain
Tel. 0121 472 4242
Fax 0121 472 7575

Charity Number 211542

4. Instruction to the twelve

The people of God are a community created by the gospel, formed by the promise and gift of abundant life, and living by faith, hope and love. We are the harvest of God's compassion for the world. This common source unites us even when we are bitterly divided by doctrine, politics or ethical issues. Jesus' first disciples were also a disparate group – diverse in education, experience, temper and character, and with very varied attitudes to money, ambition and the occupying power. But when they went out on mission, they became a movement of grace, empowered by the Spirit.

Sunday July 3   *Matthew 9:35 – 10:4*

God calls us to work for the harvest

When we feel the burden of others' needs, we should remember that the weight of the world's pain bore down heavily on Jesus, too. This is why he chose and trained others to share the task of proclaiming God's abundant life to the crowds. The ones he chose as his disciples shared his compassion for the ordinary people, and understood their problems, feelings, situation and context. The disciples were, themselves, ordinary, fallible people, but compassion drew them out. Love led, and they followed.

Love led Jesus to the type of people who could understand his way of prayer and work, and who would, given time, learn how to live God's life as he, Jesus, lived it. To such people, Jesus gave authority to heal and exorcise, because they were not to be his assistants but his deputies, full partners in the work. He invested everything in them. He invested in them all, even Judas.

✳ *Read Psalm 23.*

✳ *God of the harvest, fill us with your compassion for those who do not – or cannot – enjoy the abundance you desire for all people. Grant us your Spirit as we care for your flock.*

Monday July 4   *Matthew 10:5–15*

God provides the resources we need

Ultimately, Jesus gave his followers authority to make disciples of all nations (Matthew 28:16–20) as the basis of their mission to the end of the age. But in the first instance, he gives them a smaller task, better fitted to probationers. However, the narrowness of the focus obscures the depth of the work, and the demands that it will make upon them. They will learn that this mission is quite enough to stretch and deplete their resources.

They are not only to proclaim God's abundance, but depend upon it for their own sustenance, by travelling light and relying on the hospitality of others to provide what they need. Their mission is to be marked by generosity, power, freedom and grace, but they will only understand this as they learn the ability to receive, connecting with the good wherever it is to be found. With nothing to commend them but themselves and their message, they are to live as travellers, migrants, exiles. With no resources to 'pay their way', they are to practise grace as the guests of others, and forge a new community by itinerancy and integrity.

✳ *Read Psalm 145.*

✳ *God of the harvest, fill us with your joy that we might learn to travel lightly through the world, receiving your bounty, offering your peace, trusting your goodness to provide what we need.*

Tuesday July 5   *Matthew 10:16–23*

God promises to speak through us

As travellers without resources or power, the disciples are vulnerable. Jesus' words are echoed by the experience of Christian saints, martyrs and missionaries ever since. Yes, we have to be clever and wary, like the serpent that keeps out of sight when its enemies are close by. But too much caution is counter-productive. We are proclaiming truth, not fostering conspiracy. So we are to remember that even if we are caught, tried, beaten or persecuted, this will give us opportunities for telling others the good news.

The warning is not given to make us fearful, but to prepare us for the shock of finding ourselves despised. Furthermore, we are promised the presence, power and creativity of the Spirit in our moment of need. However much hostility we face from other people, even from members of our own families or our closest friends, God still loves us. This assurance is the source of our personal and corporate endurance.

✳ *Read Psalm 138.*

✳ *O God of the harvest, fill us with confidence that we are held in your love, even when we are surrounded by enemies.*

Help us to face our fears, that we might speak your truth in moments of crisis.

Wednesday July 6   *Matthew 10:24–36*

God calls us to faith, not fear

As Christians, we should not be surprised if, in difficult times, our lives reflect the experience of Jesus. Without seeking enemies, we can acquire them. However, that does not permit us to copy their methods. There is a difference between discretion and deceit.

We are to live by honesty and trust, even in the face of hostility, speaking openly and risking physical danger to remain loyal to spiritual truth. The inner light of the Spirit must be allowed to shine through our actions.

Three promises sustain us. First, all secrets will be revealed. No action to silence the gospel, however cruel, can be covered up for ever. Second, whatever happens to us, God loves us. Our value does not lie in the way that we are viewed – or treated – by the world, but in our status as God's children. Third, those who remain faithful to Jesus at moments of great danger will be acknowledged and commended by Christ in the presence of his Father.

✳ *Read Psalm 112.*

✳ *O God of the harvest, fill us with faith that whatever forces are working against your compassion and generosity, the peace and power of your truth will be revealed at the last, and that, until that time, we are held in your steadfast love.*

Thursday July 7   *Matthew 10:37–42*

God is creating a new community (1)

God's desire is for all people to enjoy life to the full, but not everyone is able to hear and receive this message, and as a result, the formation, and re-formation, of the Christian community is accompanied by divisions as traditional loyalties are tested and new alignments forged. This is a time of creativity, energy and excitement, as relationships are made in new ways, but it is also a time of great loss, grief and pain.

Discipleship requires us to flow with this process, rather than resisting it, because this is the way that God's life is activated in the world. Nevertheless, our acceptance is costly, and can make us anxious, tense and defensive. It is as we work through our fears, willing to give all, offer all, commit all to this ferment, that we discover our true life, the life that is hidden with Christ in God.

And while we do this, what can we cling to? Small actions of spontaneous kindness, receiving and being received, the joy of faith shared, the generosity of friends.

✳ *Read Psalm 146.*

✳ *God of the harvest, fill us with your strength, that we might be generous and loving to friend and foe. Help us to be resilient in hardship and buoyant in adversity, for Christ's sake.*

Friday July 8   *Matthew 12:1–8*

God is creating a new community (2)

For God's new community, love takes precedence over forms of piety or ideas of holiness that work against the welfare of human beings. It is God's desire that everyone enjoy abundant life: this is not possible if people are hungry. Our worship and devotion mean nothing if they prevent us meeting the essential needs of others.

In anxious times, human beings find security through enforcing the law, but when this is religious law, it soon becomes a means of oppression, running counter to the gospel, which is God's word of generosity and hope. It may surprise us that this can happen, but to those who are afraid, the freedom inspired by the gospel threatens the foundation of sacred life.

Jesus assures us that, when the old rules no longer apply, we can remain loyal to the principle of mercy, compassion and grace – speaking of how God is doing a new thing, and listening to the voices we do not want to hear.

✳ *Read Psalm 147.*

✳ *O God of the harvest, fill us with your patience, that we might learn to live from love and not from fear. Help us to take love as our guide to what is right, that we might offer your life as bread and hope.*

Saturday July 9   *Matthew 13:1–17*

God is creating a new community (3)

Jesus reminds us that the sower scatters the seed indiscriminately over all types of soil, then waits for a response, without having any control over whether or not the seed will germinate. Though the parable is extended into an allegory that suggests some reasons why people might hear the good news but fail to receive it, there remains much that is mysterious about this process.

We proclaim good news, but we do not control the outcome. The harvest depends on the way that others respond to our work. But the process is also partly hidden within the mystery of God. We may refine our methods, as Jesus himself spoke in stories to reach those who could not be reached otherwise. However, the success or failure of the mission is not our responsibility. We are partners with Jesus in God's work. Our part is faithfulness to our calling, and trust in the abundant love and sovereign power of the One who has called us.

✳ *Read Psalm 150.*

✳ *God of the harvest, fill us with your peace, that we might grow like healthy plants in fertile soil, yielding good fruit in due season, and in our maturity witnessing to your abundant love.*

FOR REFLECTION – alone or with a group

● How does God invest in Jesus' disciples today, training us for the work of mission?

● What are the challenges, rewards and dangers of an itinerant lifestyle? Can modern disciples follow Jesus' instructions to travel light?

● Reflect on the lives of Christian saints, martyrs, missionaries and evangelists. What can we learn from their achievements – and their mistakes – about the discipline necessary to follow Jesus?

FOR ACTION

Meet with a Christian friend to pray for the church in your neighbourhood, and to encourage one another in your faith.

LAMENTATIONS –
THE LONELINESS OF THE CITY

Notes based on the Hebrew text by
Albert H Friedlander

Rabbi Dr Albert H Friedlander OBE is the Dean of the Leo Baeck College in London and the Rabbi Emeritus of the Westminster Synagogue. He was a Fellow of the Wissenschaftskolleg in Berlin and has served as visiting professor at many universities. His books on theology and history have appeared in various languages. He is one of the Presidents of the Conference of Christians and Jews alongside the Archbishop of Canterbury, the Cardinal of Westminster, and the Chief Rabbi; the President of the London Society for the Study of Religion and Philosophy, an Honorary President of the World Conference of Religions for Peace, and co-editor of European Judaism. Among his current books are the new, revised edition of Out of the Whirlwind: the Literature of the Holocaust; Leo Baeck: Teacher of Theresienstadt; *and* Riders towards the Dawn: Jewish and Christian Thinkers after the Holocaust. *In 2004, he was a visiting professor at the University of Munich. These notes are based upon the Book of Lamentations in* The Five Scrolls *(New York, CCAR Press, 1984; translation of text by Albert H Friedlander; introduction by Albert H Friedlander and Herbert Bronstein).*

The Book of Lamentations is part of biblical Wisdom literature (*Chochmah*) which explores the meaning of life. It is the text for our time of destroyed cities and a slaughtered populace in the aftermath of war – a universal text of human suffering. It deals with an historical event, the destruction of Jerusalem in 580 BCE by the Babylonians. Tradition views Jeremiah as the author of these laments for the destroyed city and its exiled citizens. The author represents the total loneliness of an abandoned city and its lost people. Loneliness seems to sum up the mood of Lamentations: the physical loneliness of a besieged city and the spiritual loneliness of a people who seem to have been abandoned by God. Somehow, these laments must bring the mourners back to God and must restore purpose and meaning to the city itself. The grief breaks through the structure of this acrostic poem to remind us that the way to God often comes through pain and suffering.

The burning cities of our time

Alas, how solitary does the city sit that was so full of people,
How is she become a widow.
Bitterly does she weep at night, and her tears are on her
    cheeks.
Among her lovers she has none to comfort her.

Most of us live in large cities where we are often afraid and lonely.
The streets are no longer safe and the fear of terrorists lingers in
our mind. War has destroyed many cities in our past: Coventry
and Dresden, Hiroshima and Nagasaki, Mostar and Rwanda,
Deir Yassin and the twin towers of New York are the bleeding
wounds of our society. Lamentations describes the burnt-out
places of our own lives – there is a destroyed Jerusalem in each
one of us. Our text sees that God 'has afflicted her for the
multitude of her transgressions' (verse 5) and we cannot disclaim
responsibility for the suffering that fills the world around us. Social
injustices also destroy the world, and we can sense guilt within us
when we see people sleeping rough in our streets and read the
graffiti on our trains in our travels. We are alienated from those
around us; we feel very much alone with our shattered dreams.
Psychiatrists speak of 'the inability to mourn'; but we must mourn
for that past in order to rejoin others and hope for a future.

✳ *God, help me to break through my loneliness and to return*
to you. Then, I can work with others to help to repair the
damages of our suffering world.

Lonely dreams in the night

Night visions have your prophets seen of you,
of vanity and delusion…
Oh, those who pass by clap their hands at you,
they hiss and shake their head.

At night, in our pain, we reach towards God, particularly when we
feel ourselves surrounded by false friends and enemies. Nights
can be so lonely. But we see only how our world has been
destroyed, pretend that we are faultless, and prescribe the
actions which God must now take: the others must be destroyed,
our possessions must be restored, we must be justified. We see
only ourselves.

The people of the destroyed Jerusalem were not totally
guiltless. The poor were oppressed, the rulers were selfish, and

the people no longer worshipped in truth. Still, the nations around them were heartless and cruel, and God's justice would ultimately prevail against them. Jerusalem's prophets - Jeremiah and Ezekiel – were there to teach Israel, before and after the exile, that it had to change and return to God. Slowly, for more than a century, they learned this truth and then returned to rebuild Jerusalem. We have less time; but we can also learn that we have to rebuild ourselves and thus move from pain to joy.

✴ *God: make me appreciate that my awareness of the pain in the world, my encounter with injustice and the search for peace have to begin within myself. Help me!*

Tuesday July 12   *Lamentations 3:1-20*

The sorrows of Everyman

Ah, I am the man who has seen affliction by the rod of his wrath.

Am I not driven on by him in darkness and not in light?

Against me does he turn his hand, over and over again all the day.

The Hebrew text here is a triple acrostic, searching out all the hidden crevices in the human soul, showing men and women in their ultimate loneliness. We have all seen affliction and entered the heart of darkness which continues to overshadow our days as well. We see others who suffer, including our families; but we feel that 'God turns his hand towards me'. Is there any hope for me? Others seem to overcome their problems and move on. Where can we find help? Reading our Bible, we come to see that it speaks to us as well, that those who are entrapped in the destroyed city begin to feel the dawning light of faith.

Visiting Hiroshima, I saw a people whose children were still affected by that poisonous light of a thousand suns; but their prayers were of peace, and reached out towards their neighbours from the West.

✴ *God has given all of us courage: we fall down, we rise, and start again.*

Wednesday July 13   *Lamentations 3:21-51*

The hope after darkness

How can the Lord's mercies be consumed? Surely, His compassion

does not fail.
Has not each dawn new hope? Great is your faithfulness!
Has not my soul said: The Lord is my portion,
therefore I hope in him.
Is not the Lord good to those who trust him,
To the soul that seeks him?

Those who survived the destruction of Jerusalem and of the Temple still had trust; Holocaust survivors today still believe. Can we do less?

The psalmist prayed: 'Weeping may tarry for the night, but joy comes in the morning' (Psalm 30:5). What if the hours of the night stretch out interminably? The dark midnight of our soul has caused time to stop. We keep living in that time of isolation, we remain untouched by the concern of others. Doctors speak of Asperger's syndrome, of the inability to recognise emotion in others, or to find it in ourselves. We remain frozen in the Ice Age of our loneliness. We are cruel because we do not know how to be kind. So, too, suffering can destroy the warmth of our soul. Yet, when physicians may not be able to heal our souls, this Book of Life may open us to the healing which comes from God.

✳ *Heal me, O God, and I shall be healed. Save me, and I shall be saved.*

Thursday July 14   *Lamentations 3:52-66*

When evil pursues

Relentlessly, they chased me like a bird,
They are my enemies without cause.
Rancour thrust me alive into the pit,
And closed it over me with a stone.
Rushing waters flowed over my head:
I said: 'I am cut off'.
So then I called upon your name, O Lord,
Out of the pit of the nether world.

When the world around us seems to pursue us totally, we hide in the castle of our solitude. No one can help us; we are alone. But then, deep within us, there comes the knowledge that we can call upon God. We are Joseph, cast into the pit, and Jonah, thrown into the waters. Help comes to us which challenges the evils that had overwhelmed us. Some of the evil, we now see, existed within us; our own faults had brought us into darkness. The world is not changed into paradise; evil endures. Yet we are changed. We can begin to cope with our problems, and we can begin to

167

realise the powers for good which God has placed into the human soul. And then we move from the darkness towards the light.

✳ *God, let me not despair. May I find you within myself in my darkest hour so that I can serve you by day and by night.*

Friday July 15   *Lamentations 4:1-22*

Our total frailty

Alas, the gold is dulled, how tarnished is the finest gold.
The stones of the sanctuary are poured out at the top of
    every street.
Behold the precious children of Zion, comparable to fine
    gold,
How they are thought of as earthen pitchers,
The work of the potter's hands.

In the city of destruction, gold has become dross, and the walls of the Temple have melted and are flowing into the gutters. The people, also, have lost their value. Fashioned in beauty by the Potter, they are now broken shards lying in the streets.

The burned city has become a synonym for the world of today. Suicide bombers litter the streets of Jerusalem with broken bodies. Starving children reach out towards us from the doorways of our shops and in the Underground. Humans, created in the image of God, have been abandoned.

How blacker than coal is their face,
They are not known in the streets.

If we do not know the victims, if we do not help them, they will waste away. And if we do not turn to them with compassion, we have not understood the text we are reading today.

✳ *God, do not only instruct me in books. Let me learn to read the faces of the victims near and far. When we share our loneliness, we will rise above it and again become your children.*

Saturday July 16   *Lamentations 5:1–22*

Exile

Remember, O Lord, what is come upon us.
Consider and behold our disgrace.
Our inheritance has been turned over to strangers,
Our homes to aliens.
We are orphans, fatherless, our mothers are as widows.

The children of Israel went into exile when their city and Temple were destroyed. Our 21st century is also the landscape of exile, of asylum seekers and of wanderers who leave their homelands and wander through the world in search of a resting place. Sometimes, a people is granted a return to their homeland. Most times, they establish themselves in a new society in order to rebuild their lives. Coventry was such a destroyed city. A new Cathedral came to life, and its heart is a Centre of Reconciliation which is linked with Dresden. The city itself has welcomed the orphaned and the fatherless. The lesson was learned that all cities are sisters, and that the same bell tolls for all of us. The Book of Lamentations belongs to all of us.

✳ *God, spare me from exile and from wandering. May my home endure, my city prosper. Let it always be a place of compassion for everyone: 'May my house be a house of prayer for all people'.*

FOR REFLECTION – alone or with a group

● Are we ever secure in a world of war?

● Does not a far-off conflict hurt us as well?

● What have we done to help those who live alone, closed to consolation?

FOR ACTION

There are so many relief organisations. Make certain that you join one group who represents you. Also make certain that you join more than one group.

CELEBRATION
1. Celebrate the festival

Notes based on the New Revised Standard Version by

Maureen Edwards

Maureen Edwards, a former editor of Words for Today, *is now retired. Her wide experience of encounter with people of different cultures through both work and travel continues to inspire all that she writes and does.*

Celebration – whatever form it takes – is a universal experience, an occasion of great joy which brings people together as a community. Some festivals celebrate the cycle of agriculture – especially harvest. Some celebrate significant historical events: Jews celebrate their deliverance from slavery in Egypt through the Passover, Christians celebrate the coming of God's Son at Christmas... Think of others. And think of family celebrations at the birth of a child, birthdays, marriage and partnerships ... milestones of life. Think of the colour they add to the routine of everyday life. Even the poorest communities know how to celebrate: to take time to rise above their situation and be renewed in hope and strength for their struggle.

Sunday July 17   Genesis 21:1–8
Celebrate new life

In every culture special customs are observed at the birth of a child. Among the Waduruma of Kenya, the father took hold of the child's ear and, as he gave it a little shake, said, 'Your name is so-and-so; guard it and honour it.' The child would then be given small objects, e.g. a miniature hoe, as a symbol of the part s/he would grow up to play in the life of the community, and the whole community spoke of her as 'our child'. Communities who lived around Mount Kenya took the child out and held her up towards the presence of God who was believed to reside there and so dedicated the child to God. There was also feasting and great joy.

In the traditional Hebrew community, into which Isaac was born, the child was named and circumcised on the eighth day – again a symbol of the child's value to the community and special relationship to God. This too was followed by feasting with the whole community, just as Christian baptism and naming are followed by a feast or party to celebrate the child's entry into the family of God.

We think of children we know who are precious to us and give thanks.

✳ *Open our minds to listen and learn from the fresh and direct challenges children make to us.*

Monday July 18   *Exodus 23:14–17*
Celebrate harvest
Here are three Jewish festivals:
● the Feast of Unleavened Bread and the Passover in the spring;
● the Feast of Weeks, seven weeks after Passover, marking the beginning of the wheat harvest when the first fruits were offered to God;
● the Feast of Booths, Sukkot, at harvest time and the end of the dry season when they prayed for rain.

Before today's global economy, which enables us to have whatever food we want at any time of the year, people had a greater sense of closeness to the land. They ploughed it by hand, planted their own seeds and watched the mystery of growth – the tiny shoots, the thin green blades, the grain ripening through the long days of summer. They knew good, fertile years, and they knew years when the harvest failed.

Some years ago, I visited South India, just after the monsoons, when farmers were gathering an ample rice harvest. They worked with bare feet, their sandals left at the edge of the field. The harvest field is holy ground.

✳ *You crown the year with your bounty;*
        your wagon tracks overflow with richness.
The meadows clothe themselves with flocks,
        the valleys deck themselves with grain,
they shout and sing together for joy.   *Psalm 65:11,13*

Tuesday July 19   *2 Chronicles 30:1–21*
Celebrate liberation
According to the Chronicler, Hezekiah (c.715–687BC) – who had followed a long line of corrupt rulers – was Judah's best king. He began his reign by clearing the Temple of altars to gods placed there by their Assyrian rulers and then he rededicated it. This was

more than just cleaning the Temple; it was an act of rebellion against their Assyrian oppressors and the beginning of a period of freedom for his people. It was appropriate then to celebrate the Passover – the feast that celebrated the liberation of his ancestors.

There is so much symbolism in today's celebration of Passover: the bitter herbs to recall the bitterness of slavery; *charoseth* (a mixture of apple, cinnamon and ground almonds) reminds them of the mortar with which their forefathers cemented bricks together in Egypt; an egg symbolises the possibility of new beginning. The celebration is also rich with story telling and there is a lot of fun and laughter, for God turns tears into laughter and suffering into freedom.

✳ *Those who love me, I will deliver...*
       When they call to me, I will answer them;
   I will be with them in trouble,
   I will rescue them and honour them.   Psalm 91:14–15

Wednesday July 20   *Nehemiah 12:27–43*
Celebrate achievements
Nehemiah, a second generation exile in Babylon, had responded to God's call to return to Jerusalem and help his people to rebuild the city walls. They had made several attempts, but each time the Samaritans had attacked and destroyed all that they had achieved. Nehemiah had the experience, the skill and authority they needed. Within just a few months, the work was complete. To both the Jews and their enemies it appeared as the work of God. There had been much pain, time and work lost, and the loss of lives, but there was much to give thanks for. Hence the fiesta in today's reading: 'The joy of Jerusalem was heard far away.'

Think of similar celebrations today – for example, the handover of Hong Kong to China, the end of the long civil war in El Salvador, the end of apartheid in South Africa...

Think of areas of the world where people still long for freedom.

✳ *God of history, when you are disturbed by human pain,*
you raise up leaders to free the oppressed.
We pray for your people in ... that, freed from exploitation and suffering,
they may glorify you before the world.

Celebrate vulnerability

This psalm was probably written at the time when the Jews were travelling back from their exile in Babylon in the 6th century BC. It is one of a group of psalms called 'Songs of the Ascent' which were sung by the pilgrims on their way to and from Jerusalem. In this one, which may have been composed to be sung at Sukkot, we see them processing, carrying sheaves, and bursting into 'shouts of joy'. We see also the vicissitudes of rural life: sometimes, when the rains failed, they came to celebrate a feast of disappointment. Celebration alternates here with sadness and deprivation. That's real life.

During Sukkot, the Jewish family creates a rough booth with branches and other natural materials and lives in it for a week, to recall the 40 years when their ancestors lived in tents in the desert. Instead of cosy meals in the dining room, they eat under a makeshift roof with the sky visible through the gaps. It reminds them that however solid and comfortable their home may be, a house is only a shelter. They must recognise the limits of material security and, if need arises, be able to move out. The joy of Sukkot is a celebration of setting out on the road to freedom, accepting vulnerability and uncertainty about where it may lead, but rejoicing that a new start has been made.

✳ *Refresh us with your joy so that we may help build the land you have promised to the righteous, in a world where all may live in freedom and peace.*

From the Sukkot Evening Service

Celebrate worship

After the rebuilding of the walls of Jerusalem (Wednesday's reading), the Jews set about rebuilding the Temple, and this too had to be celebrated and dedicated to the worship and glory of God. More than 700 animals were sacrificed, and there was a great sense of thankfulness and joy. The trauma of their city and Temple being razed to the ground, their 40 years of exile, the desolation of their return to a ruined city – all this had come to an end. While they did not have complete political freedom, they were able to live in peace in their own land, and their city and Temple had been restored. The worship of God was central again to the life of the people.

Think of the beginnings of your church: the people who built it, their hopes for a future you now share. How is their story celebrated? How great a sense of celebration do we have each time we gather for worship and meet around the Lord's table?

✳ *Let us dream. Let us prophesy. Let us see visions of love, peace and justice. Let us affirm with humility, with joy, with faith, with courage, that you, O Christ, are the life of every child, woman and man.*   South African women

Saturday July 23   Revelation 19:6–10

Celebrate life

Here is a hymn written for a persecuted community, maybe at the end of the 1st century. It is so strong a vision that it presents the end as though it is happening now. The kingdom is fully present. It is rich in metaphors. The Lamb – a New Testament term for Christ – is an image of vulnerability and powerlessness. With the Lamb as bridegroom and the church as bride, we are invited to share in all the wonder and celebration of a marriage ceremony and feast.

This is not merely about enduring the present in the hope that one day, in the hereafter, all will be well. Rather, it is to live now in defiance of our present circumstances, celebrating life in a way which embraces the reality of our vulnerability, suffering and powerlessness.

A friend of mine, whose name was Gill, was nearing the end of her journey with cancer, and she knew it. Just two months before she died, she wanted to celebrate her birthday with her family and all her friends, near and far. She sent out invitations to almost 100 people. She wanted to cater for them and entertain them all in her home. It was not just her way of saying goodbye but also of celebrating friendship and a full life. Was it crazy? Unnerving? The weaker person taking control and doing something for us? I believe it said something very profound, something that we also glimpse in Jesus' last celebration of the Passover with his friends – that we who think we are strong can learn from the poor, the weak and the dying how to live.

✳ *God of all, give us such a sense of our closeness to your loving presence in Christ that we may truly celebrate this relationship in all that we do, both now and in the life to come.*

FOR REFLECTION – alone or with a group

● How is our sense of community strengthened when we celebrate together?

● Think of ways to bring a sense of celebration into everyday life.

FOR ACTION

Make plans for a celebration in your family or community. Share them with others and think together of ways to make it happen.

CELEBRATION
2. Peculiar parties

Notes on the New Revised Standard Version by
Karen Jobson, Rachel Mann
and Jennifer Smith

Karen Jobson is a student minister for the Methodist Church training at the Queen's Ecumenical Foundation, Birmingham, UK, and a former teacher. Rachel Mann watches lots of films and skis far too much. She has taught philosophy, worked in chaplaincy and spent long periods very ill with Crohn's Disease. She is also training for the ordained ministry at Queen's, but for the Church of England. Dr Jennifer Smith is a candidate for ministry in the Methodist Church of Great Britain also training at Queen's. A US citizen, she has previously lectured in American history and politics in the UK.

Parties are dangerous, whether they be birthday, karaoke, dinner, or even the politest of cocktail parties. For parties involve risk – the danger of meeting new people, or encountering familiar things in fresh ways. At parties plans are made, old acquaintances renewed and, sometimes, animosities rekindled. When we party we celebrate all that is good in being human, yet we face the prospect of being out of control. And just occasionally, we glimpse heaven in a momentary half-smile. Parties are always dangerous, but when heaven breaks in, our peculiar God arrives too. Here's to peculiar parties!

Sunday July 24   *Judges 16:23–31*
Peculiar peace

For those of us who grew up with a Sunday school picture of Samson as a heroic figure, the record of this 'peculiar party' makes hard reading. In the West, we are used to thinking of those who use their own deaths for the destruction of their foes as terrorists rather than superheroes. This story shows the people of Israel and the Philistines bound in a tragic cycle of retribution. There are no good guys or bad guys, just entrenched enemies. The 'peculiar' tragedy of this party is that precisely in what they think are celebrations of peace, the Philistines lay up the stores of violence that bring their own destruction. How easy it is to want to humiliate an enemy to reassure ourselves we are really safe, to copy this halfway peace without reconciliation. We see the tragic results in our newspapers and on our televisions every day. Even in our own lives (let alone those of great nations) we know that breaking a cycle of conflict requires great courage and sacrifice. Far from being a model to guide us, this story should join others that are more contemporary to repeat its tragic warning.

✳ *O God of reconciliation,*
may we learn the lessons of history
to become true peace-makers.
Grant us peace in our time, O Lord.

Monday July 25   Genesis 43:15–30
Risky reunions
Many families have breaches in their lives together, even if not quite as dramatic as the break between Joseph and his brothers. And even where there is no particular break, distance and circumstance can make the habit of being family hard to keep up. By our 'habit of family' we learn our history, the joyful as well as the painful parts of it. We do this by gathering at tables for holidays, exchanging pictures of babies and telling news, dancing at weddings and weeping at funerals. If we have fallen away from close contact, we may do these things with family members who are little more than strangers, or not at all. In Joseph and his brothers' reunion, all wear masks to hide their anxiety and need for each other's help. But Joseph still risks offering hospitality when anger would seem justified, and the brothers risk accepting it, though fearing the worst. Across the table where he is host their mutual risk is fruitful and the family bond, though far from perfect, is renewed. All true reunions are risky, and few are perfect. But where risk is shared, there may be hope even in imperfection!

✳ *Dear Lord,*
where we hide our need and anxiety,
unmask us.
Where others show us their true selves,
give us grace to see them
gently with God's eyes.

Tuesday July 26   Mark 6:21–25
Experimental parties
Herod is shown, in this passage, to be a weak man who recognised John's innocence yet felt powerless to protect him. A

parallel to this can be seen in Mark 15:14–15 when Pilate handed Jesus over for crucifixion despite knowing that he was not guilty. As with most good stories, it seems likely that spice has been added (it would have been unusual for women, particularly of a high standing, to be able to mix freely with men) but the scene is a striking one.

Swaying, swishing, shimmying
Hips, shoulders, breasts
Fingers, splayed, wide,
Intermeshing intricate patterns of seduction in the air.
The adolescent whirls.
Innocence, sensuality, power
Blur
Into the hypnotic cadence of the dance.
Pulsing, pouting, provoking
Proud mother watches,
Man with power
Succumbs.

As a teacher, I am struck by the image presented of a young woman exploring her sexuality, not fully aware of the consequences of doing so. For many young people parties present a chance to experiment with different aspects of themselves, but the emotions evoked and the ensuing consequences can feel overwhelming. Adults can often seem unable to relate or too scared by the issue to be honest. The result of our fears and silence is not heads on a plate, but is potentially unplanned pregnancy or disease.

✳ *Nurturing God, help us to stand alongside young people without judgement or condemnation, as they discover who they are.*

Wednesday July 27   *Luke 14:1–14*
Parties for all
The healing of the man appears in the same section as parables about election. The message is clear: God's mercy extends beyond any human constraints that we would like to impose upon it. The rules that humans use to govern their lives are meaningless to God, as are the limitations and values by which we judge others.

Like the Pharisees, Christians often presume that their invitation to God's banquet is guaranteed, but this parable makes it clear that there is no room for arrogance or conceit. Those who would exalt themselves will be brought low; those who are the lowest will be exalted.

In our churches, self-righteousness and pride often seem to mark our relationships. We enter into informal competition with others, be it over flower arranging, praying or visiting. We define our territory and rotas to protect our own egos. And it is not just between individuals but also between denominations: 'Methodists sing properly – not like Anglicans' or 'Anglicans respect tradition – not like Methodists'. Such competition can be healthy and fun but it often becomes a way of limiting the other.

✳ *Loving God, help us to remember that, in your kingdom, the first will be last and the last will be first. Teach us to put aside our own pride and to recognise the value and worth of all people.*

Thursday July 28   Numbers 28:16–26
A command performance

'I command you to relax and have a good time!' If anyone said that to you, I imagine it would have one guaranteed effect – to make you tense and anxious. Yet today's reading has God instructing Moses to command the Israelites to do just this – to thank God by relaxing from work and partying for a week. This festival (of weeks) is a command performance so detailed that one expects the Israelites to collapse with stress by the end of it.

What is your image of God? Perhaps it is haunted or shaped by a 'God who commands'. Certainly such a God stalks the history of Christian thinking. And how easily in human hands he becomes the God who dominates and demeans. How many traces of this idea remain in your image of God? How does it affect you?

Yet something tantalising remains: God commands the Israelites to rest. To party. And here is a challenge: to allow ourselves the risk of rest. To be open to the God who will show us how to party well. To become people whose rest infuses their work.

✳ *O God whose work is rest,*
enable us to take leave
of those images which diminish you
and diminish us.
In your peace make us restful;
out of our rest, may we work and party well.

My party is defiance

He ripped it out – calling me a baby as he laughed at my tears. But he misunderstood. The pain of having my earring gouged out was nothing. My tears were a lament for the theft of that golden sign of promise.

I received the earring long ago on the banks of the Nile – on that day when women conspired to save the baby Moses from Pharaoh's bloodlust. I was a little girl then, but I remember holding Moses' sister's hand as she made that pact with Pharaoh's daughter to keep Moses from harm. A pact sealed by the exchange of earrings between them. And I was so giddy that Moses' sister gave me that simple gold band to shut me up. A band I took as a sign of promise and hope.

And now the calf is smelted. The men grin through sooty faces. Women begin to dance, and children run, noisy and thrilled. So the party begins, but I will not dance. My party is defiance. My wound I bathe with hope – that from Sinai will return the One who was saved by a conspiracy of hope. To save us from this festival that serves no one but ourselves.

✳ ***God of Promise,***
kindle our hope;
stir our defiance;
draw us into solidarity with you.
Through Jesus Christ.

A very peculiar party

The world ends every day. Somewhere. For someone. For Luis killed at 19 in a car crash; for Simone dead from AIDS for want of medication; for Alice sliding into the beyond after a long and full life. Each day the world ends. And each day people eat and drink, party and dance, make love and act as if life were for ever.

Fragility grows through the fibres of human life. More than that, I suspect that human flourishing depends on our very fragility. For, like a great party, all that is wonderful in existence can be easily spoiled; yet without this fragility, the danger of failure, transcendence could not break into the world.

When Jesus talks of the days of the Son of Man as like the days of Noah and Lot we may be reminded of human fragility in all its banality and wonder. Yet we may also remember Jesus' promise of the heavenly banquet waiting to break into this world. A peculiar, incredible party made ready not for the righteous, but for the outcasts, at which all are welcome. A dangerous party, fragile with possibilities, but wonderful precisely because of this.

＊ *Fragile God,*
help us to be ready to serve you in your hour of need;
enable us to be vulnerable to your dangerous love.
Through Christ our host.

FOR REFLECTION – alone or with a group

● Reflect on some of the parties you have been to over the years. Which bring back memories of joy, and which memories of sadness? Why?

● How easy do you find it to rest, to play, to engage in God's Sabbath?

● What were the chief characteristics of Jesus' parties? Where do you see such parties happening today?

FOR ACTION

Think of an old friend or acquaintance, or a family member with whom you have fallen out of touch. Pray for that person and their life now, then write a letter sharing a memory and inviting them to be in contact.

CELEBRATION
3. Dance in celebration

Notes based on the New Revised Standard Version by
Kathy Foulds

Kathy is currently the co-ordinator of assistants in the L'Arche community in Cork, Ireland. L'Arche is a community founded by Jean Vanier where the emphasis is on sharing life with people who have intellectual disabilities. Kathy met her husband Mike when they were both assistants in Scotland in the 1970s. Along with their four children, they are family members of L'Arche. Kathy has given a number of retreats and is also a trained spiritual accompanier.

L'Arche is a faith community that we believe has been called into being by God as a sign of love and a witness to God's love in the world. We seek to reveal to each one that we are loved, that we are lovable and that we are a source of life for others. Therefore celebration for us is not just a way to make people feel good for a while but rather the way in which we live out our faith.

In this week's readings we are introduced to various people throughout the history of salvation who, like Jeremiah, have heard God's word: 'I have loved you with an everlasting love' (Jeremiah 31:3). Their response to this knowledge has been celebration in music and dance. Let us see if we too can find our place in the dance.

Sunday July 31   *2 Samuel 6:1–14*
Loved and chosen

Here is a people who knew the nearness and presence of God among them. They knew they were chosen by God and were not afraid to show it.

I will never forget Easter Sunday morning in 2001. My family and I had travelled with our L'Arche community from Cork to join an International Faith & Light pilgrimage in Lourdes. We were a gathering of 20,000 pilgrims from all over the world, half of whom had an intellectual disability, singing and dancing with guitars and tambourines, castanets and cymbals. What joy and freedom to be among these people whom the world labels disabled! We knew we were loved and were not afraid to rejoice in that knowledge.

This was a real celebration of thanksgiving. We knew that our Lord had truly risen and lived among us. And as if in response to all this outpouring of joy our God blessed us with extraordinary sunshine.

Surely this is how we must always gather in our worshipping communities on a Sunday morning to celebrate God's presence amongst us and that we are God's people.

✳ **Lord – open our hearts to your love and to who we are as your people. Then we too, like the Israelites, will dance before you with all our might.**

Monday August 1   *Psalm 150*
A universal call to praise God
'Let everything that breathes praise the Lord!' (verse 6). The book of Psalms concludes with this universal symphony of praise to God.

When I was growing up, one of our (Catholic) neighbours used to take great delight in telling us children that he had a 'Protestant' dog – a dog that ate meat on Fridays! There was no offence intended to anyone – Protestant or Catholic. But in its own way it revealed to us that labels could not define dogs any more than they could define or limit dogs. Among our friends were children from both the Catholic and Protestant traditions and we were hard pressed to tell the difference. Over the years I have told this incident to my own children with a twinkle in my eye, in the same spirit in which I heard it so long ago. All of creation praises and celebrates the Creator God not simply by adherence to regulations and tradition but by being fully alive and becoming who we are meant to be as children of God.

✳ **Lord, give us eyes to see you in all people, no matter what their creed or culture. Fill our hearts with love and gratitude for all your creation so that we can join in the universal symphony of praise to you our creator.**

Tuesday August 2   *Jeremiah 31:1–14*
The kingdom of God
'I am going to … gather them from the farthest parts of the earth, among them the blind and the lame … Then shall the young women rejoice in the dance, and the young men and the old shall be merry' (verses 8, 13). So speaks Yahweh to his scattered people telling them of his vision for them.

183

L'Arche seeks to be a sign of this kingdom of God. People come to us from all over the world. In each of the last few years in our community in Cork we have welcomed assistants from at least ten different countries – Trinidad, Zimbabwe, Korea and Uzbekistan, to name but a few. They vary in age, education and religious tradition. They come in answer to a call to share life with our people with intellectual disabilities. Together we build community – sharing meals and chores, joys and sorrows, prayer and celebration. Celebration is very central to all that we live in L'Arche. We need very little excuse for a party – celebrating birthdays and anniversaries, arrivals and departures, feast days and holidays.

One of our people speaks of her birthday every day of the year. Is it because this is the day when she knows how unique and special she is, loved with an everlasting love? Our God desires that we know this love always. Our God wants every day to be a celebration of God's love for us.

✳ *Lord, help me to rejoice in being your creation and delight, so that I may be a channel of your love for others.*

Wednesday August 3   *1 Chronicles 15:25 – 16:3*

The choice between gratitude and resentment

This reading from Chronicles speaks of the same event as we read about on Sunday from 2 Samuel, but here David's rejoicing is contrasted with the attitude of Michal. When she saw him leaping and dancing 'she despised him in her heart' (15:29).

When I was a student I used to visit a hospital for old people. I was always struck by the fact that some old people were happy and a pleasure to be with while others were full of criticism and resentment. I discovered that the difference lay not so much in the events of their life story but rather in how they had responded to these events. David was able to rejoice and make merry because he believed he was chosen and loved by God. And it seems the more he rejoiced and gave thanks the bigger his heart grew and the more generous he became. For some reason, Michal chose resentment and so could only criticise.

I have a choice each day either to focus on what is missing in my life or, like David, to live by faith in God's love and rejoice in all that is given.

✳ *Lord, help me today to trust in your love and to choose your way of love and gratitude.*

Thursday August 4   *Acts 3:1–10*

Disability as gift

When I first joined L'Arche back in 1977, people with intellectual disabilities were referred to as the 'mentally handicapped'. The word handicap came from the idea of someone sitting cap-in-hand begging for alms like the cripple in this story. Many of us came to L'Arche thinking we would be giving to these poor handicapped people. Instead we found ourselves being invited to look into the eyes of the individual, to enter into relationship and to receive from them as well as give. I have discovered that a willingness to enter into real relationship with someone who needs my support leads to mutual transformation.

The people with whom I chose to live have given me life. Together we have learned to walk, to leap and to praise God. Within the community we have no need to label each other. Able or disabled – who knows?

✳ *Lord, give me eyes to see the gift hidden in my own disabilities as in those of others.*

Friday August 5   *Exodus 15:19–21*

Bearers of good news

Miriam's exhortation to the Israelites to rejoice at the death of the Egyptians might sound strange to us today. But we must see it in context. The Israelites believed that God was with them on their journey and that it was he who was overcoming the evil that threatened them. Miriam, the prophetess, was the one to see God's hand in the events of the time and to call her people to rejoice.

In my community we have many such prophets who give thanks for many things: the sunshine 'so that we can go to the beach', the rain 'so the flowers will grow', the arrival of a new assistant and, most often, the meal we are about to share. All is seen as gift from God and celebrated in word and song.

Jesus often said: 'Let those who have eyes see.' As Christians, are we not called to do precisely this? We are the people who recognise and then celebrate God's good news all around us in our world.

✳ *Lord, give me eyes to see you alive in our world and a heart that opens in celebration.*

The elder son

Here we have the second part of the story of the Prodigal Son –
the hardest part to stomach? My experience is that most of us
identify more easily with the elder son. Is it perhaps because we
have reduced our faith to fulfilling duties and following rules? Like
the elder son we are baffled at the father's response to the
younger son, the waster. We ask, 'What about me? I have been
obedient, dutiful, and responsible all my life. What is my reward?'

One of the gifts of our people in L'Arche is that they have no
illusions about being dutiful. Many of them have experienced
themselves as failures, particularly in that they have not lived up
to others' expectations. Their hearts are wide open to receiving
love. I remember Marie, to whom I had just given a hug, looking
me straight in the eye and saying, 'Can I have another hug?' The
words of Jesus echoed in my ears, 'Do you love me?' Does my
response come out of duty or out of love? Yes, another hug. 'Of
course I love you'.

The challenge for us all is to hear and believe Jesus when he
says to us, 'You are always with me and all that is mine is yours'
(verse 31). If we can really hear this we will long to join the
celebration.

The invitation is there – the choice is ours. The Father
continues to wait.

✳ *Lord, give me a heart that sings with gratitude for your*
   constant love and presence.

FOR REFLECTION – alone or with a group

● In what ways do you experience God's love and presence in
   your life?

● Name a few people/events in your life for whom/which you are
   grateful.

● Imagine yourself in the story of the prodigal son. With whom
   can you identify most easily? Can you join in the father's
   celebration?

FOR ACTION

Choose a time of prayer – either personal or communal – and
turn it into a time of celebration. Be creative!

READINGS IN MATTHEW

Notes on the New Revised Standard Version by
Jim Cotter

Jim Cotter is an ordained minister of the Church in Wales, engaged in a project at Llandecwyn, near Harlech in Snowdonia, to see if small, little-used churches can come alive as 'breathing spaces on the pilgrim journey', places of quiet prayer, simple hospitality and thoughtful conversation. He also writes, and publishes as Cairns Publications, as well as travelling to lead retreats, preach, and speak at conferences. You can find out more about his work at www.cottercairns.co.uk.

Two weeks of stories, a mixture of what historically happened and what came from the imagination of Jesus and the first two or three generations of his followers. I can hear a storyteller's opening line: 'I'm not sure if the events in this story ever happened quite like this, but I know the story is true.' Some of these stories we call parables, some we call miracles, and each of them can bring us to the brink of another world where we have a choice. We can either back away from the brink in shock and dismay or take a step forward as we gasp in surprise and wonder.

What is this 'other world'? Remember, right at the beginning of Matthew's gospel, in the stories he tells surrounding the birth of Jesus, in what we might call the 'overture' or the 'prologue' to his main work, he comments that the wise men, having been warned in a dream not to return to Herod, departed for their own country 'another way' (Matthew 2:2). Of course, that can mean 'by another route', but there may also be the hint that anybody who has realised that Jesus can open eyes and ears to 'another world' will follow 'another way'.

Now this 'other world' is not 'the next world' (after death); nor is it 'the inner world' of prayer and personal faith. Both of these worlds may be real enough, but they have sometimes been portrayed as the only reality that Jesus was concerned with, in other words the world of those who were brought up to believe that Christianity was only about 'souls' going to 'heaven'. No, there is something else going on. The 'other world' of the gospels is very close to the world of families and everyday events, indeed can be glimpsed, even touched, within the familiar and the everyday. The worlds overlap, but both can be here and now, not only there and then. But it isn't easy to let ourselves be brought to the edge of this 'other world': we have to remove the cataracts from our eyes and the wax from our ears. We are so often lazy and unaware.

When we do wake up, it can feel as it must have done for the spies who were sent ahead of the main body of travellers to scout out the 'promised land' (Numbers 13). After such a long time with the browns and the greys of the desert their eyes must have rejoiced at the colours of 'a land flowing with milk and honey' (Joshua 5:6) – 'another country' of sparkling silver and myriad greens. The response? Gratitude. Wonder. Delight. These glimpses of 'another world' bring human beings nearer to the liberation, the healing and the justice which at our best we seek and share in, in the Spirit of Jesus and after the pattern of Jesus. There is something more profound going on in these stories called 'parables' and 'miracles' than the cure of a disease or the enjoyment of a good story, however welcome that cure and that enjoyment may be. Jesus' touch and Jesus' words, the deeds and the pictures, brought people the dish of honey and the cup of milk. Trapped by disease, oppressed by a foreign power, gnawed at by hunger, bedevilled by debt, they were given a taste of 'salvation', which, in the Hebrew language was always associated with wide open spaces of freedom, here and now as well as there and then.

The challenge to us is to renew that vision and take part in that programme. Ask yourself these questions: What is the vision? What surprise and wonder is opened up here? Have I, without realising it at the time, glimpsed this 'other world' already? What prompts gratitude and delight? How can this story bring me now to the brink of 'another world' and encourage me to step across into it?

A prayer for each day:

✴ *Spirit of the Living God, open my heart, open my mind, open my eyes, open my ears, that I may rejoice in the glimpses you give us of the new world of Jesus.*

5. Parables of the kingdom

Sunday August 7   *Matthew 13:24–30*
Can you tell them apart?
Wheat and weeds, a crop of corn for food and a crop of darnel for fuel. As they are growing you can't easily tell them apart, and

when they are harvested they're both useful. Weeds are plants in the place you don't want them, isn't that so? They cause grumbles and backache, but if you're hungry you're glad if the weeds (whenever in the growing season you dig them up) can be dried and used for a fire to heat the cooking pot.

So which part of the story do you emphasise? Do you use it in religious dispute to say that we are the chosen ones and they are the rejected ones? (Only we will inhabit the 'new world'.) Or are you making the point that human beings rush to judgement (meaning condemnation) quicker than a wise and patient God whose judgement means discernment, and who has a place for those we would reject? Indeed they may already have glimpsed 'another world' before we do.

I might want an argument with Matthew that the God of Jesus is more generous and inclusive than he thought. Two generations on from a visionary, and most followers fall back into the assumptions with which they grew up.

Do you believe that God will reject most human beings or that God will welcome all human beings?

Monday August 8   Matthew 13:31–32

Is this the plant you really want in your garden?

Here's an encouraging story in hard times. You may not realise it, but the small seed of this 'other world' really is doing its work and will grow into a great tree, like a magnificent Cedar of Lebanon under which many people can shelter. Such a cedar would remind Matthew's community that the great tree stood for a universal, all-embracing hospitality, the time when everybody would be aware of 'another world'.

I wonder if Jesus himself was more realistic, less tempted to believe that the vision of a 'new world' would be fully realised soon? Perhaps he recognised that though indeed we are invited to trust in the 'glimpses', it is only glimpses that we are going to get. The 'other world' will continue to be hidden, and even to put the vision into practice from time to time will make huge demands and there would seem to be little reward. For not many people would be glad if the mustard seed did grow all that well. Botanically, it grew not into a tree but into a bush, in fact lots of them, for it was like a weed that spread rapidly and threatened to take over the whole garden. And the kingdom of God is like that. It doesn't seem like good news to landowners or to the day labourers who had to do the weeding for a pittance.

189

Where might there be a glimpse of 'another world' in front of your eyes that you would prefer not to recognise?

Tuesday August 9   Matthew 13:33

A real eye-opener of a one-liner

Of course it is possible to be open to 'another world' simply by contemplating the everyday and being moved to wonder. Leaven works away, hidden from view, and has an extraordinary effect. And if your own life has been touched by the 'new world' but the 'old world' is still very much with you, well, leaven can encourage you: it takes time for results to show. (And you can expect fifty pounds' weight of loaves from this amount of leaven: enough for a celebration.) Remember that Matthew was trying to encourage his community through testing times for their faith.

But the parable does more than that. For Jesus' listeners, leaven was unclean, and here was Jesus comparing God's kingdom to something your law told you to keep your distance from – and men could breathe a sigh of relief because baking bread was woman's work. Leaven was corrupting, not holy. So Jesus challenges his hearers: Where is God to be found?

There's something else. The woman hides the leaven. She is secretive, concealing it. Perhaps this 'other world' isn't too obvious, not to be found with the morally upright and the holy.

Where do you least expect to have your eyes opened to 'another world'?

Wednesday August 10   Matthew 13:44–46

Would you really like to win the lottery?

To find a pearl worth more than gold! To dig up a treasure hidden in a field! To win the lottery! Wow! What a new world that would open up for us. How often we fantasise about it. But wait a minute. There's many a story that tells of how, for instance, a great diamond provokes envy, robbery, and murder. And if you dig up a treasure in a field, how can you be sure it belongs to you? Who owns the land? Who owns what is underneath it? Treasure and lawsuits go together.

What is more, how do you sell it? Hardly on the open market. Who can you trust among dealers? Are you going to be cheated? Put the other way, you may have glimpsed something of such great import to you that you are willing to sell everything in your house, clear away the clutter, even sell the house itself, in order to buy it. But that something may be 'another world' of no monetary value. You might have to become destitute to live in it. This 'other world' may be beyond buying and selling.

What would you put on a list as your three greatest treasures?

Thursday August 11　　　　　　　　　　　　　　　*Matthew 13:47–50*

Bad fish equals bad people?

Wheat and weeds on Sunday. Good fish and bad fish today. It's another turn of the same screw, and this time you might think that Matthew would win the argument with me. After all, if the fish are bad there is nothing you can do but throw them away. Or if you think the bad fish are bad people, they are thrown into the furnace to burn.

But wait a minute. A Jewish fisherman who was scrupulous about keeping the Law would know that fish without scales were unclean and therefore not to be eaten. Such were catfish, often caught in a dragnet in the Sea of Galilee. But can you imagine a very poor fisherman with hungry children at home throwing such a fish away?

By the way, Matthew uses a Greek word meaning 'rotten', which is hardly likely for a fish freshly caught. You can tell he is particularly concerned to emphasise a last judgement of final separation. But the question remains, as it did before. What is the character of the God of Jesus?

Friday August 12　　　　　　　　　　　　　　　*Matthew 13:51–53*

Matthew's signature

Something extraordinary and new has begun to happen, even if not in the village where Jesus was brought up. As with all new movements it is too much for those in charge. The leaders want to control it, the teachers want to understand it. (It's true of those who plan and write Bible reading notes – you've got to have some kind of order!) And the rest of us collude. Too much energy, too much freedom, and you create political disturbance. We can't do without the law. Make it all safe. We find it hard to get the balance right.

I don't suppose Matthew was too clear about what treasure from days of old was worth keeping and what new treasure needed bringing into the light. But he writes in an orderly way, very much the scribe. And indeed it is a noble calling to lead or to teach, and it is a necessary task to keep the treasure safe. But it is so difficult to stop the 'other world' from slipping away from us, its freedom and promise and glimpses of justice fading from our vision and from our work, especially if we think that God has rejected those who used to be our companions in faith.

In your own community, who honours the old and who welcomes the new, and who discerns what really is treasure?

Saturday August 13   *Matthew 13:54–58*
Happy families?
Matthew seems to be saying that some people are never willing to open themselves to the possibility of 'another world', not least if a prophet is issuing the invitation and he was brought up round the corner. The grumble is that Jesus is doing nothing to help his family keep hunger and debt at bay, the struggle that keeps nearly everybody tied to ever-repeated back-breaking routines. He should be at home helping the other members of his family. He never stays long, always off somewhere else: the least he could do is make his home his headquarters, and his words and deeds would attract visitors and help the local economy a bit. And we know his family all too well: a jobbing carpenter for a father, four brothers (named, as boys are) and several sisters (unnamed, of course).

It is like that for most people who are poor, often on the edge of destitution. There is no time for being open to wonder, no point in expecting real change. The rulers may come and go, but it never makes any difference to those at the bottom of the heap. Perhaps for the children it is occasionally different, if only in the imagination. A 'new world' can break through into the everyday. Trust can be renewed. And here and there kindness and compassion soften the harshness of life.

And in your own life, in your family, in your community?

6. Signs and wonders

We turn to a different set of stories. We know that 'parables' are made up, fictional but true. We may find 'miracles' more difficult, a mixture of fact and fiction, but we may still find them true. In both kinds of stories there is much discerning to be done.

Sunday August 14   *Matthew 14:13–21*

A worker of wonders?

Later in the week we'll look at the two feeding stories, of the five thousand and of the four thousand. But today some questions about Jesus' power and these tales of power over nature, all of which amaze people. Tomorrow it will be the story of Jesus walking on water, on Saturday the story of Jesus cursing a fig tree. Also on Saturday there is a very extravagant claim: with enough faith you can move mountains, something that has never been done by anyone, though it has been well used as a metaphor for the energy released by faith to do remarkable things.

Did Jesus display remarkable power over nature? Did he multiply loaves – or did his very presence give such sustenance and inspiration that the generosity of the 'other world' spread like wildfire? Did he walk on water – or did he give his followers a glimpse of 'another world', the memory of which sustained them through storms of persecution and painful dying and the fear of drowning in the waters of chaos? Did he cause a barren tree to wither suddenly – or did he remind his followers that too many people try and block the flow of life and blessing that is characteristic of the 'new world'?

Displays of power can make people feel very small. And if I think God is very large, then even a mountain is but a speck of dust. Awe and fear can be evoked very easily. But if it dawns on us that a healing word and a healing touch and food shared around a table (or on the grass) can bring us close to one another, we may realise we are being called to be the power of God for one another.

Does not Jesus share power, give power away, become powerless to reveal the true God?

Monday August 15   *Matthew 14:22–33*

Marvellous – but in what way?

You may be buffeted by waves of persecution, but he will come to you. In the darkest hour before dawn, when you are at your most vulnerable, take courage, step out, vulnerable to the powers of death, and he will come to you. I think that was the message that Matthew and his community were giving to one another.

There is a subtext. In Mark's version of this story the disciples are dumbfounded, as they frequently are in that gospel. Matthew singles out Peter and the story raises his status as leader. I wonder which other community he was having an ecclesiastical wrangle with? At least Matthew does not give us a perfect Peter: the pattern of failure and restoration is as true now as it was then. Nobody, no church, no leader, always gets it right. Which is a relief to all of us.

One other thing. The story is imaginative but not unique. In Homer's *Odyssey*, the god Hermes walked on the waves of the sea. And there is a Buddhist story which says that you will sink into the water only if you are not deeply centred.

Which wonder touches your own heart? Walking on the water or forgiving the failures?

Tuesday August 16   Matthew 14:34–36
Touching the fringe
I don't suppose any of us find it easy to tell the whole truth about our symptoms to a doctor, especially if we're embarrassed about the part of the body in question or ashamed about the actions that have led to our reluctant feet being dragged to the surgery. Dare we look the healer in the eye? It might be very uncomfortable, makes us feel more ill at ease than the disease we suspect we may be suffering from. It would be so much easier to touch an object that has been worn by the healer. And if my disease has meant exclusion from my community (flow of blood in ancient times, isolation because of mental disturbance in our times), my touch had better not be noticed.

Jesus is not bothered by the touch of others, cloth or skin. He does not back away. You are not stigmatised and rejected. You belong. And that is healing even when your disease cannot be cured.

Who matters most when you are ill – the dispenser of pills or the hugger of the quarantined? Which is the greater sign of the 'new world'?

Wednesday August 17   Matthew 15:21–28*
Crumbs!
She is a woman alone in a man's world. She is a Gentile, hence unclean; he will keep his distance. She expects separation and

isolation. He's provocative with his name-calling. Dogs indeed. He treats her as his equal. He draws close. He holds a witty conversation with her. He is moved by her reply. Even the dogs eat the crumbs that fall from the table.

Matthew places this story between the two stories of feeding (the five thousand and the four thousand, which we'll look at tomorrow). In those they gathered the fragments so that nothing (and therefore no one) will be lost. Here Jesus the Jew includes a foreigner in his vision and practice of 'another world'.

Doubtless the argument was lively in Matthew's community. Are we another branch of the Jewish people and religion, or are we to be a mixed community of Jews and Gentiles? Are we particular (only we are privileged) or are we universal (this 'other world' is for everybody)?

The argument still rages. Whites only? Blacks only? Heterosexuals only? Homosexuals only? Even gay men only? Or lesbians only? Who can you trust?

Thursday August 18   *Matthew 15:29–39*

Five thousand or four thousand or what?

Lives open to the gift of 'another world', hearts open in generosity, backpacks open in enthusiasm, and what a crowd! Thousands, especially if you include the women and children. Someone has worked out that that meant 5% of the population of the country. What a party! An egalitarian picnic – very simple, very abundant. I wonder how many scribes and lawyers and priests sat down on the earth and laughed. Baked beans become a feast – and oh! the marvel of nature that summer when the damson tree in the garden almost cracked under the weight of the fruit.

Think of all the levels of the phrase 'life-giving' and Yes, and again Yes to Life! Marvellous, wonderful, bringing us to our knees, lifting us off our feet, in gratitude and yippee! Or Alleluia! It is indeed manna in the wilderness, a glimpse of a promised land, 'another country', a new age that is dawning. It is what happens once in a while at Eucharist, where scales fall from our eyes and we know this is the heavenly banquet. And even when faith falters there may be a few fragments to gather, a few crumbs to keep the vision alive. Well, I don't know if it happened quite like the story says, but, as the old storyteller said, I know it's true.

By the way, the best guess is that the first version (twelve baskets of leftovers – twelve tribes) was for Israel, the second (seven baskets – seven the number symbolising completion) for the Gentiles.

Remember: a word and touch that heals, a meal that warms – and a drink that cheers. What is the most recent occasion when, with another or with others, you experienced 'another world'?

Friday August 19   Matthew 20:28–34

What kind of sight?

It doesn't matter whether this 'other world' dawns through prayer, through touch, through surgery, through change of direction, or whatever, what matters is that we can give content to the exultant cry, Once I was blind, now I can see. Cataracts have to be as patiently and carefully removed from the inner as from the outer eye. And it is as much a marvel if an operation takes six hours as if a touch takes six seconds. God's timing is not always obvious.

One of Sunday's questions needs to be repeated: If you do not regain your sight, is there still another way you can become aware of 'another world'? Perhaps you become more sensitive to the ways in which touch can heal. If your society blames those who cannot see for something wicked either they or their parents have done, it might not be comfortable for a sighted person to be seen to be enjoying life and linking arms with a friend who is blind. You may get into trouble with the authorities. (Doctors rarely do.)

Do you see the point?

Saturday August 20   Matthew 21:14–22

The only destructive miracle?

Here again is that theme so characteristic of Matthew, his concern to compare his own community, which he is trying to encourage in difficult times, with those who have rejected Jesus. Last week we read of wheat and weeds, fresh fish and stinking fish, and now fruitful fig tree and barren fig tree. There is a lot of separating good from bad in this gospel.

It's a challenge to each of us and to our communities, even if we might want to argue with Matthew that God might actually like both the just and the unjust. Still, we all have to work at not getting in the way of good things happening, at not losing our savour, at a good bit of pruning and mulching if we are not to wither. It is better to look to ourselves than to project our failings onto others. And if we are to compare ourselves to fruit trees, we do well to remember that the tree is a symbol of life and that figs are a symbol of blessing. And to experience that is to live in that 'other world'.

I don't suppose that Jesus zapped a tree, any more than he ever moved a mountain. But I can hear him through this story, and not at all to my comfort. I hear his anger at the way the religious/political leaders of his people so often failed to conduct life as blessing. And that is a sober thought for scribes who write, as well as for subscribers who read.

Look out for examples of fruitfulness: they will give you glimpses of 'another world'.

FOR REFLECTION AND ACTION – alone or with a group

At the end of these two weeks pondering parables and marvels, look back and ask what it is about this 'new world' that you are going to cherish. You might like to record some of your experiences on paper so that you can recall them on difficult days. And decide on one concrete course of action that will enable you to keep on remaining open to this 'new world' that is on the edges of this world.

TEXT MESSAGES
TO THE FAITHFUL
1. From the brothers

Notes based on the New Revised Standard Version by
Edmund Banyard

Edmund Banyard is a minister and a former Moderator of the General Assembly of the United Reformed Church. He has written both plays and devotional material and for many years edited All Year Round *for Churches Together in Britain and Ireland.*

In the long process which ultimately produced the New Testament, the letters of James and Jude were only included after much debate. Were the writers related to Jesus? Should the letters they wrote be counted as scripture? We may be glad that in the end their letters were accepted and included, for these short letters, addressed to worshippers in small scattered communities who, in a hostile world, were often struggling to make sense of their new-found faith, still have much to say that is relevant to our own Christian life in the world of today.

Sunday August 21   *James 1:1-6*
Live confidently, you are in the hands of God

James writes as a servant, or more precisely, a slave of God and the Lord Jesus Christ. This is where his life is centred. He addresses his letter to the twelve tribes of the Dispersion. Jewish communities, the 'twelve tribes', had long been spread across the known world. However James is not addressing them, but widely scattered Christian churches which include many Gentiles. They are the new Israel, called to bear witness to the gospel they have received.

But bearing witness arouses opposition. The more the church is true to its calling, the more it is likely to cut across vested interest or deep-rooted prejudice. There will be trials which should be met with joy. Joy? Who is likely to feel joy when they are really up against it? But James declares that in facing the difficulties we meet day by day we grow and mature into what God has called us to be.

Feeling a little worried? Wondering whether you are really up to it? Ask God to guide and give you strength. Ask, expecting the

prayer to be answered, then go out in the confidence that it will be!
An encouraging thought, surely, to start any day.

✳ *Lord, help me to live this day confidently, in the knowledge*
that whatever the day may bring, you will never be far from
my side.

Monday August 22   James 1:16-18
God is the source of all that is good

Every generous act, every good gift, originates in God, writes
James. However, the many temples to be found where the
Christian faith was beginning to get a foothold were dedicated to
gods that were understood to be capricious, unpredictable, often
quarrelling among themselves and taking their spite out on
humans if they were not properly placated. James was fully
aware that we may well have times when we feel unfairly treated,
look up to God and cry, why? What have I done? Why should this
happen to me? However, this in no way shakes his confidence in
the goodness and the unchanging nature of the God we worship
as opposed to the gods of the pagan world. He reminds us that
the gospel, the 'word of truth', gives us such a fresh way of seeing
things that it is like a new birth enabling us to know the true nature
of God – the God who, rather than sending troubles and trials,
endures them with us. There is much about life that we cannot
understand, but one thing we can hold on to through good and
bad alike is that our God is the source of all goodness, all love, an
unchanging God who will never let us down.

✳ *Grant me, I pray, eyes to recognise the signs of your*
goodness and love round about me, and the will to reflect
that goodness and love in my daily living.

Tuesday August 23   James 2:1-4
A church with open doors?

Imagine that you are on door duty at your church one Sunday and
a well-dressed couple with an easy confident manner arrive. You
make them welcome, see that they are shown to a seat and
introduced to someone who could be relied upon to make them
feel at home. However, a few minutes later another couple arrive
with an unkempt look and a slightly unpleasant aroma about
them. Your heart sinks. Are they on drugs, are they here to beg?
You wouldn't turn them away, of course, but where can you sit

them so that others in the congregation won't be upset?

Is it possible for our churches to serve the people who lead settled respectable lives and at the same time serve those who are likely to be drop-outs? Does the church have to reach out in different ways to people at different levels on the social ladder?

There is no easy answer, but James touches on a fundamental issue for those who serve a Lord who was particularly drawn to the people on the fringe of society, a Lord who went out of his way to welcome those whom others wrote off as being excluded from the people of God.

✳ *Lord of the outcast, the misfit and the rejected, teach us how to love those you hold so dear.*

Wednesday August 24   *James 2:14-17*

Faith or works?

We have here a theme which over the centuries has caused great controversy in the church. Martin Luther was one who had little time for this letter because he saw it as undermining Paul's teaching that we are saved by faith, not works, that no one can earn a place in the kingdom of God. But when we look carefully at what James is really saying he is in no way contradicting Paul. What we read here is that unless faith shows some love in action it is not really faith at all.

We may pray to God with great fervour on behalf of the hungry, the ignorant and the oppressed of this world, but unless at the same time we are asking God to show us how we can in some measure become part of the answer, those prayers are pretty empty.

Having faith in God means having faith in the God who loves us and calls us to live lovingly in return. Does that imply works? Yes, but works that flow from our knowledge that we are already held in the love of God; works joyously undertaken because they flow from faith.

✳ *May my faith, Lord, be such that I cannot help but reflect something of your love in all my relationships with others.*

Thursday August 25   *James 4:11-12*

Watch your words

James is dealing here with a very down-to-earth failing and we sadly have to admit that this word is as necessary in the church as it is in the world outside. What this tiny passage is concerned with is unkind gossip – passing on titbits, in strictest confidence of course, about someone who is not present to speak up for themselves. Such gossip and innuendo about public figures is common-place in our newspapers and news bulletins and we can see all too clearly how destructive it can be. We can't do much about that, but we can watch our private conversations and take this much more seriously than we often do.

James appeals to the law of the kingdom that we should love our neighbour as ourselves. This law is not concerned with how much truth or falsehood there may be in the story which is being passed on, but how much love there is in the telling. If we get caught up in slanderous tittle-tattle we are denying that law of love which is basic to the Christian way of life.

✳ *May the words of my mouth and the meditations of my heart ever be acceptable in your sight, my Lord and my redeemer.*

Friday August 26   *James 5:13-18*

A supportive community

The idea of going to church, joining in the worship and going home again until next Sunday with no more than a few friendly greetings shared is really unimaginable to the writer of this epistle. For him the local church is a supportive community where you pray for one another in sickness or distress, sing joyous hymns together to express thanksgiving and sins are acknowledged and forgiveness sought.

History has seen too many examples of charismatic leaders in churches building tight-knit communities and forcing their view of good and evil on their followers so that the fellowship becomes oppressive, but there is nothing of this in the picture James paints of how a company of believers should behave. He envisages a community that is lovingly supportive in what could often be a frightening and hostile world.

'See how these Christians love another' was once said of some of the early churches and of course if we truly love within the church, that love will inevitably spread far beyond the local fellowship.

✳ *Lord, show me how to work towards making my own church a more loving community, where we love one another and reach out to share that love so that others may know and believe.*

Fight on for the faith

We end the week on a solemn note. After a greeting in which Jude prays, 'May mercy, peace and love be yours in abundance', he plunges into a warning against false teachers and a call to contend or fight on for the faith. One of the great challenges that face us as Christians today is how to be open to new truths and how to listen with a willingness to learn from the world beyond our churches, without losing our grasp on the fundamental gospel.

That gospel might be expressed as follows: the God and Father of our Lord Jesus Christ reaches out lovingly through his life, death and resurrection to save us from the destructive grip of evil and to bring us into his eternal kingdom. If we venture to hold on to that we shall not go far astray.

✳ *Now to him who is able to keep you from falling, and to make you stand without blemish in the presence of his glory with rejoicing, to the only God our Saviour, through Jesus Christ our Lord, be glory, majesty, power, and authority, before all time and now and for ever. Amen*   *Jude 24-25*

FOR REFLECTION - alone or with a group

● What should bearing witness to our faith mean in practical terms today? How far is it a personal matter and how far is it something that calls for planned action on the part of the church?

● How do you see the relationship between faith and works?

● Are you content with the way in which the basic gospel is summarised in the note above? How would you like to restate it in your own words?

FOR ACTION

As a church fellowship, review the 'works' currently undertaken to share the good news of God's love with others. Consider whether the balance in your fellowship between faith and works is right, or if it needs amending in some way.

TEXT MESSAGES
TO THE FAITHFUL
2. From the rock

Notes based on the New Revised Standard Version by
Jean Mortimer

Jean Mortimer is a minister of the United Reformed Church. After early retirement from pastoral charge following major spinal surgery she began a new ministry as a University teacher of New Testament language and literature. She has recently reached proper retirement age and looks forward to having more time for writing, research and kite-flying on the Yorkshire moors.

Water and stones, two of the most evocative images in these readings, are features of my native North Yorkshire countryside. At testing times in my life I have looked to that landscape for courage and never failed to find there 'books in the running brooks' and 'sermons in stones'. I have looked to Peter, the rock, and imagined him returning in his mind's eye to places and events which formed, tested, refined and renewed his faith.

Sunday August 28   *1 Peter 1:3-7*
The foundation stone

The foundation stone of a new church building is often inscribed with the name of the person who lays it. The recipients of 1 Peter were members of new Christian communities founded in places where they did not feel at home. Verse 6 indicates some kind of testing – overt persecution or the challenge of being a minority in a culture based on different foundations. List some of the attitudes and aspirations of others in your immediate environment or the world at large which erode your faith or dim your hope.

The eloquent rhetoric of verses 3–6 lays down several ideas as persuasive stepping-stones on which the imagery of later passages is based. The key theme here is praise to God for the resurrection. Foundation stones laid by human hands can be eroded. Their inscriptions fade. But the resurrection, the basis on which faith rests, is a stone which will never crumble, a message of hope and renewal which will never fade.

Look at your list. Read aloud verse 3.

✳ *May these words be written on my heart, inscribed so*
  deeply that no ill wind or ill fortune will ever wear them
  away.

Monday August 29   *1 Peter 2:4-10*

Living stones

Look up the following references on which the 'stone' and 'selection' images of this passage are based: Isaiah 28:16; Psalm 118:22; Isaiah 8:14 (stone); Isaiah 43:20-21; Exodus 19:5-6; Hosea 2:23 (selection) and Hosea 1:6, 9 and 2:1 (from which the images in verse 10 are derived).

The metaphor of God as the builder and the risen Christ as his living, life-giving foundation stone reminds me of the drystone walls of the Yorkshire Dales which stand out against the wild and threatening landscape, enfolding its daunting vastness and sheltering its sheep. Without any mortar, these walls stand firm against wind and weather because of the skill of the builder, who chooses and lays the first stone with a careful eye, and selects and positions the rest with a patient and experienced hand.

List both positive and negative ways in which the worship and witness of your church make it stand out in your community. Think of a member who needs your solidarity: an individual or group who might look to your church for shelter and support.

✳ *Living God, bind us together and build us up as your*
  people;
  may our sense of belonging be a source of stability and
  strength,
  but never a stumbling block to anyone else.

Tuesday August 30   *1 Peter 3:18-22*

Sermons in water and stone

The church where I was baptised stands close by a stretch of the river Swale where, according to Bede's history, St Paulinus, one of the first Christian missionaries to the north of England, baptised his converts 'in rocky pools'. Paulinus, a native of Rome, was called to defend his faith in an alien and hostile environment. But he kept a good conscience, supported the Christian wife of Edwin, the pagan king of Northumbria, converted him and some of his subjects, established a church in York and became its first bishop. In a period of harsh persecution under Edwin's successor, he narrowly escaped drowning at sea when fleeing to the south.

The story of Paulinus' faith and the few who were saved by it brings this passage to life for me. For here the story of anyone's faith and baptism is set in the context of that greater story of God's saving plan which began in the time of Noah and was brought to fulfilment in the suffering, death and resurrection of Christ. The suffering that anyone may have to endure in maintaining or defending the faith is set in the context of Christ's victory and vindication.

Upon whose good conscience was the Christian faith established in your part of the world? By whose example is your faith nourished and renewed today?

✳ *Give thanks for all whom you have recalled.*

Wednesday August 31   *1 Peter 5:8-11*
On the rocks
In my childhood a favourite place for family picnics and fantasy games was Brimham Rocks. Their size and shape have given rise to fanciful names like the Baboon's Head and the Dancing Bear. There is no lion rock, but in our games of jungle hide-and-seek many a human lion lurked amongst these boulders waiting to pounce! In today's world the image of the devil 'like a roaring lion' on the prowl is often dismissed as childish fantasy, but for early Christians it was very real. Life was no picnic for them. It was a real game of hide-and-seek in which danger and temptation were never far away.

When my childhood games were over, I returned to Brimham Rocks many times with safety helmet, ropes and experienced instructors, to learn how to climb. What real temptations and obstacles do you encounter as you try to make your faith more visible? What spiritual safety equipment and instruction do you need to overcome them?

✳ *God, save me from playing at being a Christian. Support, strengthen and establish me in faith and witness that is real.*

Thursday September 1   *2 Peter 1:16-18*
Glimpses of glory
High above the source of the river Swale is a hill called Nine Standards Rigg, so-called because of the nine drystone pillars on

its summit. They stand out against the skyline like the standard bearers of a defending army. Legend says they were constructed to repel Scottish invaders by maintaining this illusion. I prefer to think they were built to mark a place of special grandeur and beauty where many have felt the awe-inspiring and humbling experience of catching a glimpse of God's glory.

Although many scholars date 2 Peter after the apostle's death, this passage preserves tradition closely linked to Peter's experience on the Mount of Transfiguration. What he witnessed there brought past, present and future together. Perhaps this explains his eagerness to mark this special place and moment (see Mark 9:5; Matthew 17:4 and Luke 9:33), to relive it in later years and pass it on. It appears to be used here to lend apostolic authority to belief in Christ's second coming. For Peter it was a landmark experience, not a legend, myth or illusion.

✳ *Recall a special landmark on your journey of faith. Give thanks for this glimpse of glory and pray for grace to pass it on.*

Friday September 2   *2 Peter 3:8-10*

God's timescale and ours

The churchyard of my childhood has a monument to Yorkshire's oldest man, who is said to have lived 169 years. A folktale states that if you knock on the stone and run around it three times the old man will return. On countless occasions I performed this ritual, impatiently waiting for the promised return. Eventually I gave up. Now when I return to this place, I am touched by its timeless atmosphere.

First generation Christians believed that Christ would soon return in glory and with judgement. But they died before this expectation was fulfilled and this created all kinds of problems for those who came after them. Some found it hard to explain the delay and others began to question whether it would ever happen. (Note the reference to 'scoffers' in 3:3-4). This passage offers two possible reasons for the delay. First, God's timescale is different from ours. Second, God waits patiently, withholding judgement, to give everyone time to repent. How convincing do these arguments seem to you? Does the picture of a patient and merciful God fit in with the violent and destructive imagery of verses 7 and 12? What kind of second coming, if any, do you expect? When and how do you think it will happen? Christians are still divided on this doctrine. Where do you stand?

✳ *Patient and persistent God, do not give up on me, if I am*
tempted to give up on difficult doctrines or give up on you.

Saturday September 3   *2 Peter 3:14-16*

Rocking stones

This passage continues the discussion about waiting for Christ's
return. It recognises that Paul's writings on this subject can be
understood and interpreted in different ways and appeals for a
balanced view, not based on 'the error of the lawless' but on the
peace and stability of reflecting 'the patience of our Lord'. The
error to which the writer refers is probably that of using
uncertainty and ambiguity about the time and manner of Christ's
return as a justification for relaxing the moral and ethical
demands of faith.

At Brimham Rocks there are several precariously balanced
rocking stones which move alarmingly beneath the feet of all who
try to stand on them. The question of the authority of scripture, its
interpretation and application in hotly debated doctrinal, moral
and ethical dilemmas, is as challenging for us as it was for the
recipients of 2 Peter. One might think of the debate on
homosexuality which is rocking the church in so many places
today. What other issues prove 'rocking stones' in your church
community? How can we grow in grace and knowledge of our
Lord and Saviour as we live with such tensions and try to keep
our balance?

✳ *God of stability and strength, help me and all your people to*
keep our balance, as we try to stand together, even on
rocking ground.

FOR REFLECTION – alone or with a group

● Which of the week's readings and reflections have given you
most encouragement?

● Which has challenged or disturbed you most?

FOR ACTION

Choose one of the questions raised in these reflections and ask
your church to discuss it in greater depth.

TEXT MESSAGES
TO THE FAITHFUL
3. From the Elder to the Lady

Notes based on the Revised Standard Version by

Maxwell Craig

Maxwell Craig, a minister of the Church of Scotland, has served parishes in Falkirk, Glasgow and Aberdeen. From its launch in September 1990 to December 1998 he was General Secretary of ACTS (Action of Churches Together in Scotland) and, in 1999 and 2000, served as minister of St Andrew's Scots Church in Jerusalem. He is now chairman of the Scottish Churches Housing Agency, the churches' ecumenical body to combat homelessness. He is a member of the Iona Community and a chaplain to the Queen in Scotland.

The focus this week is on the three short letters of John. The Johannine letters may predate the gospel of John, but who wrote them? Was it John, the evangelist? What is clear is that the letters were written to combat heresy emerging in the early church and to declare two great Christian truths – that God is love and that, if you claim to love God, you must also love your brother and sister. A heresy appearing in Asia Minor stipulated that knowledge of God need not require commitment to the incarnation. All three letters were targeted to counteract this heresy and to restore the true faith. In our multicultural age, it is helpful to be reminded of God's revelation in Christ and God's love of all people.

Sunday September 4   *1 John 1:7-10*

Walk in the light

The contrast between darkness and light is so obvious that it hardly attracts notice. But when John writes that 'God is light and in him is no darkness at all', we're shifted onto a different plane. The light of God is open, honest living, as opposed to the darkness of wrongdoing. It's in this sense that John calls us to walk in the light.

In an age when trust in our institutions is failing and the words of our leaders fail to command respect, cynicism flourishes. One of my responsibilities is to visit Scotland's Young Offenders institutions and to spend time with teenagers who, frankly, have not walked in the light. They know that what they say may not be believed. What they want is someone who will not only listen, but will also accept what they say. And that takes time. John declares first that we all do wrong and, second, that when we walk in the light, the wrong we've done is forgiven. We need a forgiver who knows our frailty from inside our humanity, as Jesus knows it.

✳ *Come, Holy Spirit of God, give us thoughts higher than our own thoughts, prayers better than our own prayers, that we may learn to walk in the light of Christ's forgiving love.*

Monday September 5   1 *John 2:9-11*
The light of love

Is John calling us to accept a new commandment? Yes – and no. It's the old commandment to love, but it has become new in the light of Christ's love. Throughout his life on earth, Jesus trusted people. He trusted Peter; he trusted Judas. He expected the best from them. This laid him open to disappointment and, eventually, led him to the cross. But it also encouraged many to respond to his love for them with their own love, just as a ray of light banishes the darkness that may be far from the light's source.

A young lad who has never been trusted finds it hard to trust. It's only when he senses that he is being taken seriously, as a full human being, that the best in him begins slowly to blossom. That's why a prison sentence need not be the end of the line: it can be the beginning of a new journey towards trusting and being trusted. It's a journey which looks to a new horizon, the horizon of God's kingdom.

✳ *Look at your hands, with their touch and their tenderness; look at your feet, with the horizon they're heading for. They are God's hands and God's feet, leased to you for the world's sake.*

Tuesday September 6   1 *John 3:13-17*
The cost of loving

John has set out God's commandment to love. Now he declares what loving can cost. Abel trusted his brother, Cain, and it cost him his life. Imagine the torment a young offender goes through when he's on home leave for a weekend. He meets his friends: there will be drinking and maybe drugs too. When he returns to jail, his fellow prisoners expect him to have brought drugs with him. If he has decided to adopt a drug-free line and has brought nothing for them, he'll be unpopular and may get beaten up. Trying to go straight isn't easy, once you've been sentenced as a criminal. For those young offenders who want to make a fresh start, loving your fellow prisoners means doing what is best for them; and that can be hard.

Loving means accepting that the other's need comes first. That's when the true cost begins, because we're naturally self-centred. The challenge John places before all of us is to step out of what is natural and into what is Christian. There's nothing sentimental about this kind of loving. This is what our faith requires of us.

✳ *Christ the master carpenter, who at the last through wood and nails purchased our whole salvation, wield well your tools in the workshop of your world, so that we who come rough-hewn to your bench may here be fashioned to a truer beauty of your hand.*   A Celtic prayer

Wednesday September 7   *1 John 4:16-19*
Love casts out fear
What are we most afraid of? Falling ill? Losing our freedom? Being surrounded by terrorist factions or warring nations? If we become seriously ill or if we're sentenced to a long period in prison, we may lose hope.

When Nelson Mandela had been in prison on Robben Island for some 14 years, he was finally allowed a visit from his daughter Zeni and her new baby son. After embracing his daughter, he was handed his tiny grandson. Mandela takes up the story: 'To hold a new-born baby, so vulnerable and soft in my rough hands, hands that for too long had held only picks and shovels, was a profound joy. I don't think a man was happier to hold a baby than I was that day.' A grandfather's privilege was to choose a name. He chose 'Zaziwe', which means 'hope'. He was still only half-way through his 27 years in prison, but he writes: 'The name had a special meaning for me, for during all my years in prison, hope never left me – and now it never would.' (Quotations from *Long Walk to Freedom*, Little Brown & Co, 1994, ISBN 0-316-90965-3, page 482.) Mandela's fear was that he would never be free again. His love for his family cast out that fear. John declares that love, which God offers to all his children, will cast out our fears.

✳ *Lord Jesus, you call us to love – and we find it hard to love. Send your Spirit into our living, we pray, that we may learn to love you and the neighbours you have given us.*

Confidence in prayer

Prayer is born of the confidence that it is heard. John urges us to pray with that confidence. He assures us that prayers offered in accordance with God's will are heard. He then calls us to one of the most important forms of prayer – intercession, prayer for other people. This reminds us that prayer is not selfish. It is God-centred and therefore freed from the narrow bounds of self.

The young prisoners whom I visit have done wrong. Have they committed what John calls mortal sin? Mortal sin is the wrong done by the person who refuses to recognise that what they have done is wrong. They have muzzled their conscience and delight in doing that wrong. And they are determined, when they are released, that there will be a next time and next time they won't be caught! Our prayers for such young prisoners are frustrated because they are freely choosing to live a life of crime.

Most wrongdoers, however, are well aware that what they're doing is wrong. We can pray for them in confidence – and hope that we shall be prayed for, in spite of the wrong we do. Because we know God is our Father, there is confidence in our praying for others and in the assurance that our fellow Christians are praying for us.

✳ *Lord Jesus Christ, Son of God, have mercy on me, a sinner.*

The danger of heresy

John's concern is to combat the heresy, which was being peddled in Asia Minor, that it is not necessary to believe that the Son of God came in the flesh. Greek culture admired philosophy. And philosophers like big ideas. What they don't like is tying their big ideas to a person. The great truth of the incarnation is that the wonder of God can be explicable to human beings; it has to be human-sized for us to grasp it fully. John's way of combating this heresy was to concentrate on God's love, as shown in the coming of Jesus. 'He who abides in the doctrine ... has both the Father and the Son' (verse 9), echoing Jesus' words, 'He who has seen me has seen the Father'. Yet, we're troubled by the verse which follows: 'If anyone ... does not bring this doctrine, do not receive him into the house or give him any greeting'. It's important to remember the context. The Christian faith was young, its roots still forming: heresy, at this formative stage, was dangerous. That was why no compromise was possible. What John clearly states is the vital importance of the incarnation of Jesus, Son of God and son of humanity.

✳ *Abide with us, Lord, for it is toward evening and the day is far spent: abide with us at the end of this day, at the end of our lives, at the end of the world.*

Saturday September 10   3 John:1-4

The truth of God

The word 'truth' occurs four times in these four verses. The truth John proclaims with passion in all three of these letters is gospel truth, the truth of the incarnation of Jesus. This truth declares the love of God for his whole creation, that God was prepared to prove that love by sending his son. So John can pray for his friend, Gaius, with the confidence that, whatever his physical condition, for which he also prays, his spiritual wellbeing is assured – he is embraced by God's truth.

In our multicultural age, the Christian faith can be presented simply as one of the options we can choose or ignore. John would have no sympathy for such woolliness. God's love is crucial. The incarnation proves it. Jesus didn't come to inaugurate a new religion, the way a superstore opens a new branch and touts for custom. John is declaring God's truth, which transcends all the churchy mist with which the past 2000 years have obscured it. God loves the creation; Christ demonstrates that love. Therefore Christ is our Lord – the way, the truth and the life for us all.

✳ *Holy Spirit of God, the source of all truth, help us to see Jesus as our Lord, that we may walk his way, speak his truth and live his life.*

FOR REFLECTION – alone or with a group

● Can we learn from the experience of prisoners? If so, what?

● Is the quality of love described by John something you can share?

● John is passionate about the truth he sees in Jesus. What truth(s) are you passionate about?

FOR ACTION

Jesus said: '...I was sick and you visited me, I was in prison and you came to me' (Matthew 25:36). Most churches arrange visits to those who are sick. Some churches are involved in visiting prisoners. Is that something you would be prepared to consider?

SYMBOLIC ACTIONS

Notes based on the New Revised Standard Version by
Peter Privett

Peter Privett is an Anglican priest, who works freelance as an educator, artist and retreat leader. He is also the UK Trainer Consultant for Godly Play, a method of religious education that takes seriously the power of the non-verbal and symbolic dimensions of learning.

There are many symbolic actions or acted parables in the Bible. Many of those in the New Testament (for example, Jesus washing his disciples' feet) appear elsewhere in this year's readings, so most of the examples in this theme are taken from the Old Testament. The symbolic actions are usually carried out by one person, often at great personal cost, in order to convey a message from God to a group of people or an individual. In the first week we look at acted warnings of the consequence of people's current behaviour and institutions. In the second week, we focus on actions which speak of God's forgiveness and loving acceptance.

1. Warnings

Sunday September 11   *Isaiah 8:1–4*
The sign of naming a pre-verbal child

War and political crisis are immediate. Neighbours are enemies. Deals are made with the region's superpower. National religious valuables are handed over as protection money. Anxiety, disquiet, nervousness and fretfulness abound. National fear is the air that is inhaled. In such a situation the language of words fails to give expression to dis-ease.

Previously (chapter 7), the prophet has tried to reassure with the sign of the young pregnant woman. More non-verbal learning is needed, more words will not do. *Maher-shalal-hash-baz*, meaning literally 'the spoil speeds', 'the prey hastens', is spoken and written. The communication is not formal court speak, neither political spin, nor civil service nonsense, but common, everyday language.

Ratification by senior national figures is not enough. The language of words fails. Embodiment is needed. Another language is called for. The uncluttered language of 'I went to the prophetess' (verse 3) is followed by embodied language, the birth and naming of the child. The child is the language through which meaning can be made and expressed. The name of the pre-verbal child is the sign, is the message. The child who, before they can utter the primitive sounds of 'mama' and 'dada', is dependent upon others for assurance and sustenance, is learning in this pre-verbal stage of development the truth of trust and mistrust.

✴ **Thank God for your name. Sit quietly with the name of God – I AM. What other name would you have?**

Monday September 12   Isaiah 20:1–6

The sign of prophetic nakedness

Crisis increases. Desire for control, hunger for supremacy is accompanied by invasion, disintegration of boundaries, and break-up of borders. The superpower consumes all in its path. Those that are free are turned into slaves. Realities of hope and security are stripped away. The situation is dire and words cannot give voice to the calamitous condition. Something else is needed. Spoken language breaks down in such circumstances.

Isaiah strips away his shoes, his clothes, his undergarments, and becomes vulnerable, defenceless, and at risk. What offers protection and warmth, and dignity, is removed. He is exposed to the elements, to ridicule, to harm. Nothing can be hidden. His is a ministry of nakedness, not as a cheap publicity stunt but as a profound expression of what is. It is not a quick, instant message. It is a three year communication of non-verbal meaning, moving from shock to ridicule to complacency and unfeeling.

There is a difference between Isaiah's experience and that of Egypt and Ethiopia. Presumably, the prophet has an element of choice in his exposure, whereas the two countries have no choice at all, although it could be argued that the prophetic vocation might give little choice as well. The humiliation of the neighbouring allies is secured by the restriction of their options. They are acted upon and done to. They move from being subjects to being made objects, a movement from freedom into slavery. The sign of the naked, vulnerable prophet not only speaks to the situation abroad, of them, but also changes the direction of focus to include us.

The final question asks, 'With the disintegration of our objects of hope and confidence, what will happen to me, to us?'

* **Gather together objects or symbols that represent the things you hold dear – your faith, your relationships. What happens when these are removed, stripped away?**

Tuesday September 13   *Jeremiah 13:1–11*

The sign of the prophet's underwear

Where does reality lie?

Very often, words are chosen carefully and precisely. They are, sometimes, a result of long and protracted thought. Words are excluded because they are not right. What you say can be used in evidence against you, so you had better be careful, especially in a time of national crisis and war.

Signs and symbolic actions don't always work like that. Ideas, associations, memories, pictures, colours, emotions fly in all directions, defying the desire to be controlled and codified. In periods of national crisis and war those in control are often fearful of such non-verbal language.

The shocking image of Jeremiah's underwear as a symbol of the divine-human relationship and a sign of the ensuing conflict with Babylon is very strange for a western male in the 21st century. Yet underwear is an intimate piece of clothing, worn next to the sexual parts of the body, the parts that tell us about ourselves. It is clothing in close relationship with our movements, so close that it almost becomes part of us, especially if like Jeremiah we've walked 100 miles to the Euphrates. It is clothing that supports and protects. It is designed for a purpose and function.

Remove the undergarments and they disintegrate and are useless. They become detached, separate, disconnected, unable to move in relationship. They become rotten. They decompose and decay. They move in opposition to their purpose. This Western male is beginning to see things differently!

* **Choose a symbol or object that might seem to be unusual to describe your relationship with God. What new things can you discover?**

Wednesday September 14   *Jeremiah 19:1–13*

The signs of earthen flask and words

Jeremiah has a difficult national task to perform. The people must face the impending crisis. The superpower will invade and subdue. There will be no escape. The way forward is to face it and enter it. Walter Brueggemann, in his book *Prophetic Imagination* (Fortress Press, 2001, revised edition), identifies Jeremiah's task as one of proclaiming that grief must be faced, entered into, and experienced, otherwise there can be no possibility of new life. It cannot be otherwise.

Such realities are so profound, so deep, that verbal and non-verbal ways of knowing need to go hand in hand. These two language systems combine with great power to accomplish the work that needs to be done.

The verbal system in the passage is imaginative, rich in images, and poetry; the symbolic system is direct and simple. Both language systems stand counter to the language of popular theology and to consumer-led spirituality that wishes to avoid the difficult and stay in the false reality of complacency and comfort. Give the people what they want to hear.

The language of both systems is violent and powerful too, for it can be no other when people are in a state of denial. It has to shock, to disrupt the religious experience which has been diverted into a utility and commodity in order to manipulate the divine will – 'If I do this, then please, God, do this'.

The signs in this passage point to a definitive shattering beyond repair, to the point where creation works in reverse and the movement is from order to chaos. Only then can something new begin. This message demands extreme communication, a language of action and words.

✳ *Take a cup, glass or other container, then shatter it... Spend time before God with this symbol.*

Thursday September 15   *Jeremiah 27:1–18*

The sign of the yoke

The prophet persists. The message is unpalatable. There can be no compromise. There are no deals. The political meeting in which this passage is set, a meeting of ambassadors and of political delegates, would like it otherwise. Their very life and jobs, their realities depend upon spinning words, upon wheeling and dealing, upon backroom bartering, upon political manipulation. The divine nature is otherwise, and is counter-cultural. There can be no rebellion; it is not an option in the face of invasion. Jeremiah's message proclaims that submission to Babylon is the only way. Symbolic actions proclaim the message and challenge the status quo.

Popular theology, which can join the religious and political in a glittering yet dangerous marriage, wants everything nice and neat, everything in the right place, but the signs of the wooden and iron yokes proclaim that this way is unsustainable and leads to a lie. It cannot address with integrity the difficulties and despair of grief and suffering. The prophet must proclaim the unacceptable message, must be true to the integrity of the spirit, otherwise we perish.

The danger of symbol and signs is that they too can be used to anaesthetise us into a false security. The temple vessels, at the end of the passage, are signs of a false hope. A desire to ignore the disaster of the present situation, to avoid the conflict, to pretend that the calamity can be met with hugs and sweet kisses.

✳ *Choose some objects and symbols. In what ways do these keep you from facing the deep realities of human experience?*

Friday September 16   *Ezekiel 4:1–17*

The signs of the brick and immobility

Crisis happens. Boundaries are destroyed. Security has disappeared. Surely this isn't happening to us? In a while we will wake up to find it's all been a dream! The prophet in such a situation has to resort to drastic measures. Once again words just won't do in the face of profound disorientation. The offering of an object as a sign might not be enough. The intensity of the reality is so deep that other means of expression are called for. In an almost surreal enactment, Ezekiel proclaims the truth of the situation by offering the signs dramatically. Sign and action combine.

Exile is upon us, but surely it will end tomorrow, especially if we pray hard. The prophetic pastoral task is to make us face the present moment. The re-enactment with the brick reinforces the truth of what has happened. The immobility of the prophet describes the truth of the existing reality. Prophetic pastors are not immune from this experience. They are part of the disaster. They are in the mess with everybody else.

The power of symbolic language often reveals itself as it is enacted. The symbols have to be entered, explored and played with to decipher their meaning. It's by painting, modelling, acting, dancing the symbol that I discover the truths that it contains. By painting my despair I may discover what my despair is.

Ezekiel's binding and immobility, his survival on almost non-existent rations gives him an experience of the reality. He takes the symbol into himself.

✳ *Choose one of the artistic media – painting, dance, music and so on. Spend some time before God experiencing the power of the symbol.*

Saturday September 17   *Acts 21:10–15*

The sign of the girdle

The future is waiting. It seems that conflict will follow. Some pastoring is needed. Once again here is a link between prophet and pastor. Energy and time have been given, to enthuse and preach the gospel. Horizons have been expanded but for some there is a conflict of worldview. A cost is involved. The last stage of the journey is about to unfold. Issues need to be brought to light, need to be recognised, acknowledged. Words keep the transactions on the surface. Agabus understands that the situation calls for some deeper experience.

The removal of the belt and the binding of the hands shift the meaning making so that knowledge is expanded. The future is explored with the help of the symbolic action. It releases strong emotions, there is weeping and the breaking of hearts. It helps to prepare for that which is to come. The symbolic action has a twofold effect. First, on Paul who is bound, where the future is named and so can be faced. Second, on the assembled company who observe, and are then drawn into the action by their emotional response.

The two are made one. Objective and subjective understandings are bound together. The symbol unites the different participants. Agabus, the prophet and pastor, exercises a therapeutic ministry. What is hidden is revealed. The hard places are made known.

Is the practice of symbolic action an intuitive process itself? Does Agabus know what he's going to do before he does it, or is it spur-of-the-moment?

✳ *Reflect, before God, on the times when symbolic action has released the deep things in you and in your community.*

FOR REFLECTION – alone or as a group

Collect together a wide variety of pictures, images from magazines, postcards etc. Go around the house collecting

218

everyday objects, ornaments, spoons, pencils, etc. If you have them, use magnetic fridge poetry words, otherwise random words from the dictionary written on separate cards. Place all these in the centre of a room and choose an object, a picture and a word. Spend time in silence and let these speak to you. Share your thoughts with one another.

FOR ACTION

Look around your community. What symbols or actions are needed to give expression to the deep needs that are there?

---

2. Signs of hope

Sunday September 18 *Leviticus 16:20–22*

The sign of the scapegoat

There is a time and a season for every purpose under heaven, a time to name and own the deep realities of alienation, estrangement, disconnection and dis-ease, a time to acknowledge these personally, corporately and nationally. When community rituals and symbols disappear then it is all too easy to be cowed and broken by the responsibility of these unbearable burdens.

In a time when understandings of community belonging are thin and stretched, then individual responsibility comes to the fore. I now have to bear the burden of everything. Therefore, it is all too easy to project the blame onto my family, colleagues, political leaders, and even easier to blame the more marginal members of my community. Let's transfer guilt onto other people. It's now their fault. A British national paper had a recent headline, 'Ask yourself, can a nation survive without a conscience?'

The ancient custom of the scapegoat offers real hope. Ancient rituals and symbols offer a substantial opportunity to go deeper into the experience. The non-verbal power speaks to the human spirit, offering a new beginning, a new start, a new opening. It offers appropriate language to give voice to what needs to be said and completed. It expands the responsibility for sin to include both individual and corporate responsibility.

Forgiveness, atonement, restitution are not just abstract ideas and words. They are grounded in substance, in the actual sending away of the goat into the desert. They are acted out and shown as well as talked about. The burning of 'confession papers', in experimental liturgy, the throwing of the pebble into the sea from the beach are small signs of atonement. But where are the national and global rituals that offer reparation?

✳ *Find some physical way to pray today. Reflect on the individual and corporate nature of sin and redemption. Find some way to express this physically.*

Monday September 19   *Numbers 21:4–9*

The sign of the serpent

The passage is filled with ambiguity. The text overflows with paradox. The story is packed with contradiction. Serpents destroy, but are also the sources of salvation and healing. There is a homeopathic truth being proclaimed. The sources of healing and destruction are the same.

In many ancient images, as early as the 4th century BC, the serpent entwined around a pole has been understood as a sign of healing. Many ancient Greek sculptures show doctors accompanied by this symbol, and carvings of the same can be found on many ruins, especially over the doorways, of what were ancient hospices and hospitals. Medical books written in the 17th century have the same image on their title pages. For many ancient cultures the serpent was associated with creation; the Celts have carvings of foliage and greenery proceeding from the mouth of the snake. The shedding of its skin was for many people a symbol of regeneration, and the circular image of the mouth and the tail meeting was a symbol of the eternity of time. The undulations of motion often reminded people of the movement of water, the material of life, of the liquidity and changing quality of existence.

The people are healed as they gaze upon the serpent entwined around the pole. Healing may happen when contradictions are entered, when integration is offered. The pole, with its associations of rigidity and non-movement, offers the opposite to the serpent. Opposites are held together, contradictions celebrated and ambiguity heals.

✳ *Draw a simple vertical straight line on a piece of paper, then draw a wavy horizontal line. Bring before God the contradictions and ambiguities of your life, the elements that destroy and those which heal.*

The sign of the purchase

The invader is at the door and has been for 11 years. The times are volatile. Unspeakable atrocities are being carried out (see the book of Lamentations). Society is bankrupt, morally and financially. This is not the time to invest in property. Common sense says, 'Let's get rid of land whilst the going is good!' All the odds are stacked against Jeremiah. His words proclaim total and utter disaster. The superpower will invade; there will be no escape.

Hope comes from a prison cell. Freedom is proclaimed from one who has had freedom curtailed. Hope comes with a profound and prophetic sign that speaks louder than words. Jeremiah does what seems impossible, ridiculous, preposterous and absurd. He engages in what seems a folly in a collapsing world, a collapsing economy, in a state of chaos and insecurity. His action offers a future, a hope, an investment. The buying of the field points beyond the present circumstances to another time when empire is dissolved. The prophetic sign offers an alternative to the present chaotic situation.

The deal is signed and sealed as if the conditions are normal. Deeds of purchase denote stability. Everything is done properly; records are stored as they should be in the earthen jars. The sign proclaims that 'houses and fields and vineyards shall again be bought in this land' (verse 15). The sign points beyond the present reality.

✴ ***Select something quite ordinary such as a telephone bill, household document or something else that represents stability. Use it to remember before God those in chaos and confusion.***

The sign of the sticks

Exile and despair have disassembled our whole being. Land and culture have been stripped away. We are disorientated and confused. Personal and national identity has been dismantled by the superpower.

Now the bones have been assembled. That which was dismembered is made whole. Skeletons become en-fleshed, and the wind blows with life again. This is not enough. A new lesson has to be learned. The sign of the two sticks challenges the idea of 'Let's go back to the way it was'. It offers a new understanding of what national identity might mean. It enlarges the possibilities. It offers the vision of an identity that cancels old rivalries, that seeks unity and the healing of divisions.

Israel and Judah will become one. Both have encountered the same process of fragmentation, dismemberment and dispersion. The sign of the two sticks is one that connects them in a shared suffering, in common misfortune. New hopes are dreamt, but they are also glimpses of the original vision, perceptions of an initial hope. The earlier expectation of unity under David is re-energised and propelled as a vision for the future. The sign of the sticks held together in one hand is also a sign of the divine nature, of the holiness of God.

✳ *Take two sticks and hold them in your hand. Let each be a symbol of something which, when held together, make a contradictory image. In what ways may God be calling you to make them one? Where do we find signs of unity?*

Thursday September 22   *Hosea 3:1–5*
The sign of marriage

Religious understanding is in confusion, meaning is in upheaval. Past certainties are forgotten and put aside.

The relationship with the divine is abandoned and forgotten. That which was joined together has been put asunder. Hosea preaches an understanding of anger, disappointment, and commitment. Hosea is an advocate for fidelity. Hosea's is a message of constancy and love.

The sign of his message is his marriage. The symbol is his relationship with his wife. The marriage metaphor is a key element in the Canaanite fertility cult that is seducing the nation. The sexual imagery of the cult statues, the institution of sacred prostitution and sexual intercourse were all symbolic religious means of ensuring the fertility of the earth. The Baal becomes married to the earth. Hosea's preaching proclaims that the blessings of abundance and the thanksgiving for fecundity are misdirected. He then offers a shocking perception, an entirely new understanding, a prophetic moment of new conception.

The sexual metaphor proclaimed by the false understanding is used to redirect us to the divine relationship. Sex is the symbol. The marriage proclaims it. Hosea's wife is not necessarily one of a morally depraved character but probably a woman who took part in the fertility rites of the cult. The representative of the institution that is in opposition to his heart is taken into the realms of his love. This is a relationship of mutuality, which then becomes the hope for the nation. It becomes the shocking vision of God's relationship with his people.

✳ *Bring to mind a close relationship, perhaps holding a photograph or some other symbol in your hand. What might God be revealing to you and to your community through this relationship?*

Friday September 23   Matthew 19:13–15

The sign of children

The incident is virtually neglected by the writer – only two verses. Blink, and you miss it! There are hardly any words. The language is sparse. It's only the children. Obviously, there are more important matters for our concern.

If we focus on young children, they proclaim a deep truth. They find verbal language difficult; it's still being formed. Theirs is a language which is primarily non-verbal. It's the language of gesture, the language of play, through which they know the deep things of life, which words can't express. The language is sign and symbol. Theirs is the primal language that adults forget.

Disciples then and now, for whatever reason, wish to exclude them. Don't bother us now! The real business of the kingdom is concerned with adult cognitive reason. But the sign of the child changes everything, the world is turned upside down. The inclusive enfolding actions of Jesus challenge the status quo. The silent, excluded are put into the centre, for such is the kingdom of heaven.

The action is accompanied by touch. Touch is a powerful healing action. Without touch, we perish. We need physical contact and embrace for our survival. Touch, though, can be cheapened into the demeaning pat on the head and worse. Touch then leads to the diminishment of spirit, to a profound non-blessing. But touch in this passage calls us to blessing, literally to speak well of another person. The blessing touch calls out the good in us.

These non-verbal children are powerful signs of the kingdom, a kingdom that has blessing at its centre. The child and the blessing also point us to the nature of God.

✳ *Bring to mind or observe a small child playing. You could take a photograph of the child. What is she/he revealing to you about the nature of God and the kingdom? What might the child be saying to God? What might the child be saying to you? What might God say to each of you?*

The sign of the meeting

The passage gathers together many of the themes of the week. There are hints of previous comments and revelations. The persecutor becomes converted. The agent of destruction will become the minister of the gospel. Opposite views are reconciled when enemies become allies. Ministry is seen as an enfolding inclusive action, amongst those considered as outsiders. Touch is healing and calls out the good.

Paul, the intellectual man of words, is reduced not only to the non-verbal, but also to the non-visual. Even signs and symbols are taken away temporarily. He is reduced to a silent, primal pre-symbolic language, the language of inward knowing, the language of visions. This language is familiar to those who come close to God. Ananias seems comfortable with this deep way of knowing. It doesn't seem strange to him. It's become part of his being.

The natural character of the encounter means that tensions can be explored, arguments made, and alternatives expressed. There is an inner conversation about the nature of truth, and through the struggle and dialogue decisions for action are made. The language of sign and symbol and action seem to be naturally integrated. The whole language of the last verses seems to have many layers of meaning. Touch brings sight, with the falling of scales. Rising leads to baptism followed by food and a strengthening. Perhaps these may be the symbolic ingredients of *hope*.

✳ *Sit quietly with eyes closed, body stilled, and be in the presence of God. Just* be.

FOR REFLECTION AND ACTION – alone or with a group

● As an individual or as a group, gather together objects, pictures and words and create an exhibition/display of hope. Reflect on how you might start to make this a reality in your community.

● Take each of this week's readings and, with a group, see if you can find ways to communicate the truths of hope using signs and symbols and actions. Do it without spoken language.

READINGS IN LEVITICUS

Notes based on the Hebrew text by
Jonathan Magonet

Jonathan Magonet is Professor of Bible and Principal of the Leo Baeck College – a centre for Jewish education, a rabbinical and Jewish studies seminary in London. His books on biblical studies include new editions of A Rabbi Reads The Bible *and* A Rabbi Reads The Psalms *(both published by SCM Press). He runs an annual Jewish-Christian Bible study week in Germany and his inter-faith work is described in his book* Talking to the Other: Jewish Inter-faith Dialogue with Christians and Muslims *(I B Tauris).*

The Book of Leviticus has a bad reputation. It is obscure, full of the minutiae of cultic detail, with strange ideas about ritual purity and seemingly obsessed with abominations and sins! All of which is true! It is also the book at the centre of the Pentateuch, and at its heart we find one of the most enduring statements in the Hebrew Bible – 'you shall love your neighbour as yourself' (Leviticus 19:18). So how do we reconcile these seemingly unbridgeable contradictions? We shall be struggling to do so as we proceed in the next two weeks' readings.

---

1. The Law of the Lord is perfect

Sunday September 25   *Leviticus 2:1–16*
How do we draw near to God?

The first task with any book of the Bible is to take the text seriously in its own terms. Leviticus uses a coded language, which has to be deciphered – only we lack many of the keys. The different kinds of sacrifices and rituals were presumably understood in the biblical world. Indeed it is interesting that the work of the priests is made public and transparent so that they could not use the 'mystery' of their profession to control the people.

The previous chapter describes the first kind of offering to be given to God, an *olah*, one that is completely consumed by fire, so the one who gives it derives no benefit from it. The Hebrew word for a sacrifice, *qorban* from a verb 'to come near', hints at the purpose. The one who brought it wanted to come close to God. To give to God, without expecting something in return, is the first lesson offered by this intriguing book.

The rabbis noted that whereas other sacrifices are introduced by the phrase 'if a man brings...' only here is the word *nefesh*, 'soul', used. For, they said, the meal offering is the offering of a poor man, and it is as if he offers his very soul.

✴ **God, beloved of the soul, source of mercy, draw your servant to do your will.**
                                                                    Eliezer Azkari

Monday September 26   *Leviticus 4:1–35*
How do we return to God?
In the previous chapter a different sacrifice is considered, the *shelamim*. The word is related to the familiar *shalom*, 'peace', but the root meaning is 'wholeness' or 'completeness'. Unlike the olah, which is completely consumed, only part of this one is burnt on the altar; the rest becomes a shared meal.

It is a reminder that killing animals for food is to be a solemn act done with full consciousness that a life has been taken. Jewish and Muslim religious regulations about slaughter maintain this sensitive awareness, often lost in societies where meat comes wrapped and frozen.

Having established sacrifice as a way of expressing our relationship with God, our chapter extends the system. If we become estranged from God through our failures or misbehaviour, there must be a mechanism for re-establishing that connection. The word translated as 'sin', Hebrew *chet*, actually means to 'miss the target', to fail, to go off course, which leaves much spiritual and emotional space for 'getting back on course'. The sacrificial act itself is only the final step of a process that has included acknowledging what has gone wrong and desiring to find the way back to God.

✴ **Bring us back to you, O Lord, and we shall return. Renew our days as of old.**
                                                              Lamentations 5:21

Tuesday September 27   *Leviticus 5:1–13*
How do we restore our damaged relationships with one another?
Chapter four has established the system of offerings based on a hierarchy of responsible roles within Israelite society: the

226

anointed priest, the governing council, a leader of one of the tribes, a normal individual. Now it addresses the case of someone who has become ritually 'impure', that is to say unfit to be present in the sanctuary, through some accidental or other event, like coming into contact with a corpse. The value of the offering is varied according to the ability of the individual to pay.

But the system here extends to cover deliberate actions that are dishonest or cause damage to others. It allows the wrongdoer to make reparation, together with a fine of twenty per cent of the worth of what was stolen or taken.

Thus alongside repairing the relationship with God, the system restores the proper relationship amongst the people, especially between the wrongdoer and the victim. As a penal system it effectively does away with imprisonment and gives the perpetrator the chance to regain a sense of responsibility for his actions and his fate. Beneath the symbolic language are again important lessons for the spiritual health of a society.

✳ *Make us content with your goodness and let our souls know the joy of your salvation. Purify our hearts to serve you in truth.* *Jewish Sabbath prayer*

Wednesday September 28   *Leviticus 6:14–23*

How do we understand the power of God in the world?

Chapters 1–5 have focused on the preparation of the sacrifices and the reasons for them. The next two chapters focus on the role of the priests in offering them and the parts of the sacrifices that they receive for themselves as part of their support. The sons of Eli the priest of Shiloh notoriously abused this right by the way they snagged the meat with large forks while it was being cooked (1 Samuel 2:12–17)!

The detailed care with which every operation must be carried out, and the cleaning up operation afterwards, is evident. To understand this deep anxiety about mistakes being made while God is in their midst, the best analogy is that of an atomic reactor. It is a source of power if correctly harnessed, but potentially disastrous if not. Hence the need for a hierarchy of protective enclosures, and of operatives with different degrees of competence who may work within the different sections.

All of this emphasises the awe of the Israelites in serving God and their concern that a false action could have consequences for the entire community. The priests, no less than the people, share a responsibility for the welfare of the whole.

✴ *God, help us to live according to your teaching and to hold fast to your commands. Let us not come into the power of sin or wrongdoing, temptation or disgrace. Let no evil within us control us.* *Jewish daily prayer*

Thursday September 29 *Leviticus 7:11–38*

How do we fulfil our responsibility to our community?

This section reminds us that offering sacrifices is not only about repairing a broken relationship with God. The 'thanksgiving' offering was an act of gratitude for the benefits bestowed upon the worshipper, while the 'votive' and 'freewill' offerings were similarly to celebrate the relationship with God. Nevertheless the logic of the system requires that appropriate penalties exist for those who break the rules. The examples listed here relate to someone who eats part of the sacrifice set aside for God, or who consumes certain portions of the animal or any blood. Some of the regulations help maintain the distinction between the priests and the rest of the Israelites, again expressing a concern about contaminating the sanctuary.

The ultimate penalty is severe, that of being 'cut off' from the people. In some cases this means an actual death penalty, but here it seems to leave it to God to inflict an appropriate punishment for the offender, perhaps an early or unnatural death. Such activities seem remote and the penalties drastic but they belong to a world in which incorrect behaviour in the presence of God was understood to have severe consequences for the entire people.

✴ *My God and God of my ancestors, as long as the soul is within me, I will declare that you are the master of all deeds, the ruler of all creatures and the Lord of every soul.* *Jewish daily prayer*

Friday September 30 *Leviticus 8:1–17*

How do we explore the mystery that is our life?

The next two chapters tell of the anointing of the High Priest and the initiation of formal worship in the newly completed sanctuary in the wilderness. The High Priest wears unique clothing and he alone is anointed with oil, as is the altar. He is set apart from others, and this status seems to go beyond the merely ceremonial. Elsewhere we read about the 'cities of refuge' to which someone who kills another by accident may flee to await trial, protected there from members of the dead man's family who might seek vengeance. If his act was not a deliberate one of murder, he is allowed to live, but must remain in the city for the rest of his life. However the death of the High Priest provides an amnesty allowing all to leave the city, as if his death symbolically atones for the blood that has been shed (Numbers 35:25).

Following the incident of the rebellion by Korach and his followers (Numbers 16), a plague breaks out which is stopped by Aaron who literally 'stands between the living and the dead' (Numbers 16:48). Both accounts evoke the unique powers vested in that office.

✴ *God, may none of our controversies rise up like those of Korach, from ambition and self-seeking. Let them only be for the sake of heaven.*   *Contemporary Jewish prayer*

Saturday October 1   *Leviticus 10:8–20*
Are there boundaries to our religious task?
This passage follows one of the few narrative sections in Leviticus. Two of Aaron's sons, Nadav and Abihu, bring 'strange fire' into the sanctuary and are consumed by a fire from heaven, presumably the one that consumed the offerings at the sanctuary a few verses earlier (Leviticus 9:24). It is not clear what this 'strange fire' is. Perhaps behind their act is their experience related in Exodus 24:9–11 where, together with Moses, Aaron and seventy elders, they were granted the mystical experience of 'seeing' God. One result seems to have been the powers bestowed on the seventy elders to prophesy (Numbers 11:24–25). Perhaps the two sons became so enthusiastic about serving God that they acted out of turn. They were literally consumed by their zeal.

A similar fate awaited two hundred and fifty men who joined the Korach rebellion against Moses and Aaron and took censers with incense into the sanctuary, perhaps also from the desire to serve God as priests (Numbers 16:35). The rest of the chapter adds further regulations for the priests, but at the end, to balance the earlier story, Moses acknowledges that some changes to the regulations are possible in exceptional circumstances.

✴ *Our Sovereign who delights in life, remember us for life, and write us in the book of life, for your own sake, God of life.*
                                        Jewish penitential prayer

2. Rules for a holy life

Sunday October 2   *Leviticus 11:1–47*
How do we value the food that we eat?

Food is such a central aspect of life, yet so easily taken for granted when it is readily available, that it comes as a shock to see such detailed concern about what may or may not be eaten. Behind the rules in this chapter certain patterns begin to emerge. Animals with a 'split hoof' and that 'chew the cud' are all vegetarians and 'domesticated'. Conversely animals that are explicitly excluded are those that hunt or scavenge. This seems to follow the old hippy adage: You are what you eat! A people that is to hold to domestic and pastoral ways and values is to be conditioned to peaceful ways even through the food they eat.

Another principle seems to be present as well. Just as land animals are 'defined' by certain physical aspects, so are fish and birds. Behind this may lie the creation story in Genesis 1. God has created the three domains, air, land and water. The Israelites are to align themselves with this ordering of the universe so that those animals are excluded that do not possess the 'typical' characteristics of their domain or that cross over between two domains.

✳ ***Blessed are you, our Living God, sovereign of the universe, who creates different kinds of food.***
Traditional Jewish blessing

Monday October 3   *Leviticus 12:1–8*
Do we accept the equality of women and men as a religious duty?

The terms 'impurity' or 'uncleanness' for the state of a woman after childbirth used here carry a lot of negative associations in English that are not intended in the Hebrew. As this passage explains, they only refer to ritual matters and have no moral overtones.

A striking distinction is made between the length of time that ritual impurity lasts after childbirth depending on whether a boy or girl is born. All sorts of reasons have been evoked for the doubling of the time after the birth of a girl but the basis may be more to do with biology than theology. In one in ten cases a baby girl may have vaginal bleeding because the mother's hormones have been withdrawn. So there are in effect two women who have to wait for purification and the mother takes on that role for her daughter.

Whatever the reason, of much greater significance is the fact that an identical offering is to be brought to the sanctuary whether the child is a boy or a girl. The absolute equality of the two genders and the identical significance to be given to the birth of either are here emphasised.

✳ *You declare freedom to boy and girl alike, may you guard them like the apple of your eye.*
                                        Based on a Sabbath hymn by Dunash ben Labrat

Tuesday October 4   *Leviticus 13:1–8*
How do we value our body as part of our spiritual being?
We tend to recoil from passages like these with their explicit descriptions of disease. The priests are diagnosing a condition in terms of whether it renders the sufferer ritually unclean, but they are clearly thinking medically as well. The correct identification of the illness will help protect the community from infection through a process of quarantine. But this text is a reminder that caring for our bodies is also part of our spiritual task.

Though traditionally understood to be leprosy, there is much debate about what exactly are the different medical conditions described here. They require the isolation of the affected person who must cover his mouth and warn of his coming by calling out 'Unclean! Unclean!' Perhaps this is the image that lies behind Isaiah's anxiety when in a vision he 'sees' God (Isaiah 6:1–7). He laments that 'I am a person of unclean lips and dwell amongst a people of unclean lips.' He has to be purified by a burning coal taken off the altar. The concept of ritual uncleanness is here taken to its logical conclusion, that all of us are less than pure when standing in the presence of God.

✳ *God, if you should count sins, who could stand, but with you is mercy and compassion.*   *Jewish penitential prayer*

Wednesday October 5   *Leviticus 14:1–9*
How do we celebrate recovery from illness?
Having declared someone to be ritually unclean, there has to be an appropriate method for readmission once the condition has

cleared up. Moreover it needs to be as elaborate and convincing as the process that diagnosed the condition in the first place so that the person is fully accepted. Nevertheless it is frustrating that we have no direct knowledge of the meaning of the various symbolic acts described here.

The shaving of all body hair may help show that the skin condition has completely departed. It also ensures that the washing covers all of the body. But perhaps it has a further purpose. Though the formerly afflicted person may enter the camp, he must sit for seven days outside his tent before being allowed to re-enter it. On the seventh day he must shave his body again, and only on the eighth day is the process completed. Perhaps a symbolic rebirth is intended, the hairless individual being once again like a baby, the eighth day corresponding to the day of circumcision (Leviticus 12:3).

The image of the bird flying free is very powerful. It carries away the burden of the illness and the isolation, and signifies the restoration of life.

✳ **Blessed are you, our Living God, Sovereign of the Universe,**
who shows favour to the undeserving, even to me.
   Traditional Jewish prayer on recovering from severe illness

Thursday October 6   *Leviticus 16:1–19*

How and when do we repair the damage we have done to others?

The term 'scapegoat' has acquired a particular meaning, that of the innocent victim who bears the blame for someone else's wrongdoing. But it is not clear whether this fits the biblical intention behind the animal sent into the wilderness.

The biblical ritual with the scapegoat occurs on the tenth day of the month. Later Jewish tradition requires that people use these ten days to examine their deeds of the past year and take active responsibility for repairing damage, making amends and re-establishing broken relationships. Though it is not clear how far such a process might have been undertaken in the biblical period, the ceremony nevertheless begins with major confessions of sins committed. Here there is no dumping of guilt on an innocent party, the 'scapegoat', but rather an attempt, after admitting what has gone wrong, to create the possibilities of a fresh start for all concerned.

The bird that flies freely away carries with it the memory of the illness of the 'leper' (chapter 14). In the same way the goat completes symbolically a process of taking responsibility for individual and collective misdeeds of the recent past that have been acknowledged and seriously addressed.

✳ *O God, whose name I dare to utter, pardon the failures, the sins and the evil which have been committed against you by your own people, the family of Israel.*

Traditional prayer on the Day of Atonement

Friday October 7   *Leviticus 19:1–14*

How do we understand our relationship with God?

This chapter raises a question that is never completely resolved. The Israelites are invited to become 'holy' because God is 'holy'. Presumably the seemingly random list of laws that follows in chapter 19 explains how this is to be achieved, but the common thread amongst them is never explicitly stated.

The word 'holy' needs a little explaining. The basic sense of the Hebrew *kadosh* is 'set apart', 'different', 'other'. Like the God they serve, Israel is to be a separate people, bound to God, a general principle already stated when the covenant was agreed at Sinai: 'You shall be for me a kingdom of priests and a holy nation' (Exodus 19:6). That command already contains the essence of Israel's paradoxical destiny. Just as the priests act as mediators between the people and God, maintaining the purity of that relationship, so is it Israel's task to represent the nations. But as a 'holy nation' their separateness and otherness is also emphasised.

When the sorcerer Balaam was forced to bless Israel he pointed to this two-edged aspect of their destiny. The price of being close to God was that this indeed became a people 'who dwell alone' (Numbers 23:9).

✳ *You are holy and your name is holy and those who seek holiness praise you day by day. Blessed are you, the holy God.*   *Traditional Jewish blessing*

Saturday October 8   *Leviticus 19:15–37*

How is it possible to love others as ourselves?

This passage contains one of the most celebrated verses in the Hebrew Bible, about loving one's neighbour as oneself (Leviticus

19:18), but it is a verse that is often misunderstood. Firstly, who is the neighbour that is intended? The verse comes as the climax of four commands that define Israel's relationship to their 'fellow citizen', their 'people', and their 'brother', moving from 'not hating', through 'reproving' when something is wrong, to 'loving'. Clearly the 'neighbour' intended in the passage is a fellow Israelite.

But what attitude should be displayed to other people? That is spelled out in verses 33–34, which refer to the 'stranger' in your midst. The identical words to verse 18 tell us to 'love him as yourself'. We may see the world in terms of 'us' and 'them', but must behave in the same way towards 'them'.

How can you command love? Grammatically, the 'neighbour' is not the direct object of love in this sentence. The Hebrew suggests instead 'You shall act in a loving way towards your neighbour, as you would towards yourself.' That is to say, act in their best interest. The closing phrase in verse 34 could also mean: for he is just like you!

✳ *Grant us peace, goodness and blessing; life, grace and kindness; justice and mercy. Bless us all together with the light of your presence, for in the light of your presence you give us law and life, love and kindness, justice and mercy, blessing and peace.*　　　　　　　　　　　　*Jewish daily prayer*

FOR REFLECTION – alone or with a group

● How do we find our way into such a remote world as Leviticus?
● How puzzling would be the rituals of our own tradition when viewed in the distant future?
● Is it possible to translate concepts like ritual purity or impurity into today's life, and if so how?

FOR ACTION

Leviticus addresses many physical aspects of our lives – the impact of illness on our bodies, the sensitivity that should surround the killing of animals for food and so on. Voluntary work in a hospital or hospice may help us understand the spiritual significance of our physical existence.

READINGS IN MATTHEW

Notes based on the New Revised Standard Version by
Melvyn Matthews

Melvyn Matthews is the Canon Chancellor of Wells Cathedral in Somerset, UK. He has responsibility for the cathedral's programme of education and spirituality. He also oversees the ministry of welcome to the thousands of visitors who come to the cathedral each year. He has been a parish priest and a university chaplain, is married with grown-up children and grandchildren, and loves sailing.

---

7. Suffering and transfiguration

Discovering who you really are can be an enormous shock. Discovering who or what one of your closest friends really is can be a much greater shock! It's really this sort of thing that is going on in the texts we shall be exploring in the next week. They are texts about personal discovery, its surprise and shock and its implications. At a deeper level they are also texts about the way in which such a discovery about ourselves or about a friend almost always involves some sort of breaking or breaking out. New ways are certainly not old ways and the newly discovered self will almost certainly come into conflict with the self of the past and all that self represented. Moreover this newly discovered self will still be surrounded by the friends of the past who might not understand or 'see' the new self. Suffering will be involved if we are going to be true to our 'new' selves, but these newly discovered possibilities are liberating and provide a glimpse of the potential transfiguration of the self. We are always on the way from glory to glory and do not know what we shall become. What we have to do is trust the process, trust that God is the source and the goal of the journey.

Sunday October 9   *Matthew 16:13–20*
Who are you really?

Let us not waste time thinking about whether this passage gives justification or not to the establishment of the Roman Catholic papacy. Let us think about it instead in relation to ourselves and our friends. I can remember several points in my life when, in conversation with a friend, I saw them and myself in a new light. The interesting thing about this passage is that in it both Jesus and Peter find or are told their true identity. Jesus is told he is the Messiah, God's anointed one, while Peter is told that he is the rock of the coming church and holds the keys of the kingdom. Whatever else it means, such terminology indicates that both Jesus and Peter came, as a result of this conversation, to see themselves in deeply religious terms. Their identity was given them by God.

Much of the time we doubt our identity or think we have to make it or achieve it in some way. Here we have a story which shows us that our identities are already given to us – provided we can understand that both Peter and Jesus are representative figures, each representing us in some way. God gives us our selves, always. The fact of that gift is a profound surprise to most people, but is also profoundly good news.

✳ *God, give us grace to perceive that you have already given us our true identity and save us from searching for it.*

Monday October 10   *Matthew 16:21–28*

There is trouble ahead!

Immediately Jesus knows that his disciples are aware of his God-given identity, he begins to share with them something of what he sees to be in store for such a person. There's trouble ahead; indeed, not just trouble but suffering and death. It is clear that Jesus himself foresaw the trouble he would run into in Jerusalem and its terrible consequences. But if we understand Jesus as a representative figure, then he becomes the one who represents the fate of all human beings – and this passage is not only about him but about us too.

Once Jesus knew that his identity came from outside the complex of associations which made up his social fabric, then he also knew that his identity was potentially disruptive and difficult. Once you have discovered that you are free of what makes society tick then you are free to speak to society and free to try to recreate it according to a different set of values. This will be particularly disruptive if those values or ways of being come from a totally transcendent source, from God. God is utterly different and so living the identity he gives will mean an utterly different way of life. We have seen individuals take on this role and we have seen that some of them, like Dietrich Bonhoeffer and Martin Luther King, met the same fate as Jesus.

✴ *God, your saints have accepted the consequences of their true identity and have embraced the pain and disruption and crucifixion this causes. Give us grace to open ourselves to new possibilities each day.*

Tuesday October 11   Matthew 17:1–8
Changed from glory into glory
The author of Matthew's gospel sees Jesus as being a sort of new Moses and deliberately emphasises the parallels between Jesus and Moses where he can. The Sermon on the Mount (Matthew 5–7), for example, is the new law given by the new Moses on the mountain just as Moses gave the old law on Mount Sinai. There are a number of other parallels. Here, 'after six days' refers to the fact that the glory of the Lord descended on Moses on Mount Sinai for six days (Exodus 24:16). The parallels between Jesus and Moses only strengthen the view that Matthew sees Jesus as a representative person.

But the more profound question is: why does Matthew follow his accounts of Jesus and Peter discovering their true identity (16:21–28) with this account of the transfiguration of Jesus on the mountain? Indeed, he is following the tradition he received from Mark at this point, but there is more to it than that. At one point Jesus is talking about the need for the disciples to accept suffering, the next he is talking about transfiguration.

This is a peculiarly modern anxiety. For modern people, suffering is an entirely negative experience which is to be either avoided or cured. It is difficult for us to see that suffering can give us anything. But what is being hinted at here is that the call to difference, the call to live a life based upon the transcendence of God, will bring transcendence and transfiguration to the believer. The believer will suffer for their faith but also be transfigured, 'changed from glory to glory' as Charles Wesley's hymn has it. Suffering is a sign of the proximity of new possibilities.

✴ *Set us free, God, from unnecessary resistance to suffering. Enable us to embrace life in its total complexity as your gift.*

Wednesday October 12   Matthew 17:9–13, 22–23
The empty seat
At a Jewish Passover meal a seat is left empty for Elijah. In the last words of the Hebrew scriptures the prophet Malachi predicted

he would come before the great and terrible day of the Lord (Malachi 4:5–6). So space has to be left for him. His arrival will signify the end and the imminent arrival of the Messiah. At a number of points Jesus identifies John the Baptist with Elijah (see Matthew 11:13–14, for example) and plainly the disciples' question reflects the question raised by scribal critics of Matthew's church community. 'How can you claim Jesus is the Messiah when Elijah has not appeared?' The answer is that he has come, in the figure of John. This illustrates the way in which Matthew and his community saw that the end of all things had already come about in the figures of John and Jesus. What was to come had come. On the mountain Jesus is accompanied by Moses and Elijah, the ones who come from the beginning and the end of history, or at least of history as Jews understood it.

So to believe in Jesus and to have followed him is to be witnesses to an inbreaking of the beyond into time, of the beginning and the end into the now. What has been and what will be is round about us if only we could see. The one thing that this does for me is to require of me a heightened awareness of things. I feel I must not let anything pass as if it were insignificant. If the 'then' is present in the 'now', if God, the transcendent source and goal of all things, is present now in ordinary life in some mysterious way, then I must pay attention to what is because it is potentially divine. I must not miss anything. This gives value and significance to everything that happens. Nothing is ordinary.

✳ *God, heighten my awareness of all things so that I may see your presence hidden before me at all times.*

Thursday October 13   *Matthew 19:23–30*
You must change your life
The German poet Rilke wrote a poem entitled 'Archaic Torso of Apollo', which speaks of the impact upon the poet of a Greek statue of Apollo, one without head or limbs. You might have seen it in the Louvre in Paris. This statue seems to interrogate the poet, and 'sees' him. It says to him, 'You must change your life'. This poem always reminds me of the impact of Jesus' teaching about the kingdom on his disciples. This kingdom seems to come from a strange and different place and to 'see' them entirely. It asks them to be different and as a result their lives must change entirely.

This passage deals with the question of wealth. Other sections deal with the question of marriage and divorce. In the previous chapter it is the question of forgiveness. As far as the matter of wealth is concerned, in the course of the history of the church there have been a number of interpretations of this passage which have tried to lessen the strangeness of Jesus' simile, but none of them really work. Jesus was telling his disciples that there are definite obstacles to entry into the kingdom for those who are wealthy. The inbreaking of the kingdom of heaven makes enormous demands. The disciples are hardly ready for what will be required.

These 'hard sayings' of Jesus ask disciples to live their lives in the light of the inbreaking of the kingdom. Different-ness has appeared from God, demanding a total change of life. You cannot carry on now as if everything was the same. Once you have glimpsed something of God's life and its otherness, you must be different if you are to really live.

✳ *God, I like things to be familiar. Help me to be aware that your life breaks into the familiar and asks me to be different.*

Friday October 14   *Matthew 20:17–23*

The source of freedom

This passage emphasises again the strangeness of Jesus' words to the disciples and their inability to accept or understand them. He predicts his death, but immediately the mother of James and John asks that her two sons should have a place in the kingdom, in other words be given great power. Plainly neither she nor they have understood what he has been saying, and the text continues with Jesus' reproach and reminder that his kingdom is nothing to do with earthly forms of power.

Jesus seems to be saying in these passages: 'When you have been found by God and have recognised him fully in his transcendence and difference, once his wonder and mystery have opened themselves to you, then you will need nothing else, neither power nor wealth. God is sufficient.' In human terms this does not mean that the disciples will not have any wealth or any power, but that they will not need to search for them or acquire them or be anxious for them. God will be all in all.

Jesus tries to tell his disciples that there is enormous freedom in such a way of life – the freedom of the kingdom.

✳ *God, I am always praying that world leaders should exercise mercy and compassion and turn away from the corruption of power. May that also be true for me, every day.*

We are all tenants

Matthew's gospel comes out of a community which saw Jesus as the new Moses, the one who gave the new community a new law. At one level the parable of the vineyard is part of that understanding. It speaks of the new people of God to whom the vineyard has been given because the old tenants were not faithful. The old Moses has failed, Matthew declares, and so the vineyard is given to others.

At a much more profound level the story is about something else. It is about ownership. What Jesus is saying here is what he says in so many other places and what he says is lived out in the way he leads his whole life. If you think you own something completely then you have, in fact, lost it entirely. We are all tenants, says Jesus; we have been given life as gift. It is not ours; it comes from God. If we try to keep it and its produce for ourselves then we will lose it entirely. This sense of life as gift is the good news of the gospel. Once you recognise and accept life as gift then your life will be transfigured, even if you suffer. You will be set free to return life, what the parable calls 'the produce', to the real owner, God himself.

✳ ***God, I am always clinging on to things. Help me to let go and live in your freedom.***

FOR REFLECTION – alone or with a group
● Somebody said to me that seeing all of life as a gift is a very hard message. How is it hard for you?
● What are you clinging on to that prevents you living in God's freedom?

---

8. Judgement and truth

A church in Coventry, England, has recently completed the restoration of a wonderful and almost complete medieval 'doom' painting. This shows Christ sitting in judgement with some people being sent down into the jaws of hell and others being drawn up to heaven. This was a common theme of medieval theology. It was portrayed not just in wall paintings but also in stained glass windows like those preserved at Fairford in Gloucestershire and in many parts of Europe. Such pictures remain part of the mindset of some Christians, and they are certainly part of the popular view of what Christianity is all about in the minds of those who do not believe.

It cannot be denied that there is a great deal of talk in the scriptures about judgement. During this week we shall be looking at the judgement passages towards the end of Matthew's gospel. One of these is the parable of the sheep and the goats, a key passage lying behind the development of the medieval 'doom' paintings. But as we shall see, this emphasis on judgement is not what it may seem at first sight. It is not about reward and punishment, but about the realisation of possibilities and especially the realisation of the possibilities given us by God. If we do not realise these possibilities then we become less than what we really are. Being in that state is what the medievals meant when they talked about being in hellfire.

Sunday October 16 (World Food Day)   *Matthew 16:1–12*

No sign shall be given

Why is it, Jesus asks, that when Jonah preached to the people of Nineveh they repented, but when I come along and perform wonders and signs of God's power and presence, nothing happens? And all the time these people are calling for a sign! Open your eyes to what is going on. The passage bears similarities to the passage where John the Baptist sent some of his followers to Jesus to ask if he were the Messiah and Jesus says, 'Look around at what I have done: the lame walk, the blind receive their sight' (Matthew 11:2–6).

These passages are about lack of perception and hardness of heart. All you need, implies Jesus, has already been shown you, and yet you still ask for a sign. Think about Jonah and how when he preached the Ninevites repented – and no Jew could forget that the Ninevites were not Jews, which was why Jonah had been reluctant to go to them. If they can repent then so can you.

Lack of perception of the inbreaking life of God is a form of judgement because it is a refusal of possibilities – possibilities given us, ultimately, by God. In our own day the question is, 'Does the world have to stay as it is with so many suffering from hunger?' 'Do you have to accept the old teaching, the leaven of the scribes and Pharisees, that nothing much can change and everything must be left to current market forces?' Or can we repent and turn and do something which will really make a difference? That would be a sign that the kingdom was breaking in now.

241

Stop asking for God to do something; it's our hearts which need to change.

✻ *God, when I see the hunger in the world I think it has always been there and I can't do much about it. I need help and encouragement to change. Open my heart to new ways of living.*

Monday October 17   *Matthew 18:1–9*

Simplicity of spirit

Usually the reason why people cannot face new possibilities is because of the mental and psychological baggage they bring with them. The past hangs heavily so that new horizons cannot be perceived. Clarity of sight is needed, a sort of inner lightness of being. When that is present then baggage can be thrown overboard and new possibilities entertained.

The image of the child is an image of somebody who has this simplicity of spirit, this inner lightness of being, and that is why Jesus puts the child in the midst of his disciples as a sort of spiritual symbol of somebody who has no baggage.

Jesus' metaphors about cutting off your hand or tearing out your eye are shockingly violent – if only to show us what needs to happen if we are to be really free. The actual process of jettisoning your psychological baggage takes a lot longer, often a lifetime, and requires a great deal of prayer and self-offering. This process of personal purgation is done in secret by grace – provided we open ourselves to the workings of that grace in prayer, study and worship.

Going to church and saying your prayers is actually a process whereby dead hands are cut off and unseeing eyes are torn out and people begin really to see and really to walk. Devotion to God is the gateway to a grace which will lead us to new possibilities.

✻ *Lord, I do not know which bits of me are baggage and which are not. Help me to know and help me to lose the baggage I do not need.*

Tuesday October 18   *Matthew 19:16–22*

If you wish to be perfect...

It is no good saying, in response to this well-known passage, that you are not a rich young man like the one portrayed here and you have no more money to give away. All of us have many possessions; they do not need to be financial ones. Nor is there any point in saying that Jesus did not mean us to give everything up. His demand is pretty clear: 'Go, sell all your possessions...' (verse 21). You cannot 'spiritualise' this passage and infer that it is really only about our spiritual life and so long as that is focused on God alone then how rich we are does not matter. Even if it is true that some of those who have sold all their possessions have still not entered into life. They remain miserable and grudging.

When Matthew has Jesus use the phrase, 'if you wish to be perfect', he is saying the same as he says in the phrase, 'if you would enter into life'. This is not a two-stage way to salvation where once you have obeyed the law then you face the more radical demand of selling all you have. No, 'entering into life', 'being saved', 'being perfect', 'entering the kingdom of God', are all phrases for the same thing. The Greek word Matthew uses is *teleios* which, while being translated 'perfect', also has connotations of 'wholeness' and maturity about it. In other words, Jesus is saying, 'If you really want to be who you are created to be then you must give things up.' This is contrary to the usual view of modern people that they have to acquire things in order to be anything at all.

At the root of Jesus' dialogue with the young man is a discussion about whether or not he understands that life is a gift. When you know that it is a gift from God then you will be quite happy to give things up. You will already know something of what you are made for, what your *teleios* is. Our 'end' is to know that we are not our own and do not possess ourselves. When we know that, we are free to give things away because we know that all things are gift anyway and indeed that we are a gift ourselves, a gift to ourselves from God and a gift to others from God. When we know that, we do not need anything. Selling all we have is a sign that we do know that truth in ourselves.

✷ *Lord, I don't think I am a gift to anybody, and I'm often very doubtful about what others give to me. Fill my heart with a greater trust, not just in others, but also in myself and in the gift that I can be.*

Wednesday October 19　　　　　　　　　　*Matthew 20:1–16*

The grumbling latecomers

To understand this story you have to remember the parable of the prodigal son. There, the treatment of the younger son by the father is as apparently unjust as the treatment of the latecomers by the lord of the vineyard. What had any of them done to deserve mercy and generosity of this kind? Moreover the behaviour of those who grumbled at the pay given to those reprobates who had only worked for an hour is very similar to the behaviour of the elder brother who grumbled that his father was being generous to the errant son. So it is a parable about the absolute generosity of God, which stands in direct contrast to the behaviour of those who have a developed sense of fairness and are quick to resent generosity to others.

In Matthew's gospel, the story is probably told to show those who had been members of the church for some time that the grace of salvation was equally open to those who were 'latecomers', that is those who had not been Jews before they were Christians.

In modern times 'fairness' is a very overworked concept which Jesus' story challenges. He points to a different principle, a different understanding of life. All life comes from an unquenchable source, a source which does not look at the behaviour patterns of those who receive it, does not hold itself back for any cause, but simply goes on and on and on giving itself. The German mystic Meister Eckhart talked about life as constantly boiling over, as a constant ferment, something like a champagne bottle that never stops fizzing. When we do not receive this life then we shut ourselves off from God and bring judgement upon ourselves.

✳ *Lord, on some days I feel like a dried-up old pot. Seeing myself as fizzing with your life is something I only glimpse from time to time. Give me open eyes to see your life fizzing along beside me, and within me.*

Thursday October 20   Matthew 23:1–12

Possession of the law

Passages such as these are a serious temptation to the Christian. They are a temptation because they tend to activate a secret belief that Judaism was and is a corrupt religion concerned only with the externals of faith – things like long fringes, phylacteries and being called 'rabbi' – whereas Christianity is concerned with grace and freedom from legalism. It cannot be said often enough that there is nothing anti-Jewish in Jesus' teaching. He was an observant Jew as were his disciples and did not advocate disobedience to the law.

What is at stake here is not Judaism, but the human capacity to find identity in systems rather than in God alone. Christianity is no more free of these traits than any other form of faith. What Jesus found impossible was the use of faith (in his case, the Jewish faith) to bolster national or individual identity. Had Jesus been a Christian, he surely would have criticised Christianity when it encouraged the same tendencies. We do not practise our religion in order to prove who we are in the community. We practise our faith in response to the love of God, and the practice of the Jewish law is just as much a response to the love of God as is the pursuit of a morally pure Christian life.

In his letter to the Romans (chapters 1–3) Paul makes it quite clear that the mere possession of the law is no guarantee of salvation, which is close to what Jesus is saying here. In the last three verses of this passage (verses 10–12), Jesus seems to be moving a step beyond simply calling for the law to be obeyed, as if mere obedience was the answer. He seems to be calling for a form of radical simplicity of life, where no one is called master, the greatest people act as servants and those who are humble are those most valued by God. The interesting irony is that if you are truly humble you will not know that you are; rather you will have abandoned all attempts at self-worth.

✳ *O God, give me more joy, more simplicity and more mercy.*

Friday October 21   *Matthew 24:32–50*
Being ready
In many religious groups which expect the end of all things at any moment, there is a call to abandon earthly pursuits and to await the Messiah's coming by forming special communities of some kind. These communities will often move out of areas of civilisation, which are regarded as decadent, into some remote place. Occasionally they relish coming under attack from others and even, in extreme cases, commit suicide together in a sort of mass act of defiance of this world.

In Matthew's gospel, as indeed in other parts of the New Testament, the imminent return of Christ does not lead to such outlandish practices, but rather to a deepened discipleship in the place where you are. It leads to a more active practice of deeds of mercy, forgiveness and peace. Being 'ready', which is what Jesus calls people to be, means living out kingdom values in the place where you have been put with the people you have been given. Readiness means taking a long deep look at what you are doing and stripping out that which is not of God and of the kingdom in order to be more ready for it when it comes. I am sure that simply by doing that, by living in radical simplicity of means, with joy and mercy as our chief characteristics, then the kingdom actually comes amongst us.

Earlier in this gospel, Jesus taught that those who were blessed were those who were meek, merciful, pure in heart and peacemakers (Matthew 5:1–14). These were the people, he said, who would see God first. There is no encouragement in either Matthew's gospel or the rest of the New Testament for forming new communities which Christ will favour on his return. There is every encouragement to live the values of the kingdom in the community and with the people where you are.

✳ *Lord, keep me from always looking to the future. Help me to slow down, look up and around and welcome your love now.*

Saturday October 22   *Matthew 25:31–46*
Judgement day
When people respond to human need and practise acts of charity, mercy and peace, they are, in fact, responding to Christ. Presumably both groups represented by the sheep and the goats are thinking that when Christ appears he will do so in a reasonably recognisable form and they will know who he is. Some, however, continue to get on with the work of practising hospitality. Others do nothing, simply waiting for the right person to turn up. The fact that Christ is present in the poor and the needy is a surprise to them both. So the image of Christ returning at the end of time has to be softened by the realisation that he is invisibly present with us always.

Then there is the question of the destination of the sheep and the goats after the judgement. The king makes it very clear that those who are righteous are invited into their inheritance (verse 34). This is the place that has been prepared for them from the beginning of things. It is the place they were made for. Those who are condemned do not go to a place they were made for but to the place prepared 'for the devil and his angels' (verse 41). This is significant, for it clearly gives the lie to those who believe that human beings are somehow inherently evil and will be condemned by God unless they can prove themselves otherwise. Hell fire is not the natural place for anybody, heaven is.

In this parable, Jesus is using a traditional religious conceit, namely the notion of Judgement Day (if indeed this parable comes from his mouth). He uses this notion to convey to his disciples not only the need for readiness, but also the need to see that Christ is already present in the world, calling us to a life of mercy and peace, and to see that condemnation is not what we were made for. The judgement imagery is no more than a vehicle for more profound teaching.

✳ *Lord, help me to believe that you have made me for yourself and not for death, and help me to see that you are already here in the small things of life.*

FOR REFLECTION – alone or with a group

● Which of the characters you have read about this week do you identify with most? The rich young ruler? The labourers who came first? Why do you identify with them and what does this mean for your life?

● What does the parable of the sheep and goats mean for you?

FOR ACTION

Go to your nearest great cathedral or large abbey church. Stand in the nave for at least 15 or 20 minutes in silence and then ask yourself what difference this glorious building makes to your life. Then put that difference into practice.

PRISONS AND PRISONERS
1. The faithful imprisoned: Joseph

Notes based on the New Revised Standard Version by
Pauline Webb

Pauline Webb is a Methodist local preacher and a freelance writer and broadcaster. Before her retirement she worked as Organiser of Religious Broadcasting in the BBC World Service and previously as Caribbean Secretary for the Overseas Division of the Methodist Church. She is a member of a multiracial church in North London.

'Stone walls do not a prison make', wrote the poet and prisoner Richard Lovelace to his beloved Althea. For those who have love in their hearts, he affirmed, there is a freedom of the soul that no iron bars can hold captive. Throughout the centuries, people of faith have found that even imprisonment cannot rob them of their confidence in God's presence with them. For Joseph the dreamer, whose story we follow this week, even the prison cell itself became a place of vision and of hope.

Sunday October 23   *Psalm 105:16–22*
Sent ahead
In recalling the story of Joseph's imprisonment, the psalmist echoes the confident words of Joseph himself who, as he told his brothers, could see God's hand at work even in their treachery and his subsequent imprisonment (see Genesis 45:5, 7 and 50:20). A West Indian friend of mine spoke in a similar way about his own experience of being unjustly accused of wrongdoing and subsequently imprisoned. Eventually, after a long campaign on his behalf, he was on appeal exonerated from all guilt and released. He then publicly thanked God for all that he had learned through the experience in jail, which has led him since to undertake a ministry of prison visiting which he now sees as God's vocation for him.

As we look back on our own lives, are we able to see God's hand at work even in those events which seemed to us to be frustrating and preventing us from fulfilling what we believed to be God's purpose for us? Remember that the word 'prevent' originally meant 'go before'. God often goes ahead of us into unlikely places.

✳ *Go ahead of us, Lord, all the way, so that even events that happen apparently by evil intent may be transformed into your good purpose for our lives. For your name's sake.*

Monday October 24 (United Nations Day) *Genesis 37:3–4, 12–28*

Family pitfalls

Many common pitfalls of family life are evident in the lead-up to this story of the brothers' criminal behaviour and Joseph's subsequent imprisonment: tale-telling (verse 2), favouritism (verse 3), jealousy (verse 4), deceit (verse 20), callousness (verse 25), greed (verse 26), hypocrisy (verse 27). Though two different accounts are interwoven here – one suggesting that Reuben tried to save his brother, and the other putting the spotlight on Judah – all the brothers are guilty of disloyalty. Conscious as they are of their blood relationship, that bond is not strong enough to restrain them from evading their responsibility and excusing their cruelty.

Many who are in prison today can tell of trouble caused by family feuds and lack of support from those closest to them. What is true of families is also true of nations. On this United Nations day we are reminded that we are all made of one blood whatever our nationality. God calls us, as members of one world family, to work for the day when all nations shall cease from internecine warfare and learn to show sensitivity, respect and responsibility for one another.

✳ *God our Father, teach us in our own family life to show to one another a love that reflects your love for each of us, a love that is without fear or favour. Lead us in our national life to show mutual respect for our brothers and sisters of all races, and through the work of the United Nations, guide all peoples into the ways of peace and of international justice, for your name's sake.*

Tuesday October 25 *Genesis 39:1–25*

Leadership in prison

Joseph's innate gifts of leadership are quickly recognised in the royal court. The story of the temptation that assails him there is told with all the graphic detail of a plot in a soap opera. Jonathan Magonet, in his book *A Rabbi's Bible* (SCM), points out that in the rabbinic version of this story, there's a special, rare punctuation mark in verse 8, suggesting some hesitation on Joseph's part before he refuses to submit to the temptation offered by Potiphar's wife. He is entrapped by her lies and false evidence, and is unjustly imprisoned. But still his good character wins him a special place in the prison community, which has its own kind of hierarchy.

On a recent visit to preach in a prison chapel, I was amazed to discover that the steward who had made all the preparations for worship and looked after me before and after the service was actually a 'lifer', in prison for murder. He had long repented of his crime and hoped to make reparation through a lifetime of service.

✴ *We pray for all prisoners who are victims of unjust accusation or of irresistible temptation. Grant that even in prison they may be encouraged to achieve the full potential of their gifts. For your name's sake.*

Wednesday October 26   *Genesis 40:1–23*

Sympathy with others

Prisoners often develop a sensitivity to each other's needs. In a letter from Robben Island, the prison in South Africa where Nelson Mandela and many of his colleagues were held for over twenty years, one of his fellow prisoners described what he called 'the closed regimented world of adult, uniformed males, cut off from the real world. Fortunately for us', he went on to say, 'we live among some of the most wonderful fellow-prisoners, whose humanity, care, selflessness and patience have greatly eased our incarceration.'

Joseph showed that kind of humanity when he quickly noticed the anxiety on the faces of two fellow-prisoners. When they shared their dreams with him, he assured them that even dreams can bring messages from God. He did not hesitate to give both the bad news and the good news. The person of faith can bear to face reality and share the truth with others, however unpalatable it might be.

✴ *Lord, we pray for all who minister to those in prison, that they may be sensitive to the inner fears and hopes of those cut off from the world outside. May they enable prisoners to face up both to the reality of their present predicament and to the hope which God offers them for the days ahead.*

Thursday October 27   *Genesis 41:1–45*

Long-term planning

'The reward of faithfulness', says a Jewish proverb, 'is faithfulness.' Joseph's faithfulness throughout his stay in prison is rewarded by long years of responsibility. Note how his kindness to a fellow prisoner becomes the recommendation which eventually brings him to the king's notice and launches him on his full vocation as one who is able to interpret God's will and to translate dreams into practical planning. Through his far-sighted vision he enables the whole nation of Egypt to make proper provision during years of plenty for the years of poverty that follow.

The Egyptian name given to Joseph literally means 'God speaks; he lives'. The names he gives to his sons are a testimony to the way in which God has turned what seemed like his misfortune into blessing, which was to affect the lives of many, not only in Egypt but throughout the whole world.

✳ *Lord, forgive the short-sightedness of those of us who live in plenty. Give us the vision of a world where none shall go hungry; where the resources you supply are shared out fairly among your whole world family. Raise up among us far-sighted politicians and economists who will make wise provision not only for our future but for the welfare of all peoples. For your name's sake.*

Friday October 28   *Genesis 45:3–28*

The family reconciled

In a broadcast on the BBC World Service, the late Rabbi Hugo Gryn was once so moved as he read an extract from this chapter in Genesis that he broke down in tears. The question, 'Is my father still alive?' brought back such poignant memories to him. As a child he had himself lost all trace of relatives who had disappeared in the concentration camps. He went on to reflect on the tragedy of families and communities divided through old enmities or quarrels, and on all the joy that can come through reunion and reconciliation. He told a memorable story of a special day in 1960 when the saintly Pope John XXIII met 130 Jewish leaders in Rome. As if to bridge the centuries of misunderstandings and suspicion, inquisitions and hatred, the Pope – whose baptismal name was Angelo Giuseppi (Joseph) Roncaldi – said in his first words of greeting, 'I am Joseph, your brother'.

✳ *We pray for all divided families and communities, that they may not allow real or imagined hurts to fester to the point where bitterness and hatred gain the upper hand, but may draw near to one another again and find healing in reconciliation. We pray particularly for families reunited after times of imprisonment, that they may rediscover the love that once held them together, for Christ's sake.*

251

A role-model of magnanimity

'The evil that men do lives after them', according to Shakespeare. But so too does the good. The story of Joseph's magnanimity and of his brothers' jealousy has lived on in Jewish history for over 3000 years. So, when the early apostles of Jesus became the victims of jealousy themselves (Acts 5:17), the experience acted like a cue to Stephen, who drew inspiration and courage from the story of Joseph as he himself faced martyrdom.

Every generation has produced its heroes and heroines who have become role-models of the ways in which enemies should be treated. Among many twentieth century heroes have been men like Bishop Wilson, who, in jail in Singapore, learned to look on his torturers as though they were children and years later met and actually gave communion to one of them. The heroine Corrie Ten Boom found the grace that enabled her after church one day to shake hands even with an SS guard who had once held her captive. She wrote, 'When Christ tells us to love our enemies, he gives, along with the command, the love itself.'

✳ *Lord, it hurts too much to be bitter. Sweeten any bitterness I hold in my own heart against those who have wronged me, by the sweetness of your grace and the empowering of your forgiveness. In the name of Christ.*

FOR REFLECTION – alone or with a group

● What other 'role-models of magnanimity' can you think of whose stories have been told in contemporary history?

● What would you list as the main causes of family quarrels, and how can they be avoided?

● What lessons can Joseph's running of the economy in Egypt teach modern national leaders about international economics?

FOR ACTION

Make sure that your local church has up-to-date information about campaigns for fair trade and world development issues.

PRISONS AND PRISONERS
2. The faithful imprisoned: others

Notes based on the Revised English Bible by
Peter Phillips

Peter Phillips is a retired Anglican prison chaplain living in England. He ministered in large local prisons and in smaller specialist units. Much of his work was with prisoners serving life sentences and those imprisoned for sex offences. Before entering full-time ministry he was deputy head of an inner-city secondary school.

Prison is a difficult and testing experience for nearly all prisoners. It can be hard to maintain faith in the face of media condemnation at the time of arrest and trial. For those condemned to a prison sentence the ridicule from other prisoners and the scepticism of staff can tempt even the most faithful to compromise. Yet most maintain their faith, even develop and deepen it and sometimes, by God's grace, bring others to faith. For, as we see in this week's readings, God sees through the prison wall, bringing reassurance and release to his faithful followers.

Sunday October 30   *Daniel 6:1–24*
False accusation

Daniel is a person of honour and integrity, qualities which King Darius rewards by promoting him to the country's third most powerful position. This by itself would be enough to enrage other promotion hopefuls. He is also a foreigner, which makes him an even easier target for resentment.

Some people are unwilling to acknowledge others' qualities and will try to undermine them. If someone else can do their dirty work so much the better. These motives underlie racial discrimination and the teasing and condescension which Christians often experience.

Such are Daniel's qualities that his enemies have to resort to a plot to trap him. Unwittingly, Darius allows Daniel to be condemned by his faith, for Daniel's integrity in government is grounded in his faithfulness to God.

We know that Darius suffered agonies of conscience during the night but Daniel seems unscathed, protected by the angel of God. The judgement of humans had been corrupt and selfish.

God saw beyond this and, although he allowed him to go to prison, he ensured that Daniel was kept safe.

God has his own ways of protecting the innocent – and of punishing the wrong-doers!

✳ *Merciful God, protect and vindicate those innocent people who are in prison. Give us grace to understand others when they try to harm or discredit us.*

Monday October 31   *Isaiah 53:7–12*

Light out of darkness

So many journeys of faith begin with bright promise. When the going gets really difficult it is tempting to wonder whether all those expectations were a delusion.

Today's highly poetic passage describes suffering of great intensity. It is often like this for God's faithful people if they find themselves in prison; the words 'a grave with the wicked, a burial-place among felons' (verse 9) vividly suggest the living death prison can sometimes seem. I have known many prisoners whose words have echoed the opening of Psalm 22, which has much in common with this passage.

Perhaps we can also see here the inner anguish of God's servants who feel that they have done nothing to deserve their torment. Their suffering can seem as much of a prison as stone walls and steel cages, made worse by the mockery and scorn of the self-righteous.

Many people see this passage as a prophecy of Jesus' redemptive actions. Whatever your view, it still points to God's ultimate vindication of his faithful servants, however much the world may condemn them. God sees through the walls of the prison, both physical and mental.

✳ *Help us on our journey of faith so that we do not lose sight of your light shining before us. When all seems hopeless may we remember your promises to us and find them a source of strength.*

Tuesday November 1   *Jeremiah 37*

Imprisoned for conscience

It's not easy to tell people things they don't want to hear. King Zedekiah and his court don't want to believe Jeremiah's prophecy about the devastation of Jerusalem. They feel that God will change his mind if Jeremiah asks him. Don't we sometimes try to avoid what we think God is saying to us?

Jeremiah's arrest on suspicion of defecting may well reflect the king's displeasure at his refusal to compromise. So Jeremiah becomes a prisoner of conscience, beaten and kept in dreadful conditions without trial or earthly hope. Only subsequent events persuade the king to relent a little.

It can be difficult enough in everyday life to hold to what we know to be right as part of our Christian duty. So it was an act of huge courage by Jeremiah to maintain God's message to the king and his courtiers. So it is for all those who in faith and conscience resist rulers and armies. They may sometimes feel that they are utterly alone. They are not, of course, because we should always pray for their safety and thank God for their courageous witness.

✳ *May we be bold in speaking your truth but may we also have the courage to face all that you want us to act upon ourselves. Your will, not ours, be done.*

Wednesday November 2   *Matthew 4:12–17; 11:2–6*

Don't keep me in the dark

One of the worst aspects of imprisonment is the feeling of powerlessness. Prisoners often don't know what's happening on the outside and they begin to imagine the worst that could happen in any situation. They come to feel that important things are being kept from them.

I know one prisoner whose partner didn't arrive for a visit; he was convinced that she had left him or had an accident, possibly fatal. He took much persuading that there was probably a very ordinary reason for her non-arrival – as indeed there was.

I have often used this story about John the Baptist in prison and prisoners always recognise its truth. They appreciate – perhaps more than other people – John's doubts about Jesus. Is he really the Promised One? Why is he mixing with the poor, the sick and sinners? He doesn't behave as the expected Messiah should.

Jesus' message to John may not seem a satisfactory answer. John, though, would be more likely to appreciate the facts rather than grand words. He would surely have realised that Jesus' ministry was, at this stage, about healing and redemption rather than judgement. Unlike earthly judicial systems, our opportunity for redemption comes before, not after, our judgement.

✴ *Help us not to be brought down by imagining the worst. Difficult as it may sometimes be, may we have the confidence to trust your greater wisdom.*

Thursday November 3   *Acts 5:12–26*

Release is always a miracle

Peter and John have already been cautioned about preaching but they continue their ministry even more fervently. So the Temple authorities, fearful of civil unrest, can only imprison them.

Some writers suggest that the apostles were released by a human messenger from God, rather than an angel. Whichever it was, out of an apparently hopeless situation comes deliverance. Most prisoners would leap at the opportunity of release, wherever it came from. Whether the messenger was human or angelic, the release itself is the miracle.

Prison is often a state of mind as much as a physical reality. So release may be a deliverance, even temporarily, from the manacles of the mind. For faithful people in prison the chapel is frequently a place of such relief. So many prisoners have said to me, 'Coming into the chapel is like stepping out of prison.'

God will always find a way of reaching his faithful ones through their prayers, their reading of scripture or the actions of others. Their confidence is still incomprehensible to others, just as the chief priests were speechless at the apostles' escape.

Peter and John, however, knew exactly what they had to say and returned to their preaching, not discouraged but refreshed and emboldened.

✴ *Reveal yourself to us in prayer, scripture or sacrament. Help us to use what you give so that we become your ears and eyes, your hands and feet for other people.*

Friday November 4   *Acts 12:1–19*

Support those in prison

Today's passage may refer to the same event as yesterday's. Here, however, we are more aware of Peter's sense of wonder at God's actions. Although John is not mentioned this time there are other important characters in the story. We are told that the church people prayed fervently for Peter while he was in prison.

Christians in prison derive strength from knowing that their churches have not deserted them but are supporting them in prayer. We can only guess how much this means to them if they have been pilloried in the media and deserted by their families. When our own prayers falter we need the prayers of others.

There are cultures where released offenders are ritually welcomed back into society as reformed individuals. In western style cultures, however, this is not usual. And yet much evidence shows that prisoners are less likely to reoffend if they have somewhere welcoming to go on release.

When we think of those about to be released from prison we should remember the servant, Rhoda, who was overjoyed to see Peter, and the other Christians who 'opened the door'.

✳ *May we see a reflection of you in those around us, however unattractive they seem to be. Since you love them, may we try to love them too in ways which help and protect us all.*

Saturday November 5   *Acts 21:27–36*

Faith overcomes violence

Religious fanatics can make as threatening a crowd as any other mob, as we still see in different parts of the world. The mob around Paul have become murderous because they suspect that Paul has caused Trophimus, a Gentile, to violate the sanctity of the temple. Religious conflicts are some of the most bitter, as our critics like to remind us, and Paul needs the Romans' protection to get away with his life. Even so, it seems that he may have been injured so badly that he had to be carried up the steps.

Most of us would be glad to escape from such a dangerous situation. Not Paul. Immediately after this passage he delivers a ringing testimony and call to baptism as if the experience has strengthened him. The violence he suffers is comparable to the violent language the media use about offenders, especially if the offender happens to be a Christian.

We still live in an age of religious persecution, whether by governments, the media or individuals. When we seem to be surrounded by a threatening or sneering mob the God who loves and upholds us will not desert us. Even if we are in prison.

✳ *Protect us from those who would hurt us. And when they succeed, may we still witness to your supreme glory.*

FOR REFLECTION – alone or with a group

● How should Christians respond to those who have committed very serious crimes?

● What can we say to the victims of crime?

● Have I built a prison in my own mind which prevents me from doing some things or considering new insights?

FOR ACTION

Find out what your local churches do to help prisoners. If you can use the internet find out what organisations exist to help prisoners in your country. Find out what is involved in a correspondence or visiting link with a prisoner. Consider taking this on yourself or as a group.

PRISONS AND PRISONERS
3. The prisoner's cry

Notes based on the Revised English Bible by
Judith Phillips

Judith Phillips is a prison chaplain at a women's prison in Gloucestershire, which serves a huge geographical area. She is concerned at the way in which the media encourage us to see offenders as monsters, not as human beings as flawed as ourselves.

Being in prison suggests notions of powerlessness, of confinement, a lack of freedom, and punishment. Imprisonment as part of a penal system appears alien to the Old Testament world of the Psalms, where it seems to be the tool of arbitrary kings; at least our sentenced prisoners know when their freedom will come, and encourage each other with the words, 'They can't keep us here for ever'. But they also recognise that we all make prisons for ourselves with our habits, our behaviours, our assumptions. When will we be set free? Is there only one prisoner's cry?

Sunday November 6   *Psalm 57*
Being steadfast

Sometimes prison and confinement can seem like a kind of refuge: sometimes drug users who know that their lives need to change will refuse bail, or ask to be remanded in custody, because prison is a safer place than the world outside. The psalmist speaks of finding refuge in the shadow of God's wings until the storms are past, but the troubles are of human making – persecutors and those who try to trap and bring their victims down. Unlike some of the more vengeful psalms, here the worst that happens to the enemies is that they will be scorned and fall into their own traps.

It seems to me to be a wonderfully confident psalm. As God's love is steadfast, so my heart aims to imitate his steadfastness. Even as the storms rage – the wind outside is howling round the house as I write – we can be free to love and glorify God. The bad times blow themselves out, but God's love is unchanging, and his purpose for us will be fulfilled. Among the nations, among those who perhaps don't know God, I shall raise a psalm, offering praise. The prisoner's cry here is joyful. And a prisoner chose to put the first four verses on the chapel notice board as part of a display on faith and hope.

✳ *Grant me, Lord, the faith to praise your steadfastness and your unfailing love at all times.*

Monday November 7   *Psalm 142*

Nobody loves me

There's quite a strong sense of abandonment in this psalm. Many prisoners have become accustomed to rejection, to failed relationships, to having no refuge, to no one having any faith in them. And often it's repeated failure, repeated rejection, a terrible sense of their own inadequacies. They feel, as the psalmist does, that there's no one there, no one at their right hand in moments of crisis, no one to rescue them. 'Save me from my persecutors.'

On Sunday, as we read out the prayers the women write, we find requests, demands even, for God to make the judge set them free, in much the same tone as the psalm. But Jesus wasn't set free, and in the end nor was Paul, and neither are many thousands of good and innocent people today. So how is that prayer to be answered?

What does God's failure to answer our prayers as we feel we deserve do to our relationship with God, to our faith? Do we make bargains with God? Or do we try to make sense of his purposes instead? If some prisoners can recognise his hand even in their being in prison, separated from their families and their familiar lives as they are, what can that teach me in my relatively easy and comfortable world?

✳ *Lord, give us the discernment to recognise the answers you give us, and the grace and courage to live with those answers.*

Tuesday November 8   *Isaiah 24:17–23*

Apocalypse and glory

The whole of this chapter offers a terrifying vision of the last day, of the earth itself suffering the consequences of its own sinfulness, of inescapable judgement for all, even for kings, gathered together, shoulder to shoulder, herded like common mortals in a pit. I'm reminded of Jeremiah in his cistern, or Joseph in his dry well, with no freedom of movement, no spreading of the wings of salvation, forgotten beneath people's feet. The hosts of heaven, even the sun and moon will be ashamed, all we have looked up to and valued, all that we thought was fixed and stable and enduring in this world.

In our own moments of crisis we can feel something of this. Certainly prisoners in for the first time – away from home, children, partners, jobs, communities, all that gave them identity, all that they valued, all that gave their lives meaning and order – will recognise Isaiah's apocalypse. And yet at the end of all this comes glory. Everything else is in collapse, turmoil, all order vanished in the human, the natural and supernatural worlds. It's almost too terrifying a vision to be hopeful, yet somehow it is. At the end of all judgement is God in glory.

✳ *When everything in our ordered world collapses and chaos reigns, hold us together with the promise of your glory.*

Wednesday November 9   *Psalm 28*
Hear me, save us

Elijah's people were set apart from the Baal worshippers because their God responded, yet in the first part of this psalm there's a reluctance to grasp that silence may itself be an answer, or that action may replace words. But in the second part comes praise and thanksgiving, and then a recognition that the Rock isn't just cleft for me, but for all of us. 'Save your people and bless those who belong to you, shepherd them and carry them for ever' (verse 9).

The prophets were concerned not just for their own personal salvation, but for the people, however stiff-necked and undeserving they were. The women's prayers in the prison where I work are often for others in prison, for them to know God's love and to discover his promises. They are aware of being a community, not just within the walls of their own prison but within a national or even worldwide community of prisoners, sharing the same needs, the same pains, the same hopes. Many of our foreign national prisoners, initially bewildered by prison life in an alien culture, are well versed in the Bible, glad to share their knowledge and understanding with others, seeking to encourage and build a people who belong to God. They love praising him, even in their times of tribulation.

✳ *Help us to rejoice in our refuge with the one shepherd and in the one flock we share with all God's people.*

Thursday November 10   *Psalm 130*

Set me free from my sins

'Out of the depths...' (verse 1). For the many who come to us detoxing from the drugs that very often they took to anaesthetise some pain, the depths are where they find themselves, as feelings return and they begin to recognise what they have done to their own lives and to the lives of others – family, children, victims. 'Can I be forgiven?' they ask.

One woman said she had been encouraged by these words from a Sunday preacher: 'Nothing we can do will make God love us less, and nothing we can do will make him love us more'. With God is forgiveness, a setting free from sins, an acknowledgement that accounts are not kept – something we might bear in mind, not just for our own sins but for those of others. I came across this as a prison chaplain's prayer: 'Dear Lord, be merciful to those who must pay for their sins, and, Lord, please keep mine a secret'.

This is a wonderfully reassuring psalm, secure in the knowledge that the morning will come, and that God's loving forgiveness is unfailing.

✳ *We are your children, Lord, and we ask for your forgiveness. Please listen to our cry and keep us surrounded with your loving arms.*   *A prisoner's prayer*

Friday November 11   *Psalm 88*

The cry from the grave

Most lament psalms follow a pattern, with the initial lament followed by hope and praise. This one doesn't. It's utterly bleak and dark, a world cut off from God, populated only by the forgotten dead. The psalmist feels punished, abandoned, shut in, overwhelmed, alone, with only the dark as a companion. There can be no glib answers, no obvious comfort for those whose lives have been and continue to be blighted by abuse, neglect or bereavement, and to whom nothing good ever seems to have happened. And in the depths of their despair prisoners often feel that they're being punished, as children whose parents are divorcing feel that it's all their fault.

So what can we say to those whose lives have been so marred, to encourage them to keep faith, to proclaim God's glory? The psalm is full of images of depth, confinement by floods, darkness, the grave. And yet even at the lowest point the psalmist keeps a kind of faith. He doesn't stop believing that God is there. God's just not answering. But even in the darkness he goes on praying.

✳ *Lord, don't let us patronise the despairing with glib assurances, but give us the strength to share their darkness until the light comes.*

Saturday November 12   *Psalm 70**

The joy of seeking

Some come into prison bearing the burden, as they see it, of having found their faith lacking. Others come in seeking, or begin to seek. A working prostitute chose to tell a chapel full of women one Sunday that she knew that God existed, that her frequent stays in prison had given her faith. She's currently looking in her Bible for passages to share with other women, to bring them to the place she is finding for herself. Hers is not a Damascus situation, but a slow, hard-won growth. Others also seek and hold on, recognising that having the right words doesn't matter, that there are people in prison chapels they can speak to of faith and prayer, and know that they will be taken seriously.

There's a longing for God's saving aid, but a recognition too of the truth in their favourite poem 'Footprints', in which a dreamer sees two sets of footprints at most stages of life, but only one at crises, and accuses Jesus of abandoning him or her at those times. The reply, of course, is that the one set of prints is where Jesus was carrying the dreamer through the worst parts.

Prisoners cry out for many things, and there are no easy answers, but there are those in their midst who seek to encourage them.

✳ *Let all who seek you be jubilant and rejoice in you, and may those who long for your saving aid forever cry, 'All glory to God!'*   *Psalm 70:4*

FOR REFLECTION – alone or with a group

● Consider that prisoners are very often also victims. We are encouraged to see a neat separation between the criminal and the innocent victim, but in fact half the women in prison have been abused, and a third sexually abused. And the poor very often rob the poor.

● How often do we feel the need to sort people's problems for them, to be able to lighten their darkness, rather than simply to share it? Quick fixes, in matters spiritual as well as practical, aren't always possible. Makeovers aren't always appropriate.

FOR ACTION

Prisons operate in the name of the society that builds, maintains and fills them, so keeping ourselves informed about what is done in our name is something we should all do. In Britain the Prison Reform Trust is a valuable source of information, and informed debate on penal matters is always worth following. Prisoners are not only our fellow citizens, but our brothers and sisters in God's creation. Make some time this week to find out more about your local prison.

PRISONS AND PRISONERS
4. Setting the captives free

Notes based on the New International Version by
Bao Jia Yuan

Bao Jia Yuan graduated from Nanjing Union Theological Seminary in 1966. Unable to work as a minister during the Cultural Revolution, he was sent to the countryside for many years. It was not until 1986 that Bao could begin full-time church work, and in 1987 he was finally ordained. Bao is currently Associate General Secretary of the China Christian Council and Director of the Nanjing Office of the China Christian Council. For many years he has been much involved in ecumenical relations with other churches, Bible publishing, church development projects and church ministries among minority nationalities.

'Challenge yourself and go beyond the limit' has become a fashionable maxim in China today. In our own day as well as in previous times, the strength of human power has been embodied in many forms, in economic, political and cultural structures. Yet, potentially life-enhancing as such structures are, we can also find ourselves imprisoned in them. Biblically speaking, human powers are all too vulnerable, and we even find it hard to direct our hearts to the good we want to do. Only when the invigorating Spirit of God dwells in us will the transforming power of God set captives free – and we are speaking here of more than a physical freedom. The Spirit of God brings a spiritual freedom that liberates us from the greed for wealth, from the profound damage of sexual abuse, and from the effects of indulgence in gambling, drugs and alcohol, and so on. This freedom brings the peace and joy of Christ's new life, and also empowers Christians to give witness in society through service of others, including reaching out to the poor, helping the needy, and doing social welfare. As John 8:36 tells us, 'So if the Son sets you free, you will be free indeed'.

Sunday November 13   *Psalm 107:10–16*
He does not crush the weak

Five years ago a young man wrote me a letter from prison in Fujian Province, asking me to send him a Bible. He had been sentenced to seven years' imprisonment because of his participation in mob fighting with knives. In jail, he struggled to maintain the mob's code of chivalry which kept him loyal to the hooligan gang. He was almost crushed by misery and slavery to sin. Finally, one day he was introduced to and came to know Jesus by some Christians working in the prison. He cried to the Lord, and his heart was caught by the Word of God. He knew that only the power of the gospel could change his inner heart and bring about a new life. 'A broken and a contrite heart, O God, you will not despise' (Psalm 51:17).

In a second letter he wrote a few months after he had received the Bible, he told me that Jesus had taken away his vengeful thoughts and changed his bad behaviour. Amazingly, this man had even organised a small Bible study group among the inmates. These Christian prisoners are trying to live out the Christian faith in their re-education programmes and working to be model prisoners demonstrating their newfound faith in Christ to their fellow prisoners.

✳ *O God, your love has no limit, your grace has no measure; your power knows no boundaries.*
Let the cup of joy overflow.

Monday November 14   *Psalm 146*

Come to me and I will give you rest

The last five psalms in the psalter overflow with praise; they may have been written after the return of the exiles to Jerusalem from Babylon. The psalmist emphasises that God's help is lasting and sufficient. He gives thanks to the Lord for God's deliverance of the prisoners and the salvation of the poor and oppressed.

China is today experiencing a crisis of values as we shift from a self-reliant and more closed society to a more open and pluralistic one. This has been described as an erosion of the moral fabric of society and a multifaceted sense of loss: loss of faith, loss of traditional confidence, even loss of 'soul'. Challenge and opportunity, joy and pain exist side by side. Quite a number of people have lost what they once had and have been marginalised, pushed to the edges of society. Who is on their side? What can the church do for them? They are crying for one who can lift the burdens from their bent backs, laden down by heavy loads – the pressure of work, the uncertainty of the future, the anxiety of family burdens and the tensions in human relationships.

We, like them, need to listen to the invitation of Jesus: 'Come to me, I will give you rest'. Let us trust in him and, as we do so, seek to extend that invitation to others who have been pushed to the edges of our society.

✳ *Lord, help me to seek you whenever I am weary in body; encourage me to turn to you when I am sinking in spirit. Renew my commitment to your salvation once again.*

Tuesday November 15   *Zechariah 9:11–17*

Give hope to God's people

The Book of Zechariah tells of the Messiah, the promised 'great deliverer of Israel'. These vivid details which look forward to Christ's life were written 500 years before their fulfilment. Compare today's passage with the story in Mark 11:1–11, and stand in awe of our God who keeps his promises and gives hope to God's people.

Chinese Christians experienced trial by fire during the cultural revolution (1966–1976). During that period no visible church was allowed to exist (all were closed), and no Bibles were allowed to be read publicly (most of them were burned). Amazingly, the Holy Spirit never ceased her work, and God kept his promise to his people. Chinese Christians started meeting secretly in homes or caves under the ministry of Christian lay leaders. A Chinese Christian recalling those days said, 'The time eventually passed as the tides of the sea come and go. With sorrow and silence, we've walked through the darkest valleys; with tears and laughter, we've gone through ups and downs.'

God has made a covenant with his people. He knows and controls the future and so hope is always present, however appalling the present. We may not be able to see ahead, but we can be secure if we trust in God. He will deliver us from 'the waterless pit'.

✳ *O Lord Jesus, for us you were wounded, you bled to release us. Your love is unbounded: we adore your name.*

Wednesday November 16   *Isaiah 52:1–10*

Come to seek and to save the lost

The enslaved life in Egypt, the hardship endured in the wilderness, the destruction of Jerusalem, the exile in Babylon –

all left deep scars in the heart of Israel, causing them to shout out for deliverance. Now, in this passage, the nightmare of screaming out for salvation is finally over. The time has come for the Lord to deliver his people and bring them home. The time has also come for his people to tell the news that the God of Israel reigns and to share the happy news of peace and salvation with others.

An itinerant preacher living in a poor mountainous village in southwest China knelt down to give thanks to the Lord for an unexpected gift he had received from an unknown brother at Christmas – the amount of 200 RMB (equivalent to 25 US dollars). His first thought as to how he might spend the money was to buy a newly published study Bible that might improve his preaching. His second idea was to use the money to buy a long-handled battery torch for his nightly visits to his fellow Christians, since his home-made oil lantern was easily blown out by the wind or the rain. But in the end he decided to use the money to buy some new clothes for his two school kids. What strength and riches in faith this man demonstrated, denying himself the precious items that would have made his own life easier and instead spending what he had received on his children. No wonder the Bible says, 'How beautiful on the mountains are the feet of those who bring the good news, who proclaim peace, who bring good tidings, who proclaim salvation to the people.'

* *Walking into a new day,*
My heart is full of joy.
My first words from within:
    I thank you, O Lord.

Bathing in your love
Anointed in your Spirit,
    I hear you calling my name.   *A Chinese praise song*

Thursday November 17   *Isaiah 61:1–7*
You shall have a double portion of everlasting joy
The mission to bring good news to the suffering and afflicted is the heart of the gospel. For centuries the Holy Spirit has made it possible for people to find salvation through forgiveness of their sins (Luke 1:77), reconciliation with God, and restoration of human dignity.

Several years ago, a middle-aged pastor worked together with his congregation to set up the largest church in Wuyi of Zhejiang Province, with 4000 seats. This magnificent building has become the symbol of this little commercial town. This pastor converted to Christ during the Cultural Revolution when he was a little boy. An unplanned event changed his life when he saw two Christian women being attacked and publicly tortured by a crowd of Red Guards. He was deeply moved by their faith and dared to speak out against their unfair treatment. Unfortunately his action provoked the Red Guards and he was put in jail for two years. This was the beginning of his faith journey. If you were to ask him about his experience in the prison, he would say, 'I suffered for Jesus' sake, so no wonder my heart is always overflowing with joy'.

✱ *The captive to release,*
to God the lost to bring,
        to teach the way of life and peace,
it is a Christ-like thing.   *From* Daily Watchwords

Friday November 18   *Luke 4:14–21*

No one can rob you of that joy

In the passage for today, Jesus reads the scripture from Isaiah 61:1–2 in the synagogue. His reading and the way in which he interpreted it shocked every listener present at the small synagogue in Nazareth. He makes a great announcement to Israel and to the whole world: 'God is ready to give blessings to all who come to him'. What a blessing of God has been fulfilled in Jesus! He made it possible for those who were blind to see; the lame are walking without a limp; the lepers are completely healed; the deaf can hear again; the dead come back to life; and the poor are hearing the good news.

In reality, things do not seem to happen like this. Our dear sister Xiao Ying's life is approaching the end after a long struggle with leukaemia. Her brother cried to God, pleading and asking why God had not answered his prayers to heal his sister. Her friends hurried to see her after hearing about her condition, but all experienced a lack of words to bring consolation. When they pushed open the door of Xiao Ying's home, surprisingly they found Xiao Ying sitting there calmly and busily decorating a little Christmas tree. She greeted her friends with bright eyes and a sweet smile, saying, 'I am so happy to have you here today. This is probably my last Christmas and I want to spend it with you.' After a pause, she continued: 'I have no regrets at all, though I know my time is limited, because I have Jesus in my heart. He has helped me to understand that it is not the length of life, but the meaning of life, which counts. It is Jesus who heals my broken heart and gives me an inner satisfaction and serenity that nobody can take away.' On hearing this, tears ran down her friends' faces, for who could utter anything better than what she had said?

✴ *O strengthen me, that while I stand*
    firm on the rock, and strong in thee,
I may stretch out a loving hand
    to wrestlers with the troubled sea.

O use me, Lord, use even me,
    just as thou wilt, and when, and where,
until thy blessed face I see:
    Thy rest, thy joy, thy glory share.   Frances Ridley Havergal

---

Saturday November 19   *Romans 7:21–25*

Overwhelming victory is ours through Christ who loved us

Our vulnerability to sin means that we may be more loyal to the world and self than to God. That is the reason why we need the deliverance of Jesus Christ who has conquered sin once and for all and who promises to fight by our side. To achieve victory over sin involves more than accountability, memorising scripture or resolute character. To achieve victory over sin involves God's movement in our lives and the opening of the heart to him through our love for him. It also involves our commitment to love of one another.

A barefoot doctor in the northwest Qinghai Plateau opened a clinic next to his bedroom after his return from a one-year medical training programme sponsored by the Amity Foundation (a social service organisation initiated by Chinese Christians). He named it the Amity clinic. His bedroom is often transformed into a ward, while he himself sleeps on the floor. It is also his common practice to offer free medication to the poor and the elderly. He says: 'I follow Amity, just as Amity follows Jesus' teaching: 'Freely you have received, freely give" (Matthew 10:8). Love conquers evil'.

The real victory over sin is achieved in and through love. As we allow God to fill us completely with God's love, so we shall find that love overflowing to others and the victory over sin being given.

✳ *God, fill us with love for you and for others*
so that we may overcome the sins that would bind us and
imprison us.

FOR REFLECTION – alone or with a group

● Share with someone a difficult time in your life when you experienced the joy of being set free from captivity.

● How can we become the instruments or channels of God to help those people who have been imprisoned, either literally or metaphorically?

FOR ACTION

Visit a person or persons who have been ignored or marginalised by the community; stay with them a while and listen to their story. See how you can assist them or support them.

PRISONS AND PRISONERS
5. Prisoner for the Lord

Notes based on the New Revised Standard Version by
Donald Eadie

Donald Eadie is a Methodist minister and was formerly Chairman of the Birmingham District of the Methodist Church. For many years he has lived with a degenerative disc disease. The transition from a busy, stimulating, public life into a life lived increasingly but not solely in one room has not been easy. In time there has been a sense of inner homecoming. He has been helped and encouraged in many ways, through many people including the writings of those who address cell and communion, solitude and solidarity: Thomas Merton, Henri Nouwen and Catherine de Hueck Docherty, for example. In December 2003 Epworth Press printed the third edition of Donald's book Grain in Winter: Reflections for Saturday People.

The way of Jesus is a shared way rooted in relationship with people who are often quite different from ourselves. Some speak of 'the essential we-ness of the way' and also of a companionship within which the bread of life is both broken and shared. There are those, however, who have to face an unwelcome solitude through a confinement that comes to them in a variety of ways – perhaps through physical frailty and limitation, through ME or some other illness, through bereavement or divorce, perhaps through a short or longer term served in prison. This week we will begin to explore the paradox of contraction and expansion, confinement and freedom, within such 'prison' experiences.

Sunday November 20   *2 Corinthians 10:4b-5*
Inner and outer

Each of us has our own hero whose life and writings continue to influence us. I have many and they include Mahatma Gandhi, Toyohiko Kagawa who lived for 15 years in a 6 feet by 6 hut in the Shinkawa slums in Japan, Martin Luther King imprisoned for non-violent direct action in the civil rights movement, Dag Hammarskjöld the General Secretary of the United Nations whose inner journal was published as Markings, and Nelson Mandela held for 27 years in the notorious prison on Robben Island. Each of these individuals shaped social and political events, each inhabited and paid attention to the solitary place within themselves, each lived a rigorous interiority.

Within that hub of international diplomacy that is the United Nations Headquarters in New York there is a small, silent, still, dark room with one shaft of light striking a raised rock in the centre. It is an inner place.

✳ *Free us to pay attention to the world both around us and within us.*

Monday November 21   *Ephesians 3:1–7*

Contraction and expansion

The letter to the Ephesians is thought to have been written from within the confinement of a prison cell and perhaps by Paul. Sometimes, but not always, plumbing the depths of solitude can bring us into a deeper awareness of our human interconnectedness. We can become more mindful of the world around us. Windows are opened. The confined person can be set free to reach outwards. Dietrich Bonhoeffer was arrested in 1943 and imprisoned in Buchenwald. His understanding of himself and the world was balanced by humour, compassion and faith. His letters and papers were smuggled out of the prison and are still read today. Perhaps you also know of people who cherish the art of letter writing even if their writing is almost illegible! Some prefer the different process of communication through the sending of e-mails. And others pick up the phone and also run up a bill!

✳ *Thank you for trees with their roots reaching into dark and hidden places and for their branches stretching toward the sun. Help us also in our growing.*

Tuesday November 22   *Ephesians 4:1–6*

Present and good

There is a wondrous little group in Birmingham of which I am a part, including nuns and priests, four of whom are in wheelchairs, two of whom live with depression and two of us lie semi-flat. Two spouses also belong. Most have lived with physical limitation and pain for many years and encourage those of us in the foothills to be real and not heroic, honest and not evasive.

We are learning what it could mean to receive what God offers us to live creatively within our reality. We are learning what it is to be laid bare, stripped of roles, responsibilities, masks and dignity.

We are learning the presence and providence of God within the sense of the absence of God. We are learning that the pain bearers continue to take their place within the redemptive process. We are learning to trust the one 'who is above all and through all and in all' (verse 6).

✳ *Deepen our trust in the presence and goodness of your Spirit in all things, in all circumstances and in all people.*

Wednesday November 23   *Philemon*

The mystery that we choose to call intercession

Some of us need reminding that it is the nature of God to pray. God's Spirit prays within us, among us and through us, making us aware of what is happening in the world, sensitive both to the delights but also to feel the pains and be mindful of people. The Spirit draws us into a sense of inter-connectedness.

A friend spoke of the discovery of solidarity within the plumbing of the depths of solitude. He found a way in the night hours of praying within and through his own pain to become one of the pain bearers in the world. Pain opened his ears to the night cries of humanity. He held them in the presence of God, both the ones he knew and the ones he did not know. Then he committed them all to God whose nature it is to give.

Archbishop Desmond Tutu speaks of the immense significance of housebound elderly people all over the world undergirding with intercessory prayer the struggle for freedom in South Africa.

✳ *Release in us the power of love that your Spirit continually brings into being among people.*

Thursday November 24   *2 Timothy 1:8–18*

Trusting

The big word is trust. To have faith is to trust. The Bible speaks of both the unknowable God and also the God who is my rock and my refuge. We cannot describe or define God. Some say that it is possible to trust God when totally baffled.

A teenager returning to Britain after visiting families in the Caribbean with her father was asked, 'What impressed you most?' After a pause she replied: 'Many things. I met people who trust God and not only discuss God.'

If we stand in the truth that we know, trust mercy, attempt to use good to overcome evil, seek the good of those who threaten and hurt us, then we also will get hurt. This is the context of the marking of God. This is the crucible within human experience that we are invited both to enter and trust.

✳ *Set us free within our fears to trust your life-giving presence in all things.*

Friday November 25　　　　　　　　　　　　*Matthew 27:15–26*

The handing over

Jesus is handed over and becomes a prisoner. And here lies the paradox. In the handing over to the control of soldiers, courts and the constriction of the prison cell, there is the discovery of a new freedom. Liberation within the victim. There is in the man Jesus the freedom to enter and remain in the place of confusion, conflict and chaos, to be stripped, to walk alone among the crowds towards the cross, to receive help from Simon of Cyrene, to enter the silence of God, to become the pain bearer, to seek care for his grieving mother, to forgive those who don't understand what they are doing.

The Desert Fathers said, 'Go to your cell and your cell will teach you everything'. Some in Christian tradition speak of the journey into the inner cave not as a way of escape but rather as a journey into the heart of the world. For some there is silence there, an underground river flowing and this is the place where Christ lives. For others the inner cave is like a tumble dryer! The inner cave is the heart room, the core of our being where we can be who we most truly are and this in the presence of the one who is 'other'. Here we face the fears. Here we discover freedom. Here we learn the true homecoming.

✳ *You are welcome under my roof.*

Saturday November 26　　　　　　　　　　　　*Matthew 25:31–36**

And you visited...

Those of us who receive visitors grow to value people who know how to visit. Often a short visit, between 10 and 20 minutes, is enough. Some men also like to receive flowers, as well as women! The loan of a video, CD or novel can bring joy and it helps when we return what has been loaned to the owner! Some friends offer to cook a meal in their own kitchen and bring it to our home and perhaps enjoy it with us. On some occasions it is enough to come and not to chatter but rather to sit and to share in the quiet. The question, 'How are you?' seems simple but it is often far from easy to answer. And not everyone can cope when we tell it as it is. Some visitors help us to cherish the flavour of good things – views from loved hill-tops, news of friends, humorous stories. A long prayer seldom helps, sometimes a prayer contained in a sentence does. 'Lord, grant that fruit that alone yields to frustration.' And a little eucharist that leaves out confession and absolution and our causes for thanksgiving has left out some of the essentials.

After a burglary in which our house was trashed, our young Muslim neighbours not only offered a bed for the night but also brought round a wonderful meal the following evening.

✳ *You come to us in many ways and through different people. Thank you.*

FOR REFLECTION – alone or with a group

● 'We are learning the presence and providence of God within the sense of the absence of God.' Can you understand what this person is saying?

● 'God's Spirit prays within us, among us and through us, making us aware of what is happening in the world, sensitive both to the delights but also to feel the pains and be mindful of people. The Spirit draws us into a sense of inter-connectedness.' Is this understanding of the mystery we call intercession helpful for you?

● 'Go to your cell and your cell will teach you everything.' Have you lived through significant times of solitude and what did you begin to learn there?

● Have you been visited while being ill or confined for a significant time? What have you learned from these visits?

FOR ACTION

Are there people who come to mind who may value a letter or phone call or visit?

COMINGS AND GOINGS
1. Israelites on the move

Notes based on the New Revised Standard Version by
Alison Beever

Alison Beever is a priest in the Church of England with particular interests in spirituality, disability, encouraging theological reflection as a tool for mission and ministry, and a growing interest in the role of marginalised groups in the life of the institutional church. Being female, single and a wheelchair user, she experiences at first hand some of the issues of marginalisation.

Journeys are often marked by their beginnings and ends. Although true of some comings and goings in this week's readings, a deeper thread runs throughout: that of people journeying into a developing faith relationship with God. Confronted by human choices to turn from God, on the one hand, or to choose obedience almost beyond our comprehension on the other, we are challenged to re-evaluate our relationship with God, the world and its peoples. As Israel becomes a nation and moves into a special relationship with God, the experience of this people echoes into our time and lives, requiring us to question our faith relationship and life journey.

Sunday November 27 (Advent Sunday)　　　　　*Genesis 4:8–16*
Cain: hell or hope?

Although the wilderness is sometimes a place of blessing and prayerful withdrawal, it is for Cain the place of punishment – far from God and from fruitful land. For us, beginning our Advent journey, Cain's story is a staging post on a different journey as we recall a people's history and movement away from God into a wilderness of heart and spirit. Despite the actions and intervention of God, this journey continues across millennia in a headlong rush towards destruction. We even lose our sense of humanity, with some psychologists suggesting that 65% of us will inflict pain on another and even kill, if ordered to by an 'authority' figure. Eager to please, few question such orders. Most of us are hardened to images of suffering, torture and death. So we wonder: is there a way through our wilderness to God and to the fullness of life promised to a world struggling in birth pangs? Or is this promised world to be still-born?

And yet there is Cain, punished but protected, and a question: Why? To endure his full punishment? Or to return, in the end, to God?

✴ *Guide our journey through this Advent, Lord, that we may look to your coming with renewed hope.*

Monday November 28   *Genesis 6:11–22*

A world of our making

Floods are becoming as familiar a sight and warning as their counterpart, drought, in these days of climate change. Despite warnings of impending disaster many of us – electors, consumers, politicians, victims – still refuse to own responsibility for the world we have and are creating: a world far from the stewarded balance envisaged in the beginnings of Genesis.

The familiar story of Noah presents a corrupt world: people who have journeyed so far from the ways and face of God that humanity merits destruction. Yet within this record of unsustainable life there is one faithful man who, in his hearing of and obedience to the words of God, will save the whole of humanity.

Where do we stand in this story? Are we nearer, in our corruption and refusal of responsibility, to those who scoffed and jeered at Noah than to his obedience? Is it too late for us to own both our responsibility for and power to change the state of our world – physical and spiritual? Might our obedience and listening to the word of God in our time become a turning point for us and for many?

✴ *Guide our journey in obedience. Open our ears to hear your word, our hearts to receive it, our minds and bodies to enact it.*

Tuesday November 29   *Genesis 12:1–9*

Dare to say yes

Listen to these words that curse some Western churches: 'I'm too old'; 'I've done my bit, it's someone else's turn'; 'I've my partner/children/grandchildren/savings/insurance/pension to consider'. Words that destroy effective mission and ministry, diminishing the giftedness of individuals, giving the impression that Christianity has a retirement option. How different the world's major faiths might have been, if they had existence at all, had Abram's response been to inform Yahweh he was too old for such a journey, that he had Sarai to consider, that he must take care of his flocks, his slaves, his extended family and couldn't possibly uproot them from this locality. Abram's obedience and willingness to journey in faith, whatever else was in his mind (and this is left to conjecture and imagination), is rivalled only by that of Mary in her 'yes' to bearing the Christ.

In saying 'yes', Abram receives the promise and blessing of God and begins to move towards a covenant which will move the relationship of God and people to new depths. Could you say 'yes'?

✳ *Lord, free us from overly selfish concerns; help us to organise priorities that we may travel light and journey in obedience to your call.*

Wednesday November 30   *Genesis 18:1–10a*

Exuberant or impoverished: a response to God

In this narrative, folk-tale merges with traditions of desert hospitality as Abraham moves towards the fulfilment of God's promises. We are drawn into the story as we watch Abraham's exaggerated response to his visitors: the old man runs to greet them and offers no mere 'drop of water and piece of bread' but a banquet of kingly proportions. We see the interplay between the identity of Yahweh and the three visitors; sometimes they are one and the same, sometimes distinct; and wonder at the guest who asks for Sarah, not to 'lie with her' as hospitality decreed he could, but to promise a child by Abraham.

A popular interpretation of this visitation comes in Rublev's so-called 'Old Testament Trinity'. In the icon, which depicts the three visitors sitting around the table with heads inclined towards each other in a lovely image of harmony, everything has symbolic meaning; every measurement indicates something of the interplay of divine mystery and relationship. A deep involvement in story and icon is invited as, looking into the icon, one becomes aware that a fourth presence is required to complete the circle at the table – the presence of the onlooker. Drawn into the image, we are compelled to consider our relationship and response to the three.

Return to Abraham's tent. What might your response be to the travellers, to God appearing in the unexpected? Exuberant, exaggerated, involved? Or afraid, reluctant, impoverished?

✳ *Lord, make me a willing participant in your will, not a timid-hearted saint-in-waiting.*

Thursday December 1 (World Aids Day)   *Genesis 22:1–19*

Choose life?

Each day we make choices that affect others' lives. Some choices sacrifice others on altars of greed and power. World Aids

Day is a stark reminder of where some choices have led, and stands as a double challenge to our future choices and behaviours. What are we prepared to give for change for ourselves, and for the millions infected with HIV? What are we willing to sacrifice for ideals or for gain?

This passage focuses on Abraham's faith and obedience, his willingness to give all in following the word of his God. We are left imagining the horror of mind and heart as they journeyed for three days, the pain of obedience, the flickering hope that God would provide, then the joy of reprieve and provision. Such obedience is an example for us, but we can also look beyond.

Many today travel for days without hope of life, looking towards death for themselves and their children unless there is provision of medicine or food. Our choices affect this provision, make the difference between life and death for others. This is today's challenge to our obedience and priorities. What word of God do you hear for your faith journey today?

✳ *Lord, as you make me aware of the needs of others, keep me also aware that my choices make a difference.*

Friday December 2   *Exodus 12:29–41*

Make haste

Jesus knocks on your door and says, 'Now is the time, follow me'. What do you do? I fear that my heart would rejoice, but my mind would sneak in with fear, and my mouth go into auto-mode, saying, 'Just a minute; can I just finish this?' or 'Hang on, Lord, I'm not ready.' I would not have fared well on Passover night!

As the Israelites leave Egypt, haste and opportunity go hand in hand. No time to stop, finish the baking, clean the room – just time to go. Yet there had been preparation, gathering silver and jewels from the Egyptians –a 'wise as serpents' time. The people are given a moment to move on, begin again, act on their faith in God, and in Moses. This is the opportunity for freedom – and they take it.

Our opportunities and invitations to liberation and freedom are not often as spectacular or dramatic. Will you recognise them when they come? Are you looking for opportunity? Are you ready to say, 'Yes, Lord, I'm coming' – or will you be forever bogged down in the details of life that form their own slavery?

✳ *Help us, Lord, to hear your invitation to life and seize our opportunities.*

Opportunity blocks

I was stuck at the entrance to the cathedral church in Exeter. My 'scooter' would not pass through the inner doors designed to keep draughts (and wheelchair users?) out. Fuming, rather noisily, I began talking to two other wheelchair users experiencing the same difficulty. Our conversation moved from complaint, through world events, to God, hope and the need for prayer. One of many such opportunities arising from an apparent obstacle. How often I wish that the 'high places' in life would become low, as well as the 'rough places smooth' (Isaiah 40:4) so that life might be more compatible with wheelchair travel. Yet would life without obstacles really be 'better'? Yes, of course, in a way, but it might be life with fewer opportunities and less occasion for blessing.

The journeying Israelites met many obstacles and opportunities on their journey to the Promised Land. Now, at the climax of their story of deliverance, the final obstacle is removed, ending the journey with a blessing. As they begin another stage in their God-relationship and life as a people, more obstacles and opportunities await them in their struggle towards identity and faith.

Obstacles can be opportunities waiting for interpretation and action; they hold blessings that cannot happen if life is one smooth journey.

✳ ***Where obstacles seem insurmountable, help me see opportunity and blessing.***

FOR REFLECTION – alone or with a group

● Make two 'maps': one of your life journey, one of your faith journey, drawing on each map key experiences, insights, relationships and growth points. Put the two together and reflect on which times were significant for growth. Do any patterns emerge? Discuss with others if appropriate.

FOR ACTION

Take one issue which is important in your locality – something political or social. Consider what needs to happen to make a difference. Gradually work from the largest scale of change to the 'ripple effect' change – the change that our daily choices can make. Plan to take action and create ripples for change.

COMINGS AND GOINGS
2. To and fro between heaven and earth

Notes based on the New Revised Standard Version by
Juanita D Paniamogan

Juanita (Neneng) D Paniamogan is an ordained minister of the United Church of Christ in the Philippines (UCCP) based in Surigao District Conference, Mindanao. She is at present a pastor of a village church and strives to enrich the life and work of the church and the community where she is located through active participation in issues affecting women, children and the environment. She does occasional consultancy among NGOs and church groups on development, training, women's concerns and self and organisational enhancement through MBTI (Myers-Briggs Type Indicator).

People journey for various reasons. Usually, those who are rich make trips for leisure and adventure, or for business and official reasons. The 'have-nots' often journey to far lands to earn a living, leaving behind their families and familiar environment. In the Philippines, over 5 million Filipinos work overseas braving loneliness, discrimination, abuse and even the possibility of death. Whoever we are and wherever we go, each person makes a journey in a lifetime from birth to death, from childhood to adulthood, from earth to heaven. Every one is a traveller in life: we have a starting point and an end. Our journey can be rough and tough or it can be joyful and successful. However we travel and whatever we go through on the way, may the love of God guide us, sustain us and lead us to God's presence.

Sunday December 4   *Isaiah 40:1–11**
Preparing the way of the Lord
The text is addressed to the Israelites who were exiled in Babylon. They are words of comfort to those who have been deprived of the most basic elements of their former life: temple, land, community and monarch. Those who today find themselves in foreign lands experiencing difficulties, discrimination and abuse may receive comfort from these lines. But to be able to receive the good news of this text we need to 'prepare the way of

the Lord', make the road smooth, even and straight. It's a huge job for an individual but it can be an inspiring mission for all who believe in a just God who loves all peoples.

Although we cannot prepare the way of the Lord alone, we nevertheless need to start with ourselves: with our own anxieties and fears, our selfishness and greed, our indifference to the issues around us which perpetuate injustice and the abuse of the weak and vulnerable. We need to journey into ourselves and do away with those values and motives which are not from God and do not reflect God's intention for abundant life for all. So at this Advent time we prepare for God's reign within ourselves and within the whole creation.

✳ *Comfort us, O God, in our anxieties and hopelessness. Challenge us to prepare for your coming by journeying back to ourselves. We want you to come into our lives: take away our selfishness, greed and indifference. Help us to prepare ourselves and the world for your coming.*

Monday December 5   *1 Kings 10:1–10, 13*

A fulfilled journey

People journey for various reasons. The queen of Sheba made her long journey to seek out the famous Solomon and to 'test him with hard questions' (verse 1). She did not fail in her intention. She heard and saw the profound wisdom and awesome prosperity of Solomon. Have we experienced such a happy journey? Have our journeys far and near fulfilled our hopes and aspirations?

The queen of Sheba not only met Solomon and his court, she brought ample gifts of material riches for her hosts. Today we remember especially those in foreign lands who are working and striving to earn so that they can support their families. They, too, bring with them gifts: of energy and experience and talents. May we who are visited by friends and foreigners in our homes and countries take the necessary steps to ensure that their journeys are fulfilled.

✳ *Thank you, God, for gifting us with so many material and spiritual riches as we journey through life. Enable us to be receptacles of your love and righteousness so that sojourners will find solace and joy.*

An assured journey

Elijah had just experienced victory. The showdown between the prophets of Baal and of Yahweh ended in victory for Elijah. But the followers of Baal are not finished with Elijah. Jezebel, wife of King Ahab, wants him dead. And Elijah gets afraid and goes into hiding. From one place to another he runs for his life. But in all the places where he hides, God is there to provide his needs, guiding his way.

I remember in 1972 when martial law was proclaimed in the Philippines, many activists – including some close friends – ran into hiding to escape the Marcos death squad. Some were caught and executed but others survived with the help of friends who risked their own lives to shelter them. Have we been running away because we have defended what is right, upheld what is noble and godly and fought against the Baals of our time? May we be assured that, like Elijah, we too will experience God's provision and guidance as God leads us to a safer place. Elijah was restored to his tasks and calling and was able to return to the court to anoint Hazael to be king over Syria. May we also know the strengthening of our calling through times of testing and fear.

✴ ***Companion God, help us to trust in your love and care, especially when our journeys are full of difficulties, threats and hazards.***

The journey to heaven

Elijah had been a courageous prophet, proclaiming the word of the Lord and challenging the people to be faithful to God alone and never to entertain other gods. And then, Elijah was taken up to heaven by a whirlwind! An amazing story indeed. But what makes such a journey special is having a friend who tags along! Elijah had anointed Elisha to be his successor and he travelled with him till the end of the journey. Elisha refused to let Elijah go alone.

How many of us have been like Elisha, faithfully travelling with a friend – a loved one or a colleague, in plenty or in want, in sickness or in health, in good times and bad? Whether we are the main traveller or the companion, the process of journeying together is refreshing, reassuring and confirming of our gifts and capabilities. The process also gives the companion strength and teaches valuable lessons which could not be learnt any other way.

✳ *Thank you, God, for friends and loved ones who stay by our side throughout our journey towards heaven. Make us faithful companions to each other in all seasons and circumstances.*

Thursday December 8   *Nehemiah 2:1–8, 11*

The journey back

Nehemiah has to go back to Jerusalem to rebuild the city and the temple. It had been devastated by war and by the looting and abuse of the foreign invaders. With fear and trembling he faced the king of Persia who had taken many Jews as his subjects. He asked permission to journey back to Judah, the city of his parents' sepulchres. He had a vision for his homeland and a mission which he needed to fulfil.

How many of us feel the need to go back to where we come from? For some, going back is easy and joyous, but for others it is a difficult and even dangerous process which might cost one's life. There are Filipinos who have been living abroad for some time; when they come back, they feel uncomfortable and have become aliens in their own land. They cannot cope with the heat, the traffic, the noise, the impoverished situation, and they return to their adopted country. A few, however, like Nehemiah want to journey back to help rebuild their communities. One such was Benigno Aquino, who came back from exile but was shot on the tarmac because he was a threat to the status quo. Third world countries very much need their compatriots to return home, but it needs willpower and deep commitment to do that.

✳ *Loving God, challenge those of us far away from our countries to journey back and rebuild our homelands. For those of us for whom this is impossible, enable us to offer our prayers, our thoughts and whatever support we can extend as a sign of our solidarity in making our country a place of truth and beauty again.*

Friday December 9   *Jonah 1:1–17*

Journey's stopover

Are you trying to escape from what God wants you to be? In the Philippines, we have a children's song which goes like this (the original is sung in Cebuano dialect):

You can never hide, you can never lie; wherever you are, whatever you do.
You can never hide, you can never lie, 'cause God looks all over for you.

Jonah had no love for the people of Nineveh because he thought that God cares only for his own people. He intentionally sought to escape God's command to preach to the people of Nineveh. But his journey by a different route failed.

Many of us have our own escape routes by which we may seek to evade the call of God on our lives. We have prejudices, hatred and anger for those who are different from us, whether through colour, age, educational background, economic standing, political leaning or religious affiliation. We don't want to believe or have to act on God's love for all peoples of the world; we want to retain our bigotry, our narcissistic tendencies, our racist attitudes. We become uncomfortable, withdrawn or aggressive with any others who challenge our own narrow prejudices.

Must we wait until we get a stopover in the whale's belly before we wake up and relate to, connect with and love those who are different from us?

✷ *Merciful God, you are God of all peoples, even those who do not know you or acknowledge you. Help us to reach out to those who are different from us. Keep us journeying with you towards those you want us to touch and love.*

Saturday December 10 (Human Rights Day)　　　Isaiah 35:8–10
The holy way

These verses are part of God's promise for the exiled Jewish people. They are living in a foreign land where they have been marginalised, abused and discriminated against. But God assures them that their journey to freedom, peace and abundant life is at hand. Soon, 'everlasting joy shall be upon their heads; they shall obtain joy and gladness, and sorrow and sighing shall flee away' (verse 10). This is the message for those who are victims of human rights abuse and those who work for basic human rights.

Societies around the world have often failed to uphold the basic rights of children, women, workers, farmers and indigenous peoples. Only the rights of those with power, wealth and influence have been protected. The right to abundant life is a gift of God for all. This is the imperative of the Christian faith and the mission of God's people. Though our journey may be rough and tough, we are assured that God will accompany us in all our struggles along the 'holy way' towards God's reign.

✳ *Loving God, give us the strength and courage to defend the rights of the weak, the least and the last. Righteous God, assure us of your presence for the living, loving and struggling of our journeys, and bring us at last to your everlasting presence.*

FOR REFLECTION AND ACTION – alone or with a group

● Look back on your life and make a chart or map of a significant journey, noting when it happened, where you went, the people you travelled with, the experiences you had and your feelings while making the journey as well as when you reached your destination. What do you learn from this exercise?

● Think about people who have come into your home, your church or your neighbourhood over the past year. What did you do to make their journey worth remembering? What did you learn from them?

● Think about visitors and those away from home at this time who may need support, concern and a helping hand. What can you do to make their time away a positive one?

COMINGS AND GOINGS
3. Sent out by God

Notes based on the Revised English Bible by
Owen Cole

Owen Cole has taught at all levels of education and is particularly concerned that Britain should be a people that is at one with itself, hence his commitment to multi-faith religious education. He has now retired but is still a member of several national professional and inter-faith bodies, in particular the Shap Working Party on World Religions in Education, the Religious Education Council of England and Wales, and the World Congress of Faith of which he is a vice-president. Besides being a Quaker Elder and Anglican Reader he is a Yorkshire Welshman, married with two daughters.

I can't agree with Robert Louis Stevenson who wrote, 'To travel hopefully is better than to arrive'. Meeting relatives or friends at the destination is a wonderful, loving experience. And ahead is the best journey's end of all, being welcomed by the divine love into eternity. Yet we are unwise to neglect the journey itself; those who have travelled by train from Settle to Carlisle have missed much if they did so with their heads in a book, and airports can be such fascinating places. (I have spent long winter nights waiting for delayed flights!) Sitting next to Hindu strangers on airplanes or Muslims on train journeys in England and in Pakistan has led to new friendships and to spiritual growth.

In these readings we shall come across some of the unexpected adventures that can befall travellers and, hopefully, be able to journey better ourselves, especially as we approach Christmas once again.

Sunday December 11   Luke 10:1–9
Be prepared

There is preparation and there is filling suitcases with clothes, buckets and spades and other paraphernalia. The seventy-two were sent out with an urgent message, 'The kingdom of God has come' (verse 11). The messengers were the message; they travelled light and with purpose.

Spiritual urgency seems not to fit in with our ways of life, perhaps because we have a wrong vision. We expect marvels and they do not come. Christmas lacks an angelic host. The magi and shepherds have been relegated to school nativity plays. Yet the eye of faith can still perceive the inner light of God's presence in human hearts and challenges. See people working with the needy and disabled. See the needy and disabled themselves who find spiritual hope where others looking at them can see only despair and feel that poorest of responses, pity. The seventy-two had to think beyond themselves to help those who yearned to find life. Perhaps the author of today's prayer has reached the heart of the matter.

✳ *Lord, when I am hungry give me someone to feed, when I am thirsty give water for their thirst. When I am sad, send me someone to lift from sorrow. When burdens weigh upon me, lay upon my shoulders the burden of my fellows. Lord, when I stand greatly in need of tenderness give me someone who yearns for love. May your will be my bread; your grace my strength; your love my resting place.*

(From Prière pour une Foi*)*

Monday December 12   *Acts 8:1b-8*
Scattered seed finds fertile ground
O how we wish we had seen the miracles that Jesus and his followers performed. I wish! But would they have confirmed our faith or made us ask for more of the same? Rallies, big occasions, be they religious, political or sporting, can be like a drug. We can't wait for the next fix – but the day after comes the hangover, life goes depressingly on as before. In the next paragraph of Acts 8 we read of a wonder-worker who, for a time, accepted the gospel, but soon forgot it in favour of turning the power of the Holy Spirit into a way of making money – he wanted more of his old life, only more so! Presumably there were gullible converts who would fall for his devices.

Hopefully, if Philip came to our church we would pay close attention to what he had to say, because accepting the message is the only lasting reason for great rejoicing. When Jesus was accused of casting out devils he asked his critics by whose power they cast them out (Luke 11:19). Such things seem to have been part of the world of Jesus' day. But the coming of the kingdom is far more than the performance of amazing acts! God's light and love in our hearts and lives are much more substantial than the temporary fixes that we often seek.

✳ *Lord, as we lift up our eyes to the hills from which our help comes, keep us from falling into a muddy ditch!*

Tuesday December 13   *Acts 8:26–40*

Go south, young man

The passages of the Hebrew bible that Christians regard as messianic have seldom, if ever, been interpreted in that way by Jews. In these verses Philip overhears an Ethiopian Jew reading one of the most famous passages in Isaiah (chapter 53). The official is confused, as we might be if we didn't read the passage through the spectacles of our Christian faith. Doesn't it refer to some figure in Jesus' past, already dead and buried? But scripture can be understood anew through the Spirit explaining it in the context of our contemporary situation, and therefore come to take on new meanings. So passages that endorsed slavery but required Christians to be good owners eventually challenged men like Wilberforce to ask whether to be a Christian and to be a slave owner were compatible. And there are many Muslims today who read the words: 'marry such women as may seem good to you, two, three, or four. If you fear that you will not act justly, then marry one woman only' (Qur'an 4:3) and emphasise the word 'justly' and affirm monogamy as the real meaning of the passage. Philip explains Isaiah to the courtier, who accepts the interpretation and is baptised. Can we think of new paths into which the Holy Spirit wishes to lead us as we read old and familiar words in the Bible?

✳ *Lord, as you have spoken to people of faith through the ages, speak now to us and lead us into fresh pastures.*

Wednesday December 14   *Acts 9:1–9*

To another the command was 'Go north'

Imagine how he must have felt, struck blind. Being unable to see can be distressing at any time, but so suddenly! It must also have troubled Saul's companions, now seemingly leaderless and probably afraid. And then there were the terrified Christians to whom he came in his helplessness. Perhaps they were refugees from his persecuting zeal. Surely his blindness was a trick?

It has been suggested by some that Saul was suffering from epilepsy, but all attempts at rationalisation miss the point. He was neither the first nor the last to experience the transforming presence and power of God, something that men and women of many faiths have known. With Saul it led to a change in name and direction, and very soon to an awareness that there is a place in the kingdom for all people, even Gentiles as well as members of the faith and nation to which Jesus and Saul both belonged. We might be thankful for this awareness whenever we feel concerned about other of Paul's views, perhaps on the ministry of women, for example. None of us is perfect. Sometimes conversion is to a new religion, but often to a deepening and renewal of the faith in which one already lives, as with John Wesley, George Fox or George Bell, Bishop of Chichester. What really matters is a willingness to change, and our spiritual and ethical transformation.

✳ *Thank you for the changes that took place in Paul and the other followers of Jesus. Change us now if that is what is needed; if not, preserve us from becoming complacent, self-satisfied or arrogant.*

Thursday December 15　　　　　　　　　　　　　　　*Acts 11:19–26*

Barnabas the catalyst

It takes a big heart and small ego to behave like Barnabas. King Saul couldn't tolerate David, the threat to his dynasty. Politicians, even in so-called democracies, do their best to suppress rivals in their own parties, perhaps sometimes wishing they had the executing powers of dictators. It can be the same in our churches, where women are pushed into the kitchen, professional social workers or teachers are given no opportunities by ministers fearful of their skills, and so-called 'unsound' ministers are denied preferment.

Not so in this story. Barnabas has achieved much but he realises that with Saul more can be done. Perhaps those who had fled to Antioch had been escaping from Saul. Now they, like Barnabas, are prepared to accept his leadership. Such trust! Once Barnabas's work has been done he soon vanishes from sight, but what he did will never be forgotten. Do we encourage others to come forward and are we then willing to fade into the background?

✳ *Deliver us from envy. Help us, Lord, to follow the example of John the Baptist who said of Jesus, 'he must increase and I must decrease'.*

Sent in an unsought direction

Flights cancelled, trains delayed, motorways closed – how frustrating. Yes it is. I've been there and found it hard to rein in my anger, until I remember that it isn't the fault of the company servants or police who tell me the bad news. Paul's mind was made up; he knew where he was going, but he was flexible enough to change it when someone, probably Luke, invited him to visit Europe. There is always a choice. Paul could have chosen the misery and bad temper of frustration that would come from sticking to his original plan, but instead he accepted the opportunity to risk the unknown. He did not then know it but it would lead to the writing of some of his finest letters, the creation of new friendships and his final journey, to Rome itself.

✴ *Lord and Father, we do not know what lies ahead of us, but we do know that you are our eternal companion. Grant us the faith and courage to travel with you into the unknown.*

Journey's end – and a new beginning

So after scourging, imprisonments, storms and shipwrecks, this is journey's end! No mention of a meeting with Peter in Rome but then Acts only fills in the bits that would not be common knowledge to Roman Christians. One reason the book may have been written was to introduce them to the two apostles and as an apologia, a defence, affirming that they, like Jesus – three notorious and rightly punished criminals – were wrongly imprisoned, innocent men. It may disappoint us that even the apostles' deaths are not described, for they would be well-known. Of course we know of the legend of Peter being crucified upside down – but it was a method that wouldn't have worked. And can we imagine a Roman execution squad discussing his last request with a Jew – or a Christian? In their eyes each would be as bad as the other! But it wasn't their manner of dying that mattered! Compare Acts' descriptions of Peter and Paul with some of the biographies of great historical figures that we read. They differ in many ways, one of them being that most biographies and autobiographies focus on the author while Acts points to the risen Jesus. Little wonder that instead of being called The Acts of the Apostles some scholars have suggested that it should be named The Acts of the Holy Spirit.

This week's notes were entitled 'Sent out by God'. The readings have focused our attention upon the great and the good but we should always remember that behind them was a support team of thousands and millions, ordinary people like you and me, who are also the recipients of the divine love. We too are sent by God to proclaim that love to the world by word, certainly, but much more by deeds of kindness.

✳ *May our lights shine in the world of God's love like stars adding to the radiant moon. For this world is not a place of darkness but the creation of One who saw that it was good and renews it daily* (read Lamentations 3:22–23). *May this be our calling until our love merges eternally with its inspiration and its source.*

FOR REFLECTION – alone or with a group

● What would have been the consequence for us if Philip, Barnabas and Paul had been as reluctant to change as we often are?

● Are we similarly challenged and will we be equally responsive?

● To what kind of retirement are those of us who have reached that stage of life called?

FOR ACTION

Make a map, or photocopy an existing one, of the places Paul visited. For each one choose a verse from Acts or one of his letters that might suitably be inscribed on the lintel of the church in that place.

COMINGS AND GOINGS
4. The coming of God

Notes based on the Revised English Bible by
Ruth Shelton

Ruth Shelton is a freelance writer, poet and illustrator, who has worked for many years in a variety of church and voluntary sector roles. She lives in Nottingham, UK.

Literary criticism is a good thing and, like biblical scholarship, widens our semantic perceptions, illuminates authors' intentions and deepens our awareness and knowledge. However, a poem, like a biblical text, cannot be wholly explained away but continues to live, breathe and develop in the imagination of the reader. The poetic meditations on the birth narratives below are not intended to be understood so much as to be inhabited, or experienced. It might help to read them out loud, slowly. Each day's notes have the same heading, but the variations on this theme are countless.

Sunday December 18   *Luke 1:39–45, 56*
Wait for the Lord
> It is the women who are waiting.
> The women in headscarves
> behind the guy from News at Ten,
> waiting for news.
> A name on a list; a face under a sheet;
> outstretched arms, a sudden movement
> under the rubble.

✳ ***Who am I, that the poor reach out to me?***

Monday December 19   *Luke 2:1–7*
Wait for the Lord
> It is the woman who waits.
> She gathers her robe around her
> as if preparing for journey; in her basket,
> bread and wine.
> The stars tell her nothing; she is afraid.
> Let something break the silence
> even if it is only the cry of a child.

✳ *When the time comes, where will I give him shelter?*

Tuesday December 20   *Luke 2:8–18*
Wait for the Lord
   It is the outsiders who wait.
   Through the hostels and detention centres
   light brushes like wings; strange chords
   sharpen on loneliness
   oscillate across frozen limbs.
   The lost watch out for the lost,
   the silenced will hear music.

✳ *Where will the signs find me? How will I hear the joy?*

Wednesday December 21   *Matthew 2:1–12*
Wait for the Lord
   It is the Lord who waits
   while we peruse our maps and theodolites,
   waylaid by important meetings,
   late as usual.
   I am burdened by preposterous gifts;
   too many stars to choose from
   but one keeps stopping.

✳ *Let me at last find kneeling space in the straw.*

Thursday December 22   *Matthew 2:13–15*
Wait for the Lord
   It is the refugees who wait.
   Signs and dreams are left behind.
   But Ben M'ahwa had a visitor
   with a newspaper from Rwanda
   and that was a miracle.
   When someone spoke in his language,
   it was the voice of an angel.

✳ *'Get up, take your safety and comfort, and share it with others.'*

Wait for the Lord
> Those who love are waiting.
> Silence and emptiness greet
> turned and expectant heads.
> Missing presumed dead;
> Have You Seen This Child?
> Scrabbling for hope, the search is hopeless
> But he is with them in their very tomb.

✳ ***Once found, let me treasure these things in my heart.***

Wait for the Lord
> It is the world which waits
> looking upwards at domes and pilasters,
> looking too high and not high enough.
> Here God comes;
> your homeless brother, your landless sister.
> Our great lost God slips under the door
> quiet as light.

✳ ***Every knee shall bow, in heaven and on earth,***
and in the depths –
and every tongue proclaim
'Jesus Christ is Lord'
to the glory of God the Father.

FOR REFLECTION – alone or with a group

● Who is waiting for the Lord in your home, in your street, in your neighbourhood?

● How can you wait with them?

● Where might the Lord be waiting for you?

FOR ACTION

Find a quiet place in which to wait for a while this week, amidst the busyness of Christmas. Find someone with whom you can wait – in pain, in anguish, in loneliness or in hope.

COMINGS AND GOINGS
5. The journeys of Jesus

Notes based on the New Revised Standard Version by
John Vincent

Revd Dr John Vincent develops and edits the Journey programme. He is a theologian and inner-city minister working with the Urban Theology Unit and the Sheffield Inner City Ecumenical Mission. He edited Faithfulness in the City *(St Deiniol's Press, 2003).*

Christianity – and the *Journey* programme – is based on the faith that the journeys of Jesus are of special significance. First, they are the action and practice of Jesus himself within the world and within the concrete history and circumstances of his time. Second, the journeys of Jesus are significant because they represent the way, the truth and the life which disciples follow and in which they find the meaning of their own journeys. Third, the journeys become paradigmatic and provocative for Christian groups and communities. In the *Journey* programme, these three elements are worked out in relation to contemporary discipleship and practice. (For details of the *Journey* programme, contact Ashram Press, 178 Abbeyfield Road, Sheffield S4 7AY.)

No separate prayers are offered this week – the prayer is in the reflection itself.

Sunday December 25 (Christmas Day)　　　　　*John 1:1–14**
Starting out
The Journey starts, we know not when.
Perhaps it has no beginning.
Perhaps there was always journeying
before and in and alongside all worlds.
The Journey has at its heart
meaning, depth, significance, Logos –
not speech, but what precedes speech,
reality that can only inadequately become speech,
meaning that remains present but hidden.
But now it appears.
This day it is born in the city of David,
as Saviour who is Christ the Lord.
The hints of it,

hidden already and forever in humanity
as its core reality (verse 9),
as its recurring secret (verse 16),
are now fulfilled.
Everything is not clear.
The Word is still a mystery.
People still walk in darkness
but the Word is still there (verse 5).
Christ is born today.
Word becomes flesh,
Reality becomes visible,
Truth becomes embodied.
Living in the light
is now open to all.
Be born in my heart, this day.

Monday December 26   *Luke 9:28–36*
Getting priorities
We hold to the law.
It's safe, and we need it.
We need to know what to do
and to have some foundation for it.
Moses, you're the man!
We need the prophets.
They're unsafe, but right.
We need to see realities
and how they crucify others.
Elijah! You're the man!
But now there is Jesus only (verse 36).
Not now the law –
even holiness and righteousness;
Not the prophets –
even equality and liberation;
But a new way of being human,
a humanity reflecting unseen light (verse 29),
a humanity with the law
in the inward heart –
a humanity of justice
established in community,
not in new institutions
but in the depth of the human psyche,
in the hearts of people together,
being established repeatedly

by transfigured humanity,
from here among the crowd (verse 37).

Staying with it
We're already on the road.
We're followers of the way.
Jesus is always ahead of us.
We hang on in fear and foreboding.
Only some of us know what is going on,
why we're going this way.
The inner core of disciples get told,
though they do not understand (verse 32).
It's about humanity,
it's about the dying seed
that only comes to true life
after it has died (verse 33).
There are real enemies ahead
who will crush it to death.
But what is crucified will rise
like wheat that springs up green (verse 34)!

Living it out
The Journey has already happened
in the healing and parables of Galilee.
The kingdom of heaven is here
where poor people and all people
live in the light of the kingdom.
So, whenever confronted by powers
that deny the reality of the kingdom
we recall the unridden colt
which outrides the horses of war.
Hosanna!
Blessed is the divine Journeyer!
Blessed is the divine kingdom
already in our midst –
to be established soon (verses 9–10).
The Journey is serious –
the 'little Christs' must keep to their colts.
The Journey is joyful –
everyone can join in and live in it.

Being faithful
> This they did when the wood was green,
> but today the wood is dry (verse 31).
> Not Simon of Cyrene now
> carries his cross (verse 26).
> Now the wood is dry
> we're all his cross-bearers.
> Filling up what lacks
> in the sufferings of Christ (Colossians 1:24),
> as the saviours of God
> living and dying vicariously
> throughout history:
>> in our communities
>> in our families
>> in our lives
>> in our vocations.
> The wood is dry, now.
> The way, the journey,
> has been trod by many.
> It's being trod now:
>> in the cities
>> in the third world
>> in the first world
>> in cyberspace
>> in stock exchanges
>> in computers
>> in countrysides
>> in inner hearts.
> The Journey is alive and well
> because forever
> lived out unto death.

Becoming globalised
> His Journey continues.
> The living Christ
> somewhere, withdrawn from us,
> but his Journey continues
> back in Jerusalem,
> within and in the form of his disciples.
> The Journey goes on,
> the eternal Word pounding

with the heart of compassion
through the march of history.
The Journey goes on:
new embodiments of the Word,
new enfleshments,
Word made flesh –
yesterday, today and tomorrow,
globalised.
On the street,
in the homes,
outside the city walls,
in the hungry,
the thirsty, the stranger,
the naked, the sick,
and the imprisoned –
And their Journey also
becomes part of the
divine Journey.

Saturday December 31   *1 Thessalonians 4:13–18*

Into tomorrow
The Journey Jesus took
through death and resurrection
is the Journey we shall take
in our own death and resurrection (verse 14).
Death does not separate us
from our true being
hid with Christ in God.
Whatever future there is beyond death
only confirms the reality we live now –
that Christ is our life
because his death works in us (2 Corinthians 4:12).
We do not know what Journeys await us
after the end of this life.
We only know that we cannot go
beyond his love and care.
The Journey of the Christ
and of ourselves in him
is the Journey that saves humanity
and ourselves in it.
The New Year ahead
repeats the story, with us in it.
And does it all in a new time
for the first time.

FOR REFLECTION- alone or with a group

- The 'poetic' reflections of the notes this week are intended to be themselves half-thoughts, half-prayers. But even more, leaders into thought and prayer. Does this work for you?

- How useful is the journey notion? Clearly the journeys of Jesus in the biblical texts function in a number of different ways – as descriptions of God, as descriptions of historical recollections of Jesus, as descriptions of writers' and readers' lifestyles and commitments, and as ways whereby faith gains expression and reality. Is the confusion of these elements useful? Or actual, realistic? Does it open up new pieces of journey? Which, when? Does it clarify and affirm old pieces of journey? Does it make sense of what is happening in secular history? Or in the historical development of Christian consciousness?

FOR ACTION

- What, if anything, out of your past do you see differently?
- What, if anything, in your present do you now have to treat differently?
- What, if anything, in your future do you prepare for boldly?

INTERNATIONAL BIBLE READING ASSOCIATION

– a worldwide service of Christian Education
at work in five continents

HEADQUARTERS

1020 Bristol Road   *www.christianeducation.org.uk*
Selly Oak
Birmingham
Great Britain
B29 6LB
and the following agencies:

AUSTRALIA

UniChurch Books
130 Little Collins St.
Melbourne
VIC 3001

GHANA

IBRA Secretary
PO Box 919
Accra

INDIA

All India Sunday School   Fellowship of Professional Workers
  Association   SAMANVAY
PO Box 2099, Plot No 83, 3rd cross,   Deepthi Chambers, Vijayapuri
Threemurthy Colony, Mahendra   Hyderabad – 500 017
Hills, Secunderabad – 500 026, AP   Andhra Pradesh

NEW ZEALAND

Epworth Bookshop
PO Box 6133
75 Taranaki Street
Wellington 6035

NIGERIA

IBRA Representative
PMB 5298
Ibadan
Oyo State

SOUTH AND CENTRAL AFRICA

IBRA South Africa
2 Crest View
Goedemoed Road
Durbanville 7550

Scheme of readings for 2006

Family matters
The family of God – Instructions on family life – Happy families? – The holy family – Hard sayings – Promise and blessing on families

Readings in Mark (1)
The beginning of the good news – The beginning of opposition

Key teachings of the early church
Who/what are the people of God? – Who is God? – Who is Jesus? – What has become of the Law? – The Spirit and spiritual gifts – How should Christians behave?

Readings in Mark (2)
Final days

Resurrection readings
'He is risen, he is not here!' – 'And God raised us up with Christ' – 'This man was handed over to you … but God raised him'

Images of hope in Jeremiah

Readings in Joshua
Entering the Promised Land – Fighting for the Promised Land – Settling in the Promised Land

Images of the Spirit
Breath, wind and storm – Fire – Water, pouring, abundant life – Dove, bird, wings

Readings in Mark (3)
Ministry in Galilee – Who is Jesus?

Holy days and holidays
Holy days – Holidays and rest days – The final holy day/holiday

Humour in the Bible
Unexpected and unpredictable – Caricatures and stereotypes – Wise and witty words

Titus and Philemon

Tolerance
How tolerant is God? – Are we too tolerant? – Are we tolerant enough?

Readings in Mark (4)
Training the disciples – Going up to Jerusalem

Food for body and soul
Food in the wilderness – Christ, the food in the wilderness

Readings in Ezra

Death
Mixed views in the Old Testament – The Christian hope

Wholeness and holiness
Jesus brings wholeness – The way to holiness – New life in Christ

Atonement
The gulf caused by sin and guilt – God is merciful – God and humanity made one in Jesus – God comes to humankind